owl

LAW AS COMMUNICATION

EUROPEAN ACADEMY OF LEGAL THEORY MONOGRAPH SERIES

General Editors

Professor Mark Van Hoecke
Professor François Ost
Professor Luc Wintgens

Titles in this series

Moral Conflict and Legal Reasoning by *Scott Veitch*
The Harmonisation of European Private Law edited by *Mark Van Hoecke*
On Law and Legal Reasoning by *Fernando Atria*
Law as Communication by *Mark Van Hoecke*
Legisprudence edited by *Luc Wintgens*

Law as Communication

MARK VAN HOECKE
Katholieke Universiteit Brussel

·HART·
PUBLISHING
OXFORD – PORTLAND OREGON
2002

Hart Publishing
Oxford and Portland, Oregon

Published in North America (US and Canada) by
Hart Publishing c/o
International Specialized Book Services
5804 NE Hassalo Street
Portland, Oregon
97213-3644
USA

Distributed in the Netherlands, Belgium and Luxembourg by
Intersentia, Churchillaan 108
B2900 Schoten
Antwerpen
Belgium

Hart Publishing is a specialist legal publisher based in Oxford, England.
To order further copies of this book or to request a list of other
publications please write to:

Hart Publishing, Salter's Boatyard, Folly Bridge,
Abingdon Road, Oxford OX1 4LB
Telephone: +44 (0)1865 245533 or Fax: +44 (0)1865 794882
e-mail: mail@hartpub.co.uk
WEBSITE: http//www.hartpub.co.uk

British Library Cataloguing in Publication Data
Data Available
ISBN 1–84113–341–8 (hardback)

Typeset by Hope Services (Abingdon) Ltd.
Printed and bound in Great Britain on acid-free paper by
Biddles Ltd, www.biddles.co.uk

Foreword

This is a book on all major theoretical aspects of law, using, when appropriate, an interdisciplinary approach and in that sense it offers a general overview of legal theory. On the other hand, it is not a descriptive overview, but one in which the central thesis is the importance of *communication* for and in law. Law is offering a framework for human interaction and communication. Moreover, it is made and developed through communication, whether it is a long tradition creating customary law, parliamentary debates preparing an Act, judicial decisions following or changing precedents, or scholarly debates that will form the basis for future judicial and statutory changes of the law. Moreover, in our pluralist societies, such wide communication, in which not only lawyers, but also politicians, mass media and the public at large may participate, especially when important moral or political issues are involved, is the main basis for the *legitimation* of the law. Reaching a consensus on values through a permanent open and free communication has increasingly become the alternative for "absolute truths" offered before by dominating ideologies or religions.

Parts of this book were, in a previous draft, written as early as 1979, other parts in the last few years. Some parts draw to a more or less important extent on earlier published work (although mostly not published in English), but most of the text has not been published before. Earlier versions have been used as basis for my lectures on Jurisprudence to the students in the Master's Course in Legal Theory at the European Academy of Legal Theory in Brussels, from 1992. Discussions with them helped considerably to develop my ideas further and improve this final version, including its wording, for which successively several students, who are native English speakers, have been extremely helpful. I prefer to thank all of them in general, as mentioning some names would probably do injustice to others. The same goes for all the colleagues with whom I had discussions over the years and/or learned a lot from their writings, but they will mostly find their names mentioned at least somewhere in this book. Finally, I want to thank especially François Ost, who made useful comments on the second last version of my manuscript, and with whom I have had, since 1979 when we met for the first time at the IVR World Congress in Basel, Switzerland, a long-lasting and perfect cooperation, both scholarly and organisationally, mainly within the frame of our European Academy of Legal Theory.

Contents

1

Introduction

Law has been described in many different ways. It has been seen as the incarnation of Justice,[1] and also as a pure mystification, aiming at preserving the power of the ruling class.[2] It is mostly considered as an omnipresent reality (*"ubi societas, ibi ius"*), but some have thought it to be a mere fiction, a non-reality, a myth.[3] For Kelsen it was a given set of rules, derived, at least formally, from one basic norm;[4] for others it is the power to interpret, the praxis of legal adjucation which constitutes the law.[5]

Until recently law was generally considered to derive from the will of a sovereign and/or, indirectly, from the will of the people. According to the "autopoietic" theory of law, law creates itself.[6]

The German "historical school" saw the law as part of a people's culture, subject to a historical evolution, just like its language, and which largely escaped individual, including governmental, control. For other theorists,[7] and prominently in today's political practice, law is a tool for "social engineering", a means which could be used for any societal change.

For most people law is a rational means for ordering and controlling human relations. Postmodern thinkers, however, doubt the possibility of having such a rational control at all. They see the lawyers as prisoners of legal language, controlled by "the law", rather than controlling it.[8]

Law is often defined as being linked to a state, the state having the military power to impose the law within its territory. Today a conception of legal pluralism is widely accepted, which does not limit the law to state legal systems but broadens it to differing forms of institutionalised social organisations, such as

---

[1] As, eg, in natural law approaches.

[2] See, eg, marxist legal theories, the Critical Legal Studies movement, or feminist jurisprudence.

[3] J Frank, *Law and the Modern Mind* (Brentano's, New York, 1930); F Cohen, "Transcendental Nonsense and the Functional Approach", (1935) 35 *Columbia Law Review*, 823; A Hägerström, *Inquiries into the Nature of Laws and Morals* (Almquist & Wiksell, Uppsala, 1953); T Jaehner, *Der Mythos vom Recht und seine empirischen Grundlagen* (München, 1993), pp 2, 203.

[4] H Kelsen, *Allgemeine Theorie der Normen* (Vienna, 1979) (see eg at pp 206–7).

[5] C Grzegorczyk, "Le droit comme interprétation officielle de la réalité", (1989) *Droits* 31.

[6] See, eg G Teubner, *Law as an Autopoietic System* (Blackwell, Oxford, 1993).

[7] Most prominently, R Pound (see, eg, his work *Jurisprudence*, 5 vols (West, St Paul, 1959)).

[8] eg J Broekman, "Rechtsphilosophie" in J Ritter and K Grunder (eds), *Historisches Wörterbuch der Philosophie* (Basel, 1992), vol VIII (R-Sc), pp 315–27; and "Rechtstheorie", in *ibid*, pp 342–53.

international law, sports associations, or numerous forms of "unofficial law".[9] For some, law is a system of rules;[10] for others it mainly organises the exercise of political power,[11] or it is a "narrative",[12] or predominantly a "profoundly traditional social practice"[13] or a sheer psychological phenomenon,[14] or an element of the economic system.[15]

If one would ask the average (practising) lawyer in which approach(es) (s)he recognises the phenomenon they are calling "law", it is not unlikely that the answer would be: "all of them to a greater or lesser degree". Law, indeed, has its roots in history, but it can also be used as a means for changing society, albeit within some limits; part of the law has been made, and is in practice also used, for purposes of justice and equity, but other parts are clearly used, mainly or even exclusively for the interest of individuals or for the group interest of people with some, or a great deal, of political power; we can use law as a, relatively neutral, tool for solving problems and for organising society, but it is also true that there is some world view hidden in the law and in legal language, thus influencing the way we look at reality; law (strongly) limits our opportunities, and, hence our freedom, but it also creates opportunities, it offers a framework for human action, thus guaranteeing some freedom we otherwise would lack; law is (to a certain extent) a logical system of rules, but it can also be seen as a matter of psychology, of acceptance in society.

We can indeed tell different stories about the law. We may give a very flattering image of it or a very negative one. We can present it as a very rigid static body of rules or as a very flexible dynamic system of principles, etc.

Why do people, and even legal theorists, so often overemphasise some specific aspect of the law, and, by doing so, neglect other aspects?

When people compare their own experience of law with the dominant conception of law, there will sometimes be a discrepancy between them. If, for instance, having lost a case, they have the conviction that "judges defend the interests of rich people", they will have a more Machiavellian image of the law than is usual. They will have a tendency to generalise their own experience and

---

[9] On "unofficial law", see S Romano, *L'ordre juridique* (Dalloz, Paris, 1975) (1st Italian edn 1918); F Rigaux, "Le droit au singulier et au pluriel", (1982) 9 *Revue Interdisciplinaire d'Etudes Juridiques* 1–61; J Griffiths, "What is Legal Pluralism?", (1986) *Journal of Legal Pluralism and Unofficial Law* 1–41; J Gijssels, *Recht, ruim bekeken* (Kluwer Rechtswetenschappen, Antwerp, 1991), 15–21.

[10] As, eg, for Kelsen, but to some extent also for Hart (see: RS Summers, "Legal Institutions in HLA Hart's Concept of Law", (2000) 75 *Notre Dame Law Review* 1807–27, esp. at 1826–27).

[11] As, eg, for Max Weber.

[12] BS Jackson, *Law, Fact and Narrative Coherence* (Deborah Charles Publications, Merseyside, 1988).

[13] M Krygier, "Law as Tradition", (1986) 5 *Law and Philosophy* 237–62, at 239: "Law is a profoundly traditional social practice, and it must be", but to which he immediately adds: "This is not merely to say that particular legal systems embody traditions, which of course no one would deny".

[14] As, eg, for Jerome Frank, or for Axel Hägerström (see above n 3).

[15] As many writings in the area of the *economic analysis of law* seem to suggest. Also for marxist legal theory law is basically determined by economic relationships.

to overemphasise an aspect which, correctly or incorrectly, they believe to be a basic one of the law. If they had won that case, they would probably have an opposite view of law: a means to protect the poor, to do justice in society. When discussing the matter with friends, with relatives, or in the pub, they will often strongly argue in favour of their position. The argument "that generalising one experience is but a weak basis upon which to build a general theory" will probably not impress them. To a certain extent people believe what they want to believe.

Something similar is going on in legal theory. During their legal education and the years following it, (prospective) young lawyers compare their own experience with, and their view of, law with the prevailing theories. Often there will be some discrepancy.

Law inevitably follows changes in society with some delay. Prevailing theories are adapted to the changed role of law in society with a still larger delay. An example is the tenacity of the theory according to which all law (in civil law countries) is made by Parliament and only "applied" by the administration and by the judges. A theory which seemed obvious to a previous generation (often because they wanted it to be obvious: people believe what they want to believe), may seem rather odd to the present one. On the one hand this new generation has forgotten the historical reasons which made the now established theory come into being. In our example it has been a reaction against the excessive power of the courts, in France and in some other European countries, before the French Revolution. The negative reasons for keeping this theory have now faded away, at least to a large extent. On the other hand, the established theory does not seem to fit with reality. In our example, judges play a much more important role in the creation and the development of law than can be explained and accepted on the basis of the prevailing theory. This conclusion also implies that the positive reasons for keeping the theory are fading away. New theories will emerge. As a reaction, the aspect which had been underestimated by the previously established theory will often now be overemphasised. Schools like Legal Realism or the Freirechtslehre will come into being. Of course, not all theories are extreme and oversimplified, but the more extreme ones are by far the most discussed and thus, at first sight, the most "succesful".[16] Unfortunately (or fortunately?), grand theories of law very seldom have a direct influence on legal practice. In any event, it will only be after they have been "translated" into some more moderate and equilibrated theory that they will qualify for general acceptance. But also in these more moderate new theories, emphasis will, inevitably, lie on aspects which are, at that time, felt to have been lacking in the previous theory or theories.

The result of this development over time of theories (on law) is a whole range of theories and definitions of law, sometimes clearly overemphasising

---

[16] A current example is Pierre Legrand, who, over the last decade, has been vigorously attacking any idea of a possible European Civil Code or other form of legal integration.

one relevant aspect of the law, sometimes trying to find the right balance between different opposing theories. But insofar as they try to add something (relatively) new to the previous theories, they will always emphasise at least one aspect which they consider to have been, somewhat or completely, neglected before. Positivist theories in nineteenth and early twentieth century tried to separate pure fact and analysis from sheer ideology and metaphysics. This approach has been necessary to work out a more rational legal doctrine and to enable the birth of the discipline we call "legal theory" today. Meanwhile, we know that a somewhat naive belief was underlying this approach: the belief that there could be "pure facts", and that analysis would be possible without any underlying ideology. As a result, today, positivism is attacked from all sides, now that the historical reasons for, and achievements of, positivism are, to a large extent, forgotten. And in a way the victory is easy, even without first making a caricature[17] of the opponent[18]: on the one hand, the historical reasons for the rise of positivism have disappeared, and on the other the weak points of a pure positivist approach to the law have become apparent.

Moreover, as Robert Alexy has shown, it is much easier to argue that there is at least some connection between law and morals, than to "prove" that there is no link whatsoever[19]. Just as in the example above of the theories about the role of courts in the creation of law, this example of the theories on positivism also shows how every theory (in law) has to be located and understood in its historical, societal context.

Karl-Heinz Ladeur has rightly criticised another aspect of an a-historical approach in (legal) science:

> "Accordingly, a decided tendency exists to de-historicize a theory to such an extent that its historical 'conditions of discovery' are only brought up to explain that the theory in itself had always been valid but had not been recognized earlier. Conversely, there is also a widespread tendency to detach the 'old' theories from the context of establishment in which they were 'discovered' and to measure their 'context of establishment' using the criterion of the 'new' theory which has, so to speak, raised itself to the level of a meta-theory, and to discard it as ideological."[20]

---

[17] Which in general is a very common and very unscientific method, but which can easily be successful, also in jurisprudence.

[18] One should be very grateful to scholars, like Norbert Hoerster in Germany, who keep defending, and in a very skilful way, an outdated theory, such as, in his case, pure legal positivism. Such scholars are acting as "sparring-partners", forcing their colleagues to improve their technique and argumentation, and thus, paradoxically, playing a major, albeit indirect, role in the elaboration of new (non-positivist) theories. The same goes for Pierre Legrand, who seems to be the only opponent of European legal integration who underpins this position in a scholarly way and who does it with talent.

[19] R Alexy, *Begriff und Geltung des Rechts* (Karl Alber Verlag, Freiburg/München, 1992).

[20] K-H Ladeur, "Perspectives on a Post-Modern Theory of Law" in G Teubner (ed), *Autopoietic Law: A New Approach to Law and Society* (Walter de Gruyter, Berlin/New York: 1988), pp 242–82, at p 247, where he also adds: "German constitutional positivism in particular has been a privileged victim of such a procedure".

From such an approach transpires the influence of positive sciences on social sciences, with the illusion of some eternal truth that is present in reality and just has to be "discovered". But, even in positive sciences the development of theories is much more linked to a way of looking at reality and interpreting it than we are mostly aware of. In social sciences theory building is mainly the construction of a framework for the interpretation of reality, not the result of a discovery of "facts".

In fact, only few theories go beyond their historical context and keep some value, in the broader perspective of time and space, for future generations and for other (legal) cultures. It suffices to glance, for example, through the journals publishing articles in the field of legal theory between the First and the Second World Wars. Not only are the names of the authors mostly unknown to us today, but even the most prominent, widely discussed authors of the time are now in many cases reduced to a footnote in our memory. For example, in Germany literally nothing was left of "national-socialist" legal theory the day after the collapse of the Nazi regime, and the same holds for the so-called "socialist" legal theory of the former German Democratic Republic: the whole body of jurisprudential literature collapsed together with the Wall.[21] Authors such as Josef Esser, who were at the core of every discussion about the role of the judge and about statutory interpretation during the 1960s and 1970s[22] (and most discussions at that time, in continental Europe, were about these topics), seem to be completely forgotten today. At the opposite of the examples of Nazi or GDR legal theory, authors of the kind of Esser have been very influential, even after their deaths. In a way their influence explains why they are no longer, or hardly, discussed today. The point they had to make in their time is no longer a point of major relevance. New problems have arisen; old problems are discussed from new perspectives and in a different context.

Independently from their historical and cultural contingency, theories are always reducing and simplifying reality. They construct reality from one specific perspective: legal reality thus becomes a "normative system", or a "sociological interaction", or an implementation of the "idea of justice", or a quest for "the right answer", or "a language", or a psychological phenomenon, etc.

Every simplification means that one does not give a full account of (legal) reality, but nevertheless such simplifications are necessary to enable us simply to "see" any reality, to understand it, to grasp it. Describing reality means structuring reality. Description is not possible without underlying theory. One needs a framework to be able to describe. This framework is a theoretical construct. This theoretical construct is determined in the first place by the general world view of a specific culture at that time. Law "is" something different in the

---

[21] Such experiences in their turn may explain more recent, positivistic, theories which refrain from engaging in any ideology (Niklas Luhmann's autopoietic theory of law, for instance).

[22] Mainly with his books *Grundsatz und Norm in der richterlichen Fortbildung des Privatrechts* (JCB Mohr, Tübingen, 1956) and *Vorverständnis und Methodenwahl in der Rechtsfindung* (Athenäum Verlag, Frankfurt am Main, 1970).

Chinese culture than in the Western culture. Within this Western culture, law was something very different during the Middle Ages compared with the present time. Of course, the rules were different, the structure of the legal systems was different, but the main difference lies at the level of the underlying world view. For medieval people, law was primarily a matter of authority, and this authority was ultimately a divine authority, represented on earth by the Pope and by kings. Legal science was also a matter of authority, not of rational consensus.[23]

It is very difficult for us, today, to grasp how our ancestors perceived the phenomenon called law, but we may assume that very few of the definitions we can currently find in jurisprudential literature would have made sense to them. A conception of law such as the Kelsenian one or as an autopoietic system could not fit into any medieval world view[24]—not because medieval people would have disagreed, but because they simply would not have been able to understand these approaches. They could not fit into their world view, in which there was not room for such a rational, systemic approach to reality.[25]

Of course, it is possible to construct some definition of law, covering all types of law over time, including medieval law and the law of primitive societies. But this will always remain a picture of how we perceive law today, and any definition will be constructed on the basis of characteristics we consider to be important within our world view, our view on reality, our view on "law". Such definitions will probably not give a true picture of law, as it was perceived in those alien societies. But this is not a real objection, it is, to a large extent, unavoidable. It is the only way we can grasp reality. We should only be aware of those limits of our possible knowledge of any reality. It is clearly not possible to look at the law from all possible perspectives at the same time. Offering such an "overall view" would merely mean offering a very chaotic picture. In order to get at least some insight into the legal phenomenon, a selection will be necessary: both a selection of some, time- and culture-bound perspective and a selection of some characteristics of law considered to be essential for some time-, culture- and theory-bound reasons. A definition of law is in fact nothing else than the core of a theory of law. Such a definition is a "good" definition, such a theory of law is a good theory, if it gives a better insight into the reality of law, if it offers more than previous definitions or theories did. "Offering a better insight" refers to the subjective needs of the lawyers or other people concerned. These needs are inevitably linked to some specific historical, geographical, sociological reality. If lawyers feel rather unhappy with a current relativistic conception of what "just law" could be, a "one right answer" thesis will be very appealing. If lawyers feel uncomfortable with a constant confusion of facts and values, a Kelsenian approach will be very welcome.

---

[23] GCJJ van den Bergh, *Geleerd recht. Een geschiedenis van de Europese rechtswetenschap in vogelvlucht*, 2nd edn (Kluwer, Deventer, 1994), pp.29–30.

[24] Nor can they in current non Western world views.

[25] C Taylor, *Sources of the Self. The Making of Modern Identity* (Cambridge University Press, Cambridge, 1989).

1.2 A COMMUNICATIONAL APPROACH TO LAW

This book will also offer a time- and culture-bound perspective on law and not something which would aim to be a "definitive" answer to the question "what is law?". It is a child of its time in that it builds on current theories and writings, and follows its lines of reasoning. Just like other theoretical approaches, it lays emphasis on some specific characteristic of law which seems worthy of highlighting, and which until now has been largely absent in jurisprudential literature: law as communication. Of course, the idea is not completely new (as ideas seldom are). The concept of communication received a lot of attention within some theories (theory of communication as applied to law by Habermas, systems theory as applied to law by Luhmann and Teubner). This book will try to structure a number of traditional topics of legal theory from a "communicational perspective". It is just another way of reading, another way of describing traditional problems of jurisprudence, hoping that this new perspective will offer some new insights into the phenomenon of law.

As argued above, theory aims at structuring reality in order to make it accessible, comprehensible, understandable for us. Just like theory, law also aims at structuring reality in one way or another. It offers a framework, not for understanding reality, as theory does, but a framework for human action. This conclusion could be considered to offer some minimal definition of law:[26] "law is a framework for human action". It seems broad enough to cover (almost) all definitions of law proposed in jurisprudential literature, be it too broad and too vague to suffice as a full definition. For the time being, however, this minimal definition may suffice. In the following chapters a more precise definition of law will be elaborated.

It will be argued that the concept of communication can be used at different levels with regard to the law.

Human action implies interpersonal relations and, thus, communication. As a consequence, if law offers a framework for human action, it also offers a framework for human communication.

But law itself is also essentially based on communication: communication between legislators and citizens, between courts and litigants, between the legislator and the judiciary, communication between contracting parties, communication within a trial. Most prominently, this communicational aspect is nowadays considered within the frame of the legitimation of the law: a rational dialogue amongst lawyers as the ultimate safeguard for a "correct" interpretation and adjudication of the law.

---

[26] The definition of law "as a game", in the sense of "moving within a framework" (*mouvement dans un cadre*) used by Ost and Van de Kerchove comes very close to this (see F Ost and M van de Kerckhove, *Le droit ou les paradoxes du jeu* (Paris, 1992), pp 10–11).

The concept of *"communication"* has the advantage and disadvantage of being polysemic.[27] In everyday language, as defined in dictionaries, it means "exchange of information, contact". In scholarly writing it may be used in the broad sense of "interaction" or in the narrower sense of an "intentional transmission of information by means of some established signalling system"[28], or as an "interaction that is symbolically structured on the basis of conventionally determined rules of meaning"[29], or as "the practice of producing and negotiating meanings under specific social, cultural and political conditions"[30]. Here, it will always bear this more specific, narrower meaning, sometimes, however, including also more visible, physical interaction.

Analysing the legal phenomenon in terms of communication seems to have several advantages. It approaches law as a means for human interaction and not as some autonomous end. The concept allows a broad, pluralist analysis, as communication can be found at different levels and under many different forms. It does not lead to the elaboration of a closed system but remains open-ended, as the emphasis lies on communication processes and not on fixed elements, eg "norms". The concept of communication as such refers to the taking into account of differing points of view and to some dialectical exchange of viewpoints. Such a dialectical approach should preserve us from one-sided analysis and conclusions.

Moreover, many problems in legal theory and legal practice are linked to the underlying philosophical concepts of rationality in these theories and practices. The logico-deductive approach of cartesian thinking in continental European legal theory and practice over the last two centuries has recently been more and more under attack from several sides.[31] As an alternative, argumentation and discourse theories have been developed in legal theory.[32]

The main contribution for working out an alternative philosophical framework, which could replace traditional natural law normativism and positivist rationalism, has been made by Jürgen Habermas, first in his book *Theory of*

---

[27] This probably is the main reason why "the various approaches and perspectives which generate writing on the subject of legal communication make such limited reference to each other", as David Nelken has rightly remarked (D Nelken, "Law as Communication: Constituting the Field" in D Nelken (ed), *Law as Communication*, Aldershot: Dartmouth, 1996, 3).

[28] J Lyons, *Semantics*, vol I (Cambridge University Press, Cambridge: 1977), p 32

[29] J Habermas, *The Theory of Communicative Action*, vol 2: *Lifeworld and System: A Critique of Functionalist Reason* (trans T McCarthy, Boston, 1987).

[30] T Schirato and S Yell, *Communication and Culture* (Sage Publications, London, 2000).

[31] See, eg, the writings of Jan Broekman and many publications in the fields of feminist jurisprudence, legal semiotics (Bernard Jackson, Roberta Kevelson) and legal methodology (François Gény, Josef Esser, Jack ter Heide, Walter van Gerven).

[32] C Perelman and L Olbrechts-Tyteca, *The New Rhetoric: A Treatise on Argumentation* (trans J Wilkinson and P Weaver) (University of Notre Dame Press, Notre Dame and London, 1969); A Peczenik, *Grundlagen der juristischen Argumentation* (Springer, Vienna, 1983); R Alexy, *A Theory of Legal Argumentation: The Theory of Rational Discourse as Theory of Legal Justification* (trans R Adler and DN MacCormick) (Clarendon Press, Oxford, 1989.

Communicative Action,[33] and, more recently, in his book *Between Facts and Norms*.[34]

Essential for Habermas is that there is nothing like an "objective truth", from which, inductively or deductively, conclusions might be inferred. Rationality is not something which is given, but something which is constantly made *through communication* with the others. There is, and there has to be, a constant search for the best possible answer through a constant dialogue with, in principle, all other human beings. Practical reason can no longer be founded in a teleology of history (as marxism did), nor in the constitution of human species (Habermas refers to philosophical anthropology à la Max Scheler or Arnold Gehlen), nor simply on the success of some tradition. Habermas, rightly, rejects the easy alternative: relativism and denial of reason. He replaces "practical reason" with "communicative reason". In this *language* obtains a paramount position:

> "what makes communicative reason possible is the linguistic medium through which interactions are woven together and forms of life are structured. This rationality is inscribed in the linguistic telos of mutual understanding and forms an ensemble of conditions that both enable and limit. Whoever makes use of a natural language in order to come to an understanding with an addressee about something in the world is required to take a performative attitude and commit herself to certain presuppositions. In seeking to reach an understanding, natural-language users must assume, among other things, that the participants pursue their illocutionary goals without reservations, that they tie their agreement to the intersubjective recognition of criticizable validity claims, and that they are ready to take on the obligations resulting from consensus and relevant for further interaction. These aspects of validity that undergird speech are also imparted to the forms of life reproduced through communicative action. Communicative rationality is expressed in a decentered complex of pervasive, transcendentally enabling structural conditions, but it is not a subjective capacity that would tell actors what they *ought* to do."[35]

Indeed, it is interesting to note that language is not only an essential tool for any human communication (including law), but that the very use of language for communicational purposes presupposes, by definition, the acceptance of some (communicative) rationality and underlying claims and rules, such as propositional truth, personal sincerity and normative rightness.

---

[33] J Habermas, *The Theory of Communicative Action*, vol 1: *Reason and the Rationalization of Society*, and vol 2: *Lifeworld and System: A Critique of Functionalist Reason* (trans T McCarthy, Boston, 1984, 1987. Original German edn: *Theorie des kommunikativen Handelns*, vol 1: *Handlungsrationalität und gesellschaftliche Rationalisierung*, and vol 2: *ZurKritik der funktionalistischen Vernunft* (Suhrkamp, Frankfurt am Main, 1981).

[34] J Habermas, *Between Facts and Norms. Contributions to a Discourse Theory of Law and Democracy* (trans William Rehg, Polity Press, Cambridge, 1996), p 631; original German edn: *Faktizität und Geltung. Beiträge zur Diskurstheorie des Rechts und des demokratischen Rechtsstaats* (Suhrkamp Verlag, Frankfurt, 1992).

[35] J Habermas, *Between Facts and Norms. Contributions to a Discourse Theory of Law and Democracy* (Polity Press, Cambridge, 1996), pp 3–4.

This has important philosophical consequences also for legal theory. Through this communicational approach Habermas tries to build bridges between facts and norms, whereas the main legal theorist of the twentieth century, Hans Kelsen, became so succesful because he seemingly succeeded in disconnecting completely fact and norm, *Sein* and *Sollen*. Habermas does not try to "purify" facts from norms or vice versa, rather he wants to understand the tension and close relationship between both.

This philosophical debate on the concept of rationality eventually leads Habermas to an elaborate theory of democracy. Such a theory is not only important for building a normative theory of law, but also for a descriptive theory of law, as law is intimately linked to political decision-making. It also strongly affects the methodology of law. Traditional legal theory and legal practice are still today strongly determined by eighteenth- and nineteenth-century concepts of democracy and theory of the state. The current links between law and state, the balance of power between the judge and the legislator, may only adequately be discussed in the light of changing paradigms.

If law is rational, and if rationality is to be understood as communicative rationality, then law *is* communication, and not only *about* differing forms of interhuman communications.

Law cannot any more be correctly understood within a paradigm of one-dimensional rationality. Law creation cannot be seen as a one-way process: "citizens-elections-parliamentary legislation-judicial application". The dramatic rise of complexity, both of law and of society, have made such a scheme obsolete. The strengthened role of the judge, especially the establishment of constitutional and supranational courts, the weakened role of Parliaments to the advantage of governments and administrations, are not just "wrong developments", which have to be corrected in order to make reality fit with traditional theory. They are new, probably unavoidable, realities for which new theories have to be developed, both descriptive ones (eg, a more pluralist conception of law, in which "law" and "state" are partly disconnected) and normative ones (eg, new theories of democracy, such as the Habermasian one, in which also the media has to be taken into account).

There is also an enhanced need for more attention to be paid to human interaction and communication in the light of new theories, which are less individualistic and emphasise some form of community, which transcend the sum of its members, such as ecological theories, that emphasise intergenerational duties of men,[36] or autopoietic theories, which shift the attention from the individual actor to society as a system.[37] In these theories the individual is seen less as an

---

[36] eg F Ost, *La nature hors la loi: l'écologie à l'épreuve du droit* (Editions La Découverte, Paris, 1995), pp 242–343; H Visser 't Hooft, H.Ph., *Justice to Future Generations and the Environment*, Law & Philosophy Library, vol 40 (Kluwer Academic Publishers, Dordrecht, 1999), p 167.

[37] eg N Luhmann, "The Autopoiesis of Social Systems" in N Luhmann, *Essays on Self-Reference* (Columbia University Press, New York, 1990), pp 1–20; G Teubner, *Law as an Autopoietic System* (Blackwell, Oxford, 1993).

atomic entity, which could be isolated from any concrete community, but rather as part of a whole, which does not only offer an added value to the sum of the isolated individuals, but is the necessary condition and framework for any form of individual good life. If this approach is correct, it means that *human inter-action* and *communication* have to be at the centre of any theory of law, rather than individuals or legal systems as such.

2

Defining "Law"

As already observed above, defining a concept is not merely a (pure) description of some reality to which the concept applies. Concept formation in sciences, and thus concept definition, is closely linked to theory formation. In fact, they are so closely interrelated as to virtually constitute two different aspects of the same procedure.[1] Just like theories, concepts are a way of looking at reality and of structuring reality. In human sciences they are always a mixture of description and construction of reality.

At the level of description one may distinguish between two types of reality which are being described. On the one hand there are a number of data which are in a certain society generally considered to be "pure facts". On the other hand description often does not emphasise "facts" as such, but the way scientists or people in general speak about these "facts". This is a description of some use of language, of some way people talk about reality.

Although this last kind of description can be made in the same "objective" way as a description of "pure facts", it is obvious that through such a language description one gives an account of some (inter)subjective approach to reality. It describes the way people construct reality. Moreover, the meaning of a concept is neither well determined for every user of the language, nor the same for all users during the period of time under consideration. When describing this usage of language one inevitably makes some choice regarding the "average" or "standard" meaning given to the concept.

One could doubt whether defining is really construction rather than description of reality. But, as Hempel noted:

"The entire history of scientific endeavour appears to show that in our world comprehensive, simple and dependable principles for the explanation and prediction of observable phenomena cannot be obtained by merely summarizing and inductively generalizing observational findings. . . . Guided by his knowledge of observational data, the scientist has to invent a set of concepts—theoretical constructs, which lack immediate experimental significance, a system of hypotheses couched in terms of them, and an interpretation for the resulting theoretical network".[2]

---

[1] CG Hempel, *Fundamentals of Concept Formation in Empirical Science* (The University of Chicago Press, Chicago, 1952), p 2.

[2] C Hempel, above n 1, pp 36–37.

In other words, informative, scientific description of reality is only possible when embedded in, and guided by, theoretical constructs. A whale, for instance, is defined as being a large mammal with certain other characteristics, and not, at least not in the first place, as being a large fish. This means that on the basis of some theory about animals, the way of reproduction is considered to be more essential when describing animals than eg the question whether they live in the water, on earth or in the air.

When one accepts that this is the case in empirical sciences, one will easily admit that the influence of theory on description will be even stronger in the field of human sciences, where reality is seldom considered to be an established fact, but is much more often seen as some human activity, which inevitably has to be interpreted in one way or another by the "describer" of the human activity.

What does this entail for the definition of law? First, at the level of legal data, generally considered to be "facts", one has to take into account the existence of "constitutions", "acts", "legislators", "courts", "states", "contracts" and other "legal facts".

Secondly, at the level of legal language, one has to take into account the meaning given to "law", to legal institutions, legal concepts and so on, both generally in ordinary language in the relevant society and, more specifically, amongst lawyers.

2.2 HOW TO DELIMIT THE EMPIRICAL REALITY WE (WILL) CALL "LAW"?

"International law" is called "law" by (almost) every lawyer (and layman), but its status as "law" has been, and still is, denied by many legal theorists. Many forms of unofficial law, ie law which is neither created nor explicitly recognised as such by a state, are not called "law" in common, legal and non-legal parlance, but nowadays more and more legal theorists acknowledge them as being real "law".

These two paradoxes show to what extent (legal) "reality" indeed is already determined by (legal) theory. There is not such a thing as "law" in reality. "Law" is the name people have decided to give to some kinds of reality. Depending upon the theory of law one starts from, this reality will (slightly) diverge.

It is interesting to note how there appears to be a dialectical relation between theory and reality with regard to the definition of "law". Law changes and theory changes in the course of time. A change in one of them may influence the other. The two mentioned paradoxes, for instance, only emerged after the rise of the centralised nation states. This, at that time new, political situation partly had been influenced by eighteenth century political philosophy. But in its turn, this new legal reality strongly influenced state theory and the concept of law linked with it: all law was presumed to originate from the state, if not explicitly, at least implicitly. This association of "law" with "state law" made it very difficult, from a purely theoretical point of view, to consider international law or unofficial "sub-state" law to be (fully) "law". Hence, after (state and legal) theory had adapted to a changed (political and legal) reality, reality was perceived and described, and in a way "adapted", on the basis of the prevailing theory of the state and theory of law.

But nowadays political and legal reality are changing again. The strong centralised state is fading away. In some countries more political power has been given to decentralised regional institutions. At the international level a lot of international institutions with, at least some, power of decision have come about. The European Union, most prominently, took over several legal competences of its Member States, without however, for the time being, offering the perspective of becoming some new centralised European state on its own.[3] This changed political and legal reality forces the prevailing theory of the state to adapt to this new situation. The result is a much more flexible attitude towards concepts of legal pluralism and a willingness to consider a broader, less state-centred concept of law. And it is likely that this changed theoretical position will, in its turn, influence legal reality, especially the societal position and authority of non-state law.

Reality partly determines theory. Theory partly creates reality. This is a continuous dialectical interaction without real synthesis: it is an open-ended process. Nevertheless, it is always possible to construct some definition of law, as offered by such a synthesis, which would, at least to a large extent, fit with our common understanding of law. If everybody calls "international law" "law", a theoretical definition of law should include it. If not, something is wrong with the theory rather than with practice.[4] A theoretical definition of law should structure our common understanding of law in such a way that it fits with practice and offers a framework for a clear, coherent and rational view of it.

In order to work out such a definition we will discuss a number of characteristics which, sometimes or often, are considered to be essential to law.

---

[3] The subsidiarity principle, laid down in the Maastricht Treaty (7 February 1992) has blocked all tendency in that direction.

[4] This of course does not mean that, in other cases, theory might not, rightly, suggest changes in the use of (legal) language in legal practice. But, if a practice is too deeply rooted, this probably will be done in vain.

3

(Possible) Characteristics of Law

Law regulates human behaviour. This conclusion seems to be the most obvious and least discussed in the context of defining the law. But what does it actually mean?

Law offers opportunities for possible human behaviour and law limits the opportunities for other kinds of behaviour. In most cases, people are confronted with externally, socially imposed rules (legislation, case law, customary law). In other cases, however, they create the rules themselves (eg when drafting a will or a contract). In a way, one could say (and some theories have emphasised this element),[1] that law is a form of self-regulation of human behaviour. This is true at the level of society, although the influence of each individual on the substance of general rules of law inevitably remains very limited. In an open, democratic, informed society there will be at least the illusion that such an influence is real. At the level of the individual person, however, this influence will almost always be negligible.

For the individual, law is more an external fact, a reality he has to take into account, than something he can determine, or even influence, himself. From his point of view, law is comparable to nature. Both offer him opportunities and limits for behaviour. Paradoxically, such limits to behaviour are necessary to be able to behave in a meaningful way. How could we enjoy food if we were never hungry? How could we have "holidays" if we never had to work?[2] The same holds true for the law: how could we enjoy freedom in a society in which there were no limits whatsoever to anybody's freedom? In such a society there is no order, only chaos. In a situation of chaos there is no possibility of freedom, at least no freedom in the sense we conceive it: a choice between different kinds of action, a liberty to do something or to refrain from it, with at least some certainty that others will not (try to) keep us from doing so. In modern times famous authors[3] have tried to show how law is necessary to prevent us from

---

[1] eg: the autopoietic theory (G Teubner, *Law as an Autopoietic System*, (Blackwell, Oxford, 1993) or the German historical school (C von Savigny, *Vom Beruf Unsrer Zeit für Gesetzgebung und Rechtswissenschaft* (Freiburg im Breisgau, 1892, 1st edn: 1814)).

[2] We know what this would mean from Russian nineteenth century literature, describing the daily life of the aristocracy of that time: an utterly boring, empty life.

[3] Such as Hobbes and Machiavelli.

chaos, from the "*homo homini lupus*" of a lawless society. We may disagree with the alternatives, the types of legal system, they proposed (and which, of course, were also answers to the specific needs and wishes of their time and culture), but it should nevertheless be clear that *some* kind of law, some kind of order we could call "law", is necessary for any society.

This law offers a framework for human action in society. By limiting some types of behaviour meaningful behaviour is made possible. For example, by preventing people from driving on the left-hand side of the road (or, in some countries, on the right-hand side), traffic rules make it possible to drive safely. Apparent limits to our freedom often serve to enhance freedom; in our example, the freedom to drive by car from one point to another without too many problems. If one could drive on any side of the road, this would prove impossible, because of constant traffic jams and accidents. From an individual point of view, such limits may sometimes be felt to be real limits to one's freedom. Parking prohibitions are very inconvenient when one does not find a parking place. Speed limits and red traffic lights can be very annoying when one is in a hurry. But it would be far worse if one could not depend upon other people to stop at a red traffic light when one is driving through a green light. "Free-riders" typically take advantage of the fact that almost everybody else is abiding by the rules. It is only because most people do so, and, eg, do not use the hard shoulder when they are blocked in a traffic jam (as it should be left free for police and medical teams) that such free-riders have the opportunity to use that very hard shoulder to avoid the traffic jam. If most car drivers were to follow their example, everybody would be blocked again, including the services that could help solve the cause of the jam.

On some occasions, moral and legal rules prohibiting murder may seem to be inconvenient, but these rules, at least the legal ones, have the invaluable advantage of creating a minimum level of security from being constantly under threat of murder oneself.

All this proves to what extent law is a *societal phenomenon*, even if rights and duties very often have a more limited and individualised (inter)personal scope.

The societal character of law also becomes clear when one tries to imagine a person living completely alone, eg on an island like Robinson Crusoë. In such a case no single legal rule would make any sense: criminal law, property law, contract law, social security law, tax law, etc.[4] On the other hand, once we imagine

---

[4] Of course, if one is willing to award "rights" to nature, there would seemingly be some "law": but when one were to try to apply legal concepts to such a situation, it would soon appear that this does not make any sense at all. How would one enforce any "right of nature" against our Robinson? As "animal rights" concepts seem nowadays not to be seriously defended by scholars in jurisprudence, I will not discuss the matter more thoroughly here (I refer to my article "Confusion on the Concept of 'Rights': The Case of the so-called 'Animal Rights'" in: A Peczenik and M Karlsson (eds), *Law, Justice and the State*, vol 1, *Essays on Justice and Rights* (ARSP Beiheft 58, Franz Steiner Verlag, Stuttgart, 1995), pp 215–25).

a second person living with our Robinson, almost all kinds of legal rules could make sense.[5] Hence, law is not primarily concerned with human behaviour, with individual human action as such, but with human *interaction*, interhuman behaviour, human communication.

3.2 LAW AS A SET OF NORMS

Law does not describe but prescribes reality, or, more precisely, interhuman behaviour. This, of course, is one of the most striking features of the legal phenomenon, a feature which allows us to distinguish law from almost everything else. There are indeed very few normative systems or sets of norms outside the law. We may mention morals, religion, ideology, customs, usages, etiquette, but probably nothing more. It is typical of norms that they tell human beings how to behave under specific circumstances. Following a norm has a positive value, violating it has a negative value. This implies that the breaking of a rule will be followed by some kind of social sanction, if others are informed about it. At least, the disapproval of others will result. One of the stronger sanctions could be the expulsion from the group.[6] It is typical of law (a) that sanctions are generally laid down in a more concrete and precise form before the breaking of the rule has taken place and (b) that the sanctioning process as such is also organised by law. We will come back to these points later, here we are only concerned with the normative character of law.

In jurisprudential literature, many different positions have been taken as regards the kind of reality which creates this normative character of law. For some, it is the will of a sovereign, the will of a law-giver.[7] For many, it is the deduction from superior norms, which ultimately are based on some (fictitious, or epistemologically *a priori*) "basic norm".[8] For others however, it is the

---

[5] Alf Ross used the game of chess as an example of a social phenomenon: it is not possible to play chess alone. This game, together with most other games, only makes sense because of a *human interaction*. This interaction is more than the sum of isolated actions of individuals (A Ross, *On Law and Justice* (University of California Press, Berkeley and Los Angeles, 1958), pp 13–14).

[6] Banishment has always, before modern times, been considered to be a very heavy punishment. In primitive societies it probably had, in the short run, a similar effect to a death penalty.

[7] eg: Austin and Bentham (J Austin, "The Province of Jurisprudence Determined" (1st edn,1832), reprinted in *The Province of Jurisprudence Determined and The Uses of the Study of Jurisprudence* (Weidenfeld and Nicolson, London, 1955), pp 1–361; J Bentham, *Of Laws in General* (ed HLA Hart, University of London Athlone Press, London, 1970). For a good summary of this point in Austin's and Bentham's thinking, see R Cotterrell, *The Politics of Jurisprudence* (Butterworths, London/Edinburgh, 1989), pp 52–82.

[8] H Kelsen, *Pure Theory of Law*, trans M Knight (University of California Press, Berkeley, 1967), esp. at pp 193–217.

acceptance of the norm by those who are expected to apply it (citizens[9] and/or judges[10]) which really confers a normative power on the rule.

It seems obvious that the normative character of a rule cannot exclusively be reduced to some psychological will or expectation or willingness from the side of either the norm-sender or the norm-receiver. The normative character clearly results from an interaction between both of them. An order or a rule formulated by someone or somebody, whose authority is not accepted by those who are expected to apply it, will remain a dead letter. A difference between "law in the books" and "law in action" may thus be explained. If the historical law-giver is denied authority with regard to determining (the most adequate interpretation of) the content of a rule in the context of a case beforehand, the law in action, ie the actually valid law, will be determined by the (non)acceptance by the citizens and/or officials and/or judges concerned, and not by the "will" of the "law-giver".

But, in practice, as long as the (would-be) law-giver has some authority, his rules will be taken into account, at least as a starting point. If, in current (Western) societies the will of the (historical) legislator is explicitly disregarded, which in fact does not happen so often, good reasons (or at least in the opinion of interpreters) are offered for doing so. In these cases there is clearly an inter-action between law-giver and (in most cases) judges: some communication process in which there is an interaction between the expression of a will and the acceptance of an authority underlying it, an interaction between power and a feeling of being bound by that power. To this point, which is essential for a cor-rect understanding of the legal phenomenon, we will come back later.

If law is a set, or collection of norms, is it also a normative *system*? Law aims at regulating, organising human interaction. In order to reach this aim at least to a minimal extent, some unity, some coherence within the set of legal norms, is an essential requirement. What one tries to achieve with one norm should not be destroyed by another one. It does not make sense to encourage some kind of behaviour by means of a legal norm, if this behaviour is at the same time dis-couraged by other legal norms. For this reason, law is necessarily a normative *system*, and not a mere unordered collection of norms. For the time being, we may leave aside the question of what kind of system a legal system is.

We may simply conclude that legal norms always form a legal *system*, at least in the weak sense of some logical relation of coherence amongst the norms.

---

[9] According to Scandinavian Realism (see eg A Hägerström, *Inquiries into the Nature of Laws and Morals* (Almquist & Wiksell, Uppsala, 1953); V Lundstedt, *Die Unwissenschaftlichkeit der Rechtswissen-schaft*, vol I, (1932)).

[10] According to American Realism (see eg OW Holmes, "The Path of the Law", (1897) *Harvard Law Review* 457–78: "The prophecies of what courts will do in fact, and nothing more pretentious, are what I mean by the law" (at p 463).

3.3.1 Formal Institutionalisation

In the past, the actual power of enforcing rules has very often been considered to be the main characteristic of a legal system,[11] compared to other systems. Today, emphasis lies much more on the institutional character of law. In Herbert Hart's wording, law is "the union of primary and secondary rules".[12]

Just like morals, etiquette and other normative systems, law contains "primary rules" allowing or forbidding some behaviour. But unlike all other normative systems, legal systems include other different types of rules which do not directly relate to the way people should behave. These "secondary rules" are rules *about* rules. They structure and regulate primary rules. They institutionalise the rules of behaviour. The law itself explicitly regulates *who* has the power to make, to change or to abolish legal rules and *how* this has to be done in order to generate valid law within the legal system. The law also determines *who* has the power to make authoritative determinations of the question whether, on any given occasion, a primary (or secondary) rule has been broken, and *how* to reach such a decision, ie which procedure has to be followed in order to get such an authoritative decision within the legal system. Together with the professionalisation of the law, this has led to the development of specialised

---

[11] In this book, "legal system" is used in a broad sense, and synonymous with "legal order". In a strict sense "legal system" implies some properties such as closure, consistency and completeness, which "legal order" does not require (see, on this distinction: J Bengoetxea *The Legal Reasoning of the European Court of Justice* (Clarendon Press, Oxford, 1993), pp 36–37).

[12] HLA Hart, *The Concept of Law* (Clarendon Press, Oxford, 1961), pp 77–96. Meanwhile the concepts "primary rule" and "secondary rule" have become current in the sense used by Hart. Generally speaking the words "primary" and "secondary" may suggest different kinds of relationship: temporal (secondary comes after primary), functional (secondary is less important than primary) or hierarchical (secondary is lower ranked than primary) (see on this variety of possible meanings, and their mutual relationship: N Bobbio, "Nouvelles réflexions sur les normes primaires et secondaires" in C Perelman (ed), *La règle de droit* (Bruylant, Brussels, 1971), pp 104–22). Here, the words are used in the sense of Hart and they bear neither a temporal nor a hierarchical meaning, but a functional one. However, not "functional" in the sense as defined by Bobbio, according to which secondary rules should be less important than the primary rules. In a way, of course, one could argue that this is the case, as primary rules of behaviour are the *raison d'être* of the law and, for this reason, of primary importance. However, without secondary rules we may have a normative system, like morals, but not a *legal* system. Thus, secondary rules are as important for a legal system to exist and to function as primary rules of behaviour are. They just fulfil a different function and in this sense only the secondary rules are a kind of meta-rules, of rules about rules. Finally, also Bobbio adheres to this meaning of the words "primary" and "secondary" in this context (above, p 112). Kelsen, in his last publication, adopts the distinction between primary and secondary rules (without mentioning Hart or any other author), but for him the sanctioning duty imposed on officials (judges, administrative officers, and the like) are to be called "primary", because the norm is in the first place adressed to them, and only indirectly to the citizen. Hence, according to Kelsen, rules of behaviour are to be called "secondary" rules (*General Theory of Law* (Clarendon Press, Oxford, 1991), pp 142–43).

institutions, particularly Parliament, the administration, the judiciary, and thus to a strong institutionalisation of the law.

Thus, this institutionalisation has two aspects: structures and procedures. It has two levels: the making of the law and the adjudication of the law.

In every legal system there are norm-creating and norm-applying institutions, even if sometimes they may both be the same person or body (eg the tribal chief in primitive societies, but also the judge in developed legal systems). These norm-creating and norm-applying functions are institutionalised, at least in the sense that in the society or social field to which the legal system applies, they are considered to be exercised by some specific individual(s) or body (bodies) on which the legal system confers this function(s). Even when both functions are exercised by one and the same person or body they are clearly distinguishable. The making, the wording, the acceptance *in abstracto* of a general rule is clearly different from the application of the rule to a concrete case. The difference does not lie in the fact that the existence of the rule would be hidden and could only appear clearly when applied by some official of the legal system.[13] Rules may have a far-reaching influence on people's behaviour solely through their enactment and without intervention by any civil officer, judge or other official. American Realists would say that this is so, because they anticipate probable decisions by such officials. To some extent this may be true, but it cannot be the only explanation for people's behaviour. Anticipating possible decisions by officials of the legal system is not the only, and probably not even the main, factor determining human behaviour. One could compare it to people's behaviour which may have an influence on their health. When eating, drinking, etc, most people will not determine their behaviour in the first place (let alone, exclusively) on the basis of a presumed answer to the question "what will my doctor say about that?" But when people follow a general rule spontaneously they also apply this rule to a concrete situation. Where then lies the difference between the application of the law by a citizen, and by a civil officer, or a judge? The difference lies not in the combination of a general norm with concrete facts and all the (factual and legal) interpretation it may entail. This in fact happens in all these cases. The difference lies in the power the legal system has conveyed to some person or body, generally called "judge" or "court", to give an *authoritative interpretation* of the law when applying it to the concrete facts. Not only is the making of the (general) rule institutionalised in legal systems, so too is the power to determine the exact meaning and scope of the rule when there is some doubt or discussion about its applicability to a concrete situation. In the development of legal systems, this power is probably the first one to be institutionalised. The power to "make" the law remains rather vague in primitive societies, organised purely on the basis of customary law (moreover, mixed with religious

---

[13] As was posited by the German scholar Mayer: "Erst durch die richterliche Entscheidung wird das Recht ein konkreter Befehl" (ME Mayer, *Rechtsnormen und Kulturnormen* (Breslau, 1903), p 45).

and moral rules). The existence and the wording of the general rule will, in such legal systems, to a large extent, be defined by the person or body having the power to give an authoritative interpretation of the law, on the occasion of a concrete discussion.[14] In fact, what is institutionalised in legal systems is not the "making of the law" or the "adjudication of the law" as such. It is, on the one hand, the power authoritatively to determine the existence, the content and the scope of rules in a general way, and, on the other, the power authoritatively to determine its applicability to a concrete case.

One may doubt whether it is possible to distinguish a third type of secondary rules, which Hart calls the "rule of recognition". For Hart this rule of recognition indicates which rules can be considered to be part of the legal system and how to identify them. This may, eg, be the fact of their having been enacted by a specific body, or long customary practice, or their relation to judicial decisions. Rules of recognition provide an authoritative mark to rules, identifying them as part of the legal system, and unifying them.[15]

What Hart has in mind is a theory of legal sources. Such a theory, of course, is necessary to every legal system, but it has an ambivalent status. On the one hand, it refers to "rules of change", empowering individuals or bodies to introduce, change or eliminate primary or secondary rules. On the other hand, it refers to some ideological position of acceptance of the legal system. In the first case, it coincides with the (internal) "rules of change", in the second case, it falls outside the legal system, just like Kelsen's basic norm. Where in several European countries, courts have accepted unwritten "general principles of law" to be a source of law, or when they accepted rules of the European Union as having a supremacy over domestic legal rules, they did not just use their power to adjudicate the law, they also changed the law, sometimes even radically. Their acceptance of these new sources of law was not the application of some pre-existent "rule of recognition", it was an ideological choice, determined by non-legal values. This acceptance of new sources of law by courts, was in its turn largely accepted in society, both by lawyers and non-lawyers, because it fits with the ideological framework of acceptance by the citizens of the State legal system in question. Is this a "rule of recognition", which is part of the legal sytem? Actually, it is not part of the legal system, but a condition for its acceptance in society. It is not an internal, but an external element. Moreover, it is not a "rule". It is a belief, an acceptance, an ideological position. Just like Kelsen's *Grundnorm,* it is not a norm, but a fact.

By definition, such "rule(s) of recognition" cannot be part of the institutionalisation of the law. It belongs to the societal breeding ground of the legal system, not to the legal system itself. This "societal breeding ground" is not institutionalised at all, but constantly moving. What is accepted as a source of

---

[14] The same holds for the chairman of some private club with no written rules, when he denounces the behaviour of a junior member, telling him "this is against the rules of our club".

[15] HLA Hart, above n 12, pp 89–96.

law today may not be accepted tomorrow, and vice versa. The societal acceptance of a legal system is not a matter of some belief in, or acceptance of, one single basic norm. There is some interaction between a formal acceptance of a legal
system, as institutionalised through its secondary rules, and an ideological
acceptance of the content of the outcome of the formal procedures. Neither of
them will suffice for the acceptance of a legal system. If, eg, courts would decide
that all rules enacted by the Pope of Rome would henceforth be part of the legal
system, they would never really become part of the legal system, because of the
non-acceptance of the court's decision in society for reasons of the content of
that decision, even if the formal power of the courts to determine legal rules is
fully accepted. If, on the other hand, the Pope of Rome were to decide that
European rules have supremacy over domestic rules of the state legal systems
within the European Union, his decision would not be considered to be part of
the national system either, for formal reasons: the Pope is not empowered to
change the law or to take authoritative decisions about the law of European
Member States. The fact that the content of his "decision" would be generally
accepted will not suffice.

3.3.2 Sociological Institutionalisation

The "sociological institutionalisation" of the law refers to the acceptance of the
legal system by the people to whom it is meant to apply. From the point of view
of the legal system, it is the efficacy of the law which is in question.

Even those scholars who have tried to separate norm and fact, *Sein* and
Sollen, the normative validity of legal rules and their actually being followed,
could not escape this factual, sociological question. So, Kelsen stated that

> "(scientific) jurisprudence regards a legal norm as valid only if it belongs to a legal
> order that is by and large efficacious; that is, if the individuals whose conduct is regu-
> lated by the legal order in the main actually do conduct themselves as they should
> according to the legal order".[16]

Any theory about the nature of law should indeed have a criterion to distinguish purely fictitious legal systems from "real" ones. Or, to put it in another
way, we conclude that in common usage the terms "law" or "legal system"
always refer to some normative system which has (had) at least some effective
functioning. If someone says "that's the law!" (s)he will always be speaking
about a legal system in force, not about some fictitious normative system. The
consequence is that we need some criterion or criteria to define the minimum
conditions under which a legal system may be considered to be sociologically
institutionalised, ie to be efficacious and to be accepted in society.

---

[16] H Kelsen, *What is justice?* (University of California Press, Berkeley, 1960), p 268.

That minimum degree of efficacy, as an element for defining the law, is generally seen as the requirement that most rules of the legal system be generally practised.[17] This point of view, however, entails several problems.

First, one has to decide which rules belong to the legal system and which ones do not. This is actually very hard to determine as it is related both to the question of the sources of law (eg unwritten general principles of law) and to the whole problem of interpretation of the law.

Secondly, even if this identification problem could be solved, it would be very difficult to measure the degree to which the rules were being practised: a very large sociological inquiry would be necessary for each rule.

Lastly, in order to conclude that a legal system is efficacious, and therefore that it exists, it would be necessary to agree upon a minimum degree of efficacy to be satisfied by an agreed minimum number of rules. Such agreement would be difficult, if not impossible, to achieve. Would one have to give more weight eg to rules of marriage, contract, murder, theft, than eg to traffic rules? And if so, to what extent?

It should be clear that the "existence" of a legal system cannot be determined in this way, by the multiplication of x per cent of the rules being practised at an average of y per cent.

On the other hand, one intuitively feels that some degree of being "in force" is required, in order to differentiate between some "real" legal system and some imaginary system, considered "legal" by some writer or lunatic.

The point is that the efficacy of a legal system is something other than the sum of the efficacy of the legal rules it contains. A legal system may be in force, even if a large number of its rules are disregarded (eg when there is a great deal of delinquency, tax evasion, traffic offences, etc). Efficacy relates to the efficacy of the legal institutions, of the secondary rules of a legal system and not of the primary rules of conduct.

But what does it mean when one says that the secondary rules of a legal system are "generally practised"? It can only mean that some institutions and officials are generally recognised as having the power to make valid law or to make legally valid decisions. Thus we are much more at the level of (social) psychology than at the level of sociology, which creates further problems for empirical measurement. Some social psychological climate of belief in the existence and validity of a set of secondary rules is indeed necessary for the actual "existence" of a legal system. The minimum degree of acceptance required, however, can only be fixed somewhat arbitrarily.

The distinction between the extent to which rules of conduct are practised on the one hand, and the degree to which secondary rules are accepted on the other hand, also allows us to distinguish between a legal system and pure force. When asking "who controls society in southern Italy: the Mafia or the Italian state?", the answer will probably be: "the Mafia". However, the Italian legal system will

---

[17] See, eg, the quotation from Kelsen above.

generally be considered to be valid in the whole of Italy. Even when many of its primary rules of conduct do not seem to be followed very often, the Mafia cannot control the belief of the people in the validity of the secondary rules. The only power the Mafia has is to influence the conduct of people at the level of their compliance with primary rules. Even if the Mafia satisfies all the other criteria which define a legal system, it lacks a social psychological climate of acceptance of the secondary rules of this "legal system" (in contrast eg to nazi Germany, whose legal system also fulfilled this requirement).

So, we may conclude that the sociological institutionalisation of a legal system means the *generalised acceptance* in the society to which it applies,[18] *of the formal institutionalisation* as developed within the legal system.

3.3.3 Professional Institutionalisation

Professional institutionalisation is not a condition for the existence of a legal system. Functional institutionalisation suffices and is, in primitive or other more limited non-state legal systems, possible without any professional institutionalisation: the chieftain, acting as a judge, is in the first place the leader of the group; the members of a committee, which makes the rules within some sports club and/or has the power to make authoritative interpretations and applications of them, may all have their full-time professional activity outside the field of sports.

However, the degree of professional institutionalisation allows us to determine the level of development of legal systems.[19] A fully developed legal system embodies three categories of legal professions: professional law-makers (eg members of Parliament), professionals of the administration of justice (eg judges) and professionals of legal doctrine (eg legal academics).[20] Each category may also have different degrees of professionalisation. International law, for example, has a high professionalisation of legal doctrine, but a low one as regards law-making and law-applying: treaties are generally drafted by professionals from state legal systems; courts, such as war tribunals, are often made ad

---

[18] The recognition by other groups, societies, states is as such irrelevant, but it is obvious that such a (non)recognition may strongly influence the (non)acceptance within the society concerned.

[19] Interesting analyses on this point have been offered by Max Weber, for whom a legal profession, including scholarly, doctrinal work, is typical of most developed legal systems (M Weber, *Wirtschaft und Gesellschaft* (JCB Mohr, Tübingen, 1972), pp 503–13, esp. at p 504.

[20] As a jurisprudent one would be tempted to add a fourth (and of course highest) level of professionalisation: professional scholars in jurisprudence. Unfortunately, however, this is not possible. The three abovementioned categories of legal professionals have a direct influence on the content of the law. They are part of the legal system concerned, they are "sources of the law". Theorists and philosophers of law, from their side, study law from an external point of view. Their writings are not exclusively linked to some specific legal system, as is the case for the three other professions. They do not, as such, co-determine the content of the law within any legal system (although they may have an influence on other law professionals; but this is not substantially different from the way non-lawyers may have such an influence).

hoc, with people who are not professional judges of other international courts, and even not professional judges in another legal system. Roman law had a rather high level of professionalisation of the adjudication of the law and of legal doctrine, but a low one as regards law-making. Some international sports organisations may have a rather developed professionalisation as regards the power to enact rules and to decide cases, but there is a complete absence of a professional legal doctrine.

In general, only modern state legal systems have a fully developed professional institutionalisation at those three levels.[21] But there are notable exceptions: the ecclesiastic legal system of the Roman Catholic church also has a highly professionalised staff for the creation and the adjudication of the law, and for canon law doctrine as well.

A characteristic of developed legal systems is the professionalisation of legal scholarship in schools of law, as a rather elaborate legal doctrine is an essential condition for such a development.

3.4 LAW AND STATE

The concept of law is often closely linked to a concept of a centralised state, it being considered to be the only source of law.[22] Both changes in practice[23] and changes in theory[24] have greatly weakened the position of these theories. At the level of theory, studies in legal anthropology and sociology, discussions on international law, and the like, have convinced many lawyers that one should adopt a more pluralist approach to law.[25]

---

[21] For differences *among* developed legal systems, related to the different position of the legal professions, most notably English common law when compared to continental law, see Weber, above n 19, pp 509–10 and RC van Caenegem, *Judges, Legislators and Profesors. Chapters in European legal history* (Cambridge University Press, Cambridge, 1987).

[22] Most notably Hans Kelsen (*Pure Theory of Law* (University of California Press, Berkeley and Los Angeles, 1967), pp 279–319), for whom any idea of dualism between law and State was considered wrong (see esp. at pp 318–19), let alone a pluralism of legal orders within one and the same territory (p 315).

[23] As for pluralist developments in Europe, see especially: AJ Arnaud, *Pour une pensée juridique européenne* (Presses Universitaires de France, Paris, 1991).

[24] Benoît Frydman rightly notes that the current views as to the pillars of modernity, ie individual liberty, equality, democracy and the rule of law, have one point in common: the state has lost its central role; law is no longer seen as the law of the State: economic approaches take a more globalised position, communitarian theories concentrate on homogeneous communities with common values and a common project, whereas procedural theories emphasise the importance of the civil society, also in a more globalised framework (B Frydman, *Les transformations du droit* (Story-Scientia, Brussels, 1999), p 97)

[25] See eg J Griffiths, "What is Legal Pluralism?", (1986) 1 *Journal of Legal Pluralism and Unofficial Law* 1–55(38); F Rigaux, "Le droit au singulier at au pluriel", (1982) 9 *Revue interdisciplinaire d'études juridiques* 1–61; B de Sousa Santos, "Droit: une carte de la lecture déformée. Pour une conception post-moderne du droit", (1988) 10 *Droit et société*, 1988 363–390; R Verdier, "Le droit au singulier at au pluriel. Juridicité et cultures juridiques", (1990) *Droits* 73–76; J Gijssels, *Recht, ruim bekeken* (Kluwer Rechtswetenschappen, Antwerp, 1991).

At the level of political developments, one could think of human rights discussions, and especially in Europe, of the rise of some idea of "state pluralism" within one and the same territory. National states have lost some of their powers by decentralising and giving more autonomy to provinces, regions or otherwise (ie not necessarily territorially) defined cultural entities. On the other hand, parts of, traditionally national, sovereignty have been transferred to the EU level.

Thus the central position of the state has been greatly weakened. Since they are no longer closely linked to a centralised state, legal systems can hardly still claim to be supreme and comprehensive.[26] National legal systems are no longer supreme when they are bound by decisions of larger legal systems (eg the European Union). Nor can the European Union be considered to be supreme since it still has limited power and is certainly not yet a European super-state. Moreover, a voluntary, even partial, withdrawal (eg as regards the Maastricht Treaty) from the EU still seems to be possible for each of the Member States at any time. Nor are these legal systems comprehensive: economic life is governed by the EU, military affairs are national matters, cultural affairs, eg in Belgium, are a regional matter (eg the national Belgian Parliament no longer has the power to interfere in education).

National and international sports organisations, organised minorities, churches, etc are increasingly seen as legal systems in their own right. When in conflict with "national" legal systems there is a practical problem of power rather than a theoretical problem of normative hierarchy. It is becoming increasingly accepted that the opportunity to form a contract is prior to a legal system, rather than derived from it—just as, in international law, treaties may be "valid" without reference to some international "state".

International law is fully "law", without an international state, without international government, because it is an institutionalised normative system, although it is institutionalised to a lower degree than national legal systems. All theories linking law to some state organisation have problems with the concept of "international law". Either it is considered not to be law at all, or, at best, it is defined as an "incomplete" legal system for as long as there is not a "world state".

Of course, until now state legal systems are by far the most complete ones, in that they cover almost all aspects of societal life and have the most advanced institutionalisation. This stronger institutionalisation is not to be found at the level of the *formal,* or functional, institutionalisation. The existence of structures and procedures for the creation and the adjudication of the law, besides the primary rules of conduct, can be seen as typical for every kind of legal system and as part of its definition.

The *sociological institutionalisation* allows us to distinguish most state legal systems from, eg, Mafia "legal systems", but, in practice, some state legal systems

---

[26] Two of the three features which according to Raz would characterise legal systems (J Raz, *Practical Reason and Norms* (Princeton University Press, Princeton, 1990), pp 150–54).

are not different from them, in that they almost completely rely on pure coercion to be accepted in practice. On the other hand, international law or numerous sub-state legal systems are sociologically institutionalised as well, and often without any coercion.

The difference in fact lies at the level of *professional institutionalisation*. State legal systems have the most advanced professional institutionalisation, most prominently as regards legal doctrine. But even here, it cannot be used as a clear cut criterion, as appears from the above example of canon law.

So, ultimately, there seems to be no criterion available which could allow us to limit the concept of "legal system" to state legal systems. Moreover, there is no reason why we should try to do so. Once we have a definition of "state" we can automatically distinguish between both types of legal systems. On the other hand, we should take into account the common usage of the concept of "law". If everybody calls international law "law", then we have to construct a concept which is broad enough to encompass it, unless we have strong reasons for not doing so. Besides, we need a concept to cover both state law and all those normative systems which are very similar to it. Finally, it could also be argued that the concept of "state" is itself a legal concept,[27] necesssarily based on some, national or international, legal system. It does not offer an external criterion or concept, allowing us to grasp the concept of legal system from an external point of view.

The only way to achieve this last aim is to locate law in its societal context and to offer criteria which allow us to define certain kinds of structured social relations as "legal systems". Inevitably, this approach also leads to "legal pluralism", to a disconnection of law from state law:

> "Legal pluralism is a concomitant of social pluralism: the legal organization of society is congruent with its social organization", notes John Griffiths, and he adds: ". . . social action always take place in a context of multiple, overlapping 'semi-autonomous social fields', . . .".[28]

This brings us from a *legal* concept of "state", as a starting point for the definition of "law", to a *sociological* concept of "community". We come back to the old adage "*Ubi societas, ibi ius*" (which, in fact, had been restricted by many lawyers (and non-lawyers as well) to "*Ubi civitas, ibi ius*"). "*Societies*" were not seen as just any kind of community, but as the main political community within a given territory.

A much broader, and much more convincing, concept of "community" in relation to law is offered by John Finnis. According to him a community can be said to exist

---

[27] A Hägerström, *Inquiries into the Nature of Laws and Morals* (Almquist & Siksell, Uppsala, 1953), pp 101–2.
[28] J Griffiths, "What is Legal Pluralism?", (1986) 1 *Journal of Legal Pluralism and Unofficial Law* 38.

"wherever there is, over an appreciable span of time, a co-ordination of activity by a number of persons, in the form of interactions, and with a view to a shared objective".[29]

Finnis seems to limit the concept of legal system to "complete communities", in which "the initiatives and activities of individuals, of families, and of the vast network of intermediate associations" are co-ordinated.[30] Obviously, he has in mind a form of societal organisation which comes very close to a concept of state, but it is not a priori limited to the legal construct of a "state". Nevertheless, his definition of "community" seems to be a very appropriate starting point for defining legal systems. One could say that a legal system is an *"institutionalised community"*. The element of co-ordination in Finnis' definition already partly implies some functional (formal) institutionalisation, but not, as such, the distinction between primary rules of conduct, on the one hand, and secondary rules of structures and procedures, relating to the making and the adjudication of the law, on the other. The element of "a shared objective" clearly refers to a sociological institutionalisation. Maybe it is even somewhat too strong. In small communities, with a limited power to enforce the rules by coercion, such a shared objective will be necessary for the coming into being and the maintenance of the community, and, hence, of its legal system. In larger, more anonymous and more encompassing communities, the shared objectives might be very limited (maybe just the need for *some* societal organisation) and far from being shared by every member of it. In those cases, however, tradition, education, the lack of realistic alternatives and the knowledge that the legal system ultimately may use coercion, will strongly influence the actual acceptance of the legal system amongst (almost) all the members of the community.

In the taxonomy of Roger Cotterrell there are four ideal types of "community", which together encompass all the distinct types of collective involvement that can be components of community: (a) *traditional community*, with, sometimes accidental, habitual or traditional forms of interaction (eg, a linguistic community), (b) *instrumental community*, a community of interest, with a shared goal (eg, a sports club), (c) *community of belief*, with a sharing of beliefs or values that stress solidarity and interdependence (eg, a religious community), and (d) *affective community*, in which individuals are united by their mutual affection (eg, a family).[31]

We may assume that any concept of "affective community" is alien to the common conceptions of "legal system". Even if law regulates the working of such affective communities, it is not an "affective community" itself,[32] although

---

[29] J Finnis, *Natural Law and Natural Rights* (Oxford University Press, Oxford, 1980), p 153.

[30] Finnis, above n 29, p 147.

[31] R Cotterrell, "A Legal Concept of Community", (1997) 12 *Canadian Journal of Law and Society/Revue Canadienne Droit et Société* 80–81.

[32] It could be argued that they are rather opposites: when law has to intervene (eg, with a divorce), the affective community generally ends. Affective communities are based on mutual trust, with a complete lack of institutionalisation or coercion, whereas law is not only institutionalised, including some idea of coercion (see below 3.5), but also largely based on distrust of human behaviour.

affective positive feelings towards the law, the state, and the like, may be very useful for the efficacy of the law.

At least some shared beliefs and values are a necessary condition for the existence and working of all legal systems (eg, the acceptance of the power of legal bodies and officials, and of some shared ideology, such as an underlying common religious belief or human rights values). In that sense every legal system may be considered to be a "community of belief". However, whether this belief plays an important role or rather a weak one, it is never the core of the legal system, but only its (necessary) context. By definition, we only start to talk about law when it is *not* identical to religious or moral beliefs.

The two remaining ideal types of "community" are typical for different kinds of legal systems: "traditional community" for "primitive" legal systems, in which customary law prevails, "instrumental community" for current international legal orders, such as the European Union. However, these are ideal types. In practice, any legal system will be a combination of both: tradition and instrumentalism, historically developed rules and shared goals for which new rules are worked out. One of them may be very limited, but both will always be present.

We may conclude that the degree of conformity of a legal system with underlying communities of tradition, instrumentalism and/or belief will strenghten or weaken it to a considerable extent. Islamic legal systems, for instance, have often a strong position as they are generally firmly rooted in traditional and religious communities and may also largely share common goals of the society they govern. International legal orders, on the other hand, have a rather weak position, as they are to a large extent lacking underlying traditional communities and communities of belief, and sometimes even common interests (eg, United Nations, OPEC, etc). This explains part of the problems in the building of the European Union (eg, lack of linguistic community, but common Christian tradition, variety of goals and beliefs, but shared views on democracy, human rights and economy), but at the same time the history of the last few decades shows to what extent European law has succeeded in helping to *create* a "*European community*", with an enhanced feeling of common identity, common interests and shared beliefs and values.

The kind of community which, if institutionalised, forms a legal system, can also be defined as a "semi-autonomous field". Sally Moore specifies this "semi-autonomy" as the fact that the social field (or, in Finnis' terms, "community"):

"can generate rules and customs and symbols internally, but that it is also vulnerable to rules and decisions and other forces emanating from the larger world by which it is surrounded. The semi-autonomous field has rule-making capacities, and the means to induce or coerce compliance; but it is simultaneously set in a larger social matrix which can, and does, affect and invade it, sometimes at the invitation of persons inside it, sometimes at its own instance."[33]

[33] S Moore, *Law as Process: An Anthropological Approach* (Routledge & Kegan Paul, London, 1978), pp 55–56.

This is a very open and broad concept of the kinds of community which constitute legal systems. By including the elements of "rule-making capacities" and the "induction or coercion of compliance" it also contains a reference to the secondary rules of law-making and law-applying, but only a weak one: the lack of institutionalisation in it makes it impossible to distinguish law from other kinds of rules. The same objection applies to Griffiths' definition of law, which is based on Moore's analysis. He defines "law" as "the self-regulation of a semi-autonomous social field".[34] This definition could also apply to the moral code developed within such a community.[35]

But, even if these approaches to law are slightly too broad, they are at least closer to empirical reality than the ideologically determined linkage of law with state.[36]

If we understand by "community" the same kind of social relationship which Moore and Griffiths call "semi-autonomous field", we may conclude by defining "law" as *the institutionalised normative system of a community*.

A "community", here, is understood in a broader sense than a political community. It may also encompass any form of (a combination of) "traditional" and "instrumental" communities, in Cotterrell's terminology, eg, a cultural community, a leisure community, a scientific community, a religious community, etc. Nevertheless, the institutionalised normative system of a *political* community holds a privileged position among the legal systems. Political communities determine the debates about the basic organisation of society within a specific territory, including a basic choice of values and some common world view. Those communities are not only based on some common beliefs, they also play an important role in preserving, changing and creating such beliefs and values.

Apart from the abovementioned high degree of sociological and professional institutionalisation, state legal systems are characterised by the generalised acceptance of their having (a) the monopoly of legitimate military force within some territory, and (b) the power to structure the public political debate and to make choices, which are binding, not only for all persons, but also for all other legal systems, acting within their territory.

[34] Griffiths, above n 28, p 38.
[35] Griffiths considers that this self-regulation can be regarded as more or less "legal" according to the degree to which it is differentiated from the rest of the activities in the field and delegated to specialised functionaries (*ibid*, p 38). This also refers to some institutionalisation, albeit in a rather weak and vague sense. The point is that Griffiths does not agree with the view that "legal" and "non-legal" forms of social control are distinguishable types (*ibid*, 39, n 3 and J Griffiths, "The Division of Labor in Social Control" in D Black (ed), *Toward a General Theory of Social Control*, vol 1, *Fundamentals* (Academic Press, Orlando, 1984), pp 37–70). This point of view is partly due to an epistemological assumption: the belief in the possibility to construct theory purely on empirical observation. Insofar as this proves impossible, one may indeed say that many things may not clearly be distinguished from some other, similar things. But, as we need theory to describe and grasp reality, we partly construct this reality and thus we are in a position to "impose" some criteria on reality, thus distinguishing what, from another point of view, cannot be distinguished.
[36] Griffiths rightly states: "The idea that only the law of the state is law 'properly so called' is a feature of the ideology of legal centralism and has for empirical purposes nothing to be said for it." (above n 28, p 38).

By this, state legal systems have, as a rule, both the practical (military) power and principal competence to draw the limits of the competences of other legal systems. Because they are considered to represent the political community[37], it is commonly accepted that State legal systems have the competence of imposing legal values and legal principles on non-State legal systems, as, eg in the case of the circumcision of young children[38] or in the case of transfer of football players (eg the *Bosman* Case)[39].

The same holds true for international law, although it is, by definition, not linked with some "international state", to the extent that it is accepted to structure and to govern the *international political debate*.

3.5 LAW AND COERCION

The actual power to enforce legal rules by sanctions is often seen as an essential feature of legal systems. This approach is a variant of the one previously discussed, which emphasised the efficacy of the law. To the extent that legal officials can use sanctions to force people to follow the rules, efficacy seems to be guaranteed. But, as we have seen, the efficacy of the primary rules of conduct is not at all essential for the existence of a legal system.[40]

Are sanctions thus unimportant for legal systems? Obviously not. All legal systems ultimately rely on force. All state legal systems ultimately stay in power because they are backed by military force, even if this force is seldom used. The point is, that the ability of officials to use force, the power to impose sanctions, will strongly influence the general acceptance of the legal system in society, as long as it is not, amongst large parts of society, felt to be clearly an abuse of power and/or a means to impose unjust rules.

But still sanctions are not, as such, essential for a definition of law. Moreover, the concept of "sanction" used should be very weak. In international law, as in sub-state law (eg a sports club) the application of the rules often can not be enforced by adequate sanctions. Sometimes sanctions are rather weak, eg exclusion from a sports club or the breaking off of diplomatic relations, and sometimes they are completely lacking. Nevertheless, international law or other non-state legal systems are full legal systems, provided that their primary rules of conduct are backed, not in the first place by sanctions, but by a complete set of secondary rules providing structures and procedures for the adjudication of

---

[37] Raz points to the importance of law for constituting a political community. Rather than linking law to state, he prefers to link it to "political community". (J Raz, "On The Nature of Law", (1996) *ARSP* 7–9).

[38] M-C Foblets, "Salem's Circumcision: the Encounter of Cultures in a Civil Law Action. A Belgian Case-study" in *Living Law in the Low Countries*, Special issue of the Dutch and Belgian Law and Society Journal *Recht der Werkelijkheid*, 1991, pp 43–56. Foblets, however, is pleading for a more pluralist approach, with a culturally less dominating state law.

[39] C–415/93 *Bosman v KBVB, UEFA and RFC Liège*, 15 December 1995 (ECJ).

[40] See above 3.3.2.

the law. Following Austin we may say that sanctions, conceived in a very broad sense, are *analytically* essential to law, whether or not they are sociologically necessary or effective.[41]

When, eg, the law stipulates some conditions for the validity of a contract, this logically implies that a contract which does not fulfil all these conditions will be void. The "sanction" of not following the legal rules is the nullity of the contract.

But this is a conclusion at the level of the legal rules, not at the level of the legal system. Of course, insofar as every legal system, by definition, contains legal rules, it will necessarily always contain sanctions. But this does not imply that sanctions are structurally essential to legal *systems*. However, at this structural level, sanctions can also be considered essential to law, but again in an analytical sense. The secondary rules in any legal system offer the *possibility* to impose sanctions in a particular case, in order to guarantee compliance with the law. The question whether a court will indeed use these sanctions, or whether such sanctions will indeed make the person(s) concerned comply with the law, is irrelevant. The essential point is that structures and procedures, created for the adjudication of the law, structurally imply the sanctioning (in a broad sense) of breaches of the law.

It is often said that the sanctioning of a violation of the rules is typical of law, in contrast with other normative systems, especially morals. Yet, at the level of the (primary) rules of behaviour sanctions are analytically as essential to any normative system as they are to law. On the other hand, every societal normative system is backed by sanctions, be it some social disapproval, the exclusion from a community, or the threat of possible sanctions by some divine power. The only thing non-legal normative systems lack is an institutionalised organisation of this sanctioning activity. This, of course, makes law, as a rule, more effective than the other normative systems. But it is only a matter of degree, not a qualitative difference.

In a way, one could even doubt whether other systems of social norms are really less effective than law is in practice.

Rules of courtesy, for example, do not seem to be less followed than legal rules. Different forms of social influence and subtle sanctions achieve a high level of effectiveness (of these rules). The threat of divine sanctions by an omniscient God (or Gods) has a much more powerful influence over the behaviour of those who believe in it than any judicial, military or police machinery.

It is precisely because the "natural" social sanctioning of the law is so weak that it needs some institutionalised sanctioning system. When there is, within

---

[41] J Austin, "The Province of Jurisprudence Determined" (1832) reprinted in *The Province of Jurisprudence Determined and the Used of the Study of Jurisprudence* (Weidenfeld and Nicolson, London, 1955), pp 363–93 (at p 16). See, for an ananlysis of Austin's theory: R Cotterrell, *The Politics of Jurisprudence* (Butterworths, London 1989), pp 52–82, esp., as regards the aspect of coercion, pp 59–67.

the community to which the legal system applies, a large acceptance of this system, the legal system may be considered to be "effective", without having to bother about the actual effectiveness of the coercion used to force people to comply with the rules in every case.

Effective sanctioning, actual coercion, plays a limited role in law anyway. Most rules are in most cases spontaneously abided by, for different reasons.

In some cases people think that the behaviour imposed by the law is simply the way one should behave anyhow, even if there were no legal rules at all. For example, most people would never steal, even if no criminal act prohibited theft. This is a case of *complete acceptance*. No sanctions are needed, nor even legal rules explicitly regulating such a behaviour, at least as long as everybody in the community completely accepts the rule.

Some persons have a rather neutral attitude towards, for instance, tax legislation: they are prepared to pay taxes, assuming that the other people have comparable duties and are, in general, carrying them out. They *conditionally accept* the rules. They assume that some state organisation is necessary and that it requires a large amount of tax income to finance all the social services it is offering. Although they would prefer not to have to pay taxes, they agree that it is inevitable that everybody pays their contribution, in the right proportion to his means. If tax legislation is equitable and properly implemented, they are prepared to accept the rules. Here, the effective sanctioning of the *others*, when necessary, will be an essential criterion for the acceptance of the rules.

In a third category of cases, people do not share either of the previous views. Nevertheless, they do not, or almost never, evade taxes, break traffic rules, etc, for fear of penalties or other forms of punishment. Those people comply "willynilly" with tax rules. This is a case of *forced acceptance*. People will only follow tax rules, in this case, if there is adequate control and if appropriate sanctions are applied. Here the calculated risk of being punished oneself for breaking the rule is a condition for following it, together with the balance between the advantages of breaking the rule and the disadvantages of being sanctioned afterwards.

These are the three different types of acceptance of legal rules. In practice, the classification into one of those types will be a matter of degree. Moreover, the different positions will influence each other. An example is furnished by the frequency of bicycle theft in student towns or university campuses. The effectiveness of the prohibition of theft is in this case often very close to zero. Some of the thieves are "honest" students whose bicycles have been repeatedly stolen in the past, without ever getting them back or receiving any news from the police. The ineffectiveness of coercion towards others directly influences the attitude of the victim towards the rule and even his or her moral attitude. "Borrowing" someone's bicycle is hardly considered to be "theft".[42] All bicycles seem to have

---

[42] Certainly not when even police officers suggest solving the problem this way—and this is the answer students sometimes get when they complain to the police.

become some common property. If someone has already contributed to this "bicycle patrimony" by buying three or more bicycles, which are stolen but still "somewhere" available, he might consider himself entitled to make free use of this "common patrimony". This student will also start to calculate the chances of being caught and sanctioned himself. In the end he will drop most moral scruples and behave in a purely utilitarian way.[43]

But this example is obviously an exception. In most cases a large majority of the members of the community concerned accept the rules in one of those three ways: completely, conditionally or forced. In each of these cases the individual will feel bound by the rules and the rule will, to a large extent, be efficacious.

This efficacy is partly, but only partly, due to some coercion. The real coercion influences the belief of people in the potential coercion that could be exercised in other cases. Both are strongly influenced by the existence of institutionalised structures and procedures for the adjudication of the law. The sheer existence of courts, of police, of administrative control, of prisons, etc will already have served to create a belief in the power of the legal system to enforce its rules.

We must also mention the cases in which people do not as such comply with the rules in one of those three ways, but simply happen to conform with them, for other reasons, which are not linked with those rules.

Very often people abstain from criminal acts, not because they consciously back the rule which prohibits them or because of fear for sanctions, but simply because they do not see any advantage in committing such an act (eg hijacking an airplane), or because it is too complicated (eg setting up an international network of fictitious companies for organising tax fraud). Most criminal acts never would be committed by most people even without legal prohibition and independent of moral reasons, but just because of differing practical reasons. Even somebody who would try to commit *all* acts prohibited by his legal system probably never would succeed in doing so in his lifetime.[44] Inevitably he would conform to at least some rules, without complying with them in any way.

For positive acts, imposed by some legal duty, on the other hand, this legal rule will generally be the most important reason for acting in conformity with this rule. Although even here, other reasons may make a person conform with legal duty than those underlying the rule or because of fear for sanctions. Somebody could, for instance, decide to pay a debt, not because of moral reasons or because of fear for a trial (as he knows that his creditor could never prove

---

[43] Fortunately for him, every year there is a new generation of students, most of them "naive" bicycle owners. Otherwise it would be a nice example of "free-rider" which inevitably, according to the economic analysis of law, would lead to a slow disappearance of bicycles from the streets: nobody would be willing to buy a bicycle, everybody would try to steal one; and as a consequence no new bicycles would enrich the town.

[44] Even if he were to limit his ambition to offences which may be committed by any citizen and which are not linked to some specific profession or other social position. It is obvious that one could never take all such positions in a lifetime.

the existence of the debt), but because of economic calculation: he wants to keep good commercial relations with this creditor. In practice, such reasons play an important role. If they are not always the decisive ones, they often function as additional reasons for complying with the legal duty.

3.6 THE AUTONOMY OF LAW

Legal systems, unlike, for example, mathematical systems, are not independent from the society to which they apply and which they organise. Each legal system forms part of a more general system of society. A legal system is a way of organising social, economic, moral, and other patterns of behaviour. Thus, legal systems must fit with society. To a certain extent, legal systems are a form of translation of social structures and social relations. When analysing the nature of law or when applying and interpreting law, one should take this functional nature of law into account.

This dependency of law raises questions of legitimacy. The problem of social, economic, moral, philosophical, etc legitimation of law is directly linked to this lack of autonomy towards society. It also implies that some autolegitimation of legal systems is impossible, as long as one is talking about real legal systems.

Although embedded in society and strongly determined by it, modern legal systems are actually relatively autonomous systems. But, if law is intertwined to such an extent with society, with all different kinds of human interaction, how could law be "autonomous"? To answer this question, we have to distinguish between "formal" and "substantive" autonomy of legal systems; between autonomy "as a system", on the one hand, and autonomy in determining the content of the rules, on the other. First, we will discuss the formal autonomy of legal systems and afterwards their substantive autonomy as regards other legal and non-legal systems and data.

3.6.1 Formal Autonomy

(a) Circularity

According to traditional legal theory, following the approach of Hans Kelsen, legitimation is approached as a linear process, in which, step by step, a rule or a decision is based on a higher rule, until some "basic norm" is reached, which has to be introduced in order to stop a *regressus ad infinitum*. This theoretical approach entails considerable problems, mainly related to the status of that "basic norm". Moreover, it does not fit very well with legal reality. Today, legal systems have more and more a circular structure when it comes to legitimation.

"Circularity" means that the higher norms within the hierarchy of a legal system not only determine the lower ones, but also in turn, are determined by these lower ones. An example, given by Gunther Teubner, is the "fiction theory of the legal person", "according to which the State as a legal person must, like Münchhausen, pull itself up by its own bootstraps by reinventing itself".[45] He, rightly, notes that this is not an error or a failure of the legal system. This circular paradox is an essential feature of law and of reality in general.[46] Including it in a theory of law is not only accceptable, but even a productive and heuristically valuable practice.[47]

Legal practice offers, indeed, more and more examples of circularity. A first one is the hierarchy of law within the European Union. Institutions of the EU[48] have the power to impose rules and decisions on Member States, but the whole Union is based on the treaties agreed upon by these states and from which, in principle, they could withdraw at any time. Furthermore, these Member States participate directly in the creation of the European rules, with members of their respective governments constituting the European Council of Ministers, which is the main formal legislator in the EU. Thus, European law determines state law, state law determines European law: a perfect circularity.

A second example is the balance of power between the legislature and the judiciary. According to the view in nineteenth century continental Europe, there was a clear hierarchy according to which the judiciary was completely subordinated to the legislature and should rightly be so. Today, we see an increasing emergence of courts exercising the power to repeal legislation and to force the legislature to change the law. The European Court of Human Rights, the European Court of Justice, together with the administrative and constitutional courts within most states, have the power to impose on legislatures their views on law and their interpretation of international treaties and national constitutions. The legislator determines the limits of judicial law-making, but in turn the judiciary determines the limits of legislative law-making: another perfect circularity.

In this circular way, legal systems partly (but only partly) legitimate themselves, eg, approval of an Act by a constitutional court legitimates the law created by the legislator, whereas this court derives its power, and thus the legitimacy of its decisions, from the (constitutional) legislator. This is not only a circular process, but also a communicative one. Legislation is submitted to courts for approval or disapproval, the reasons for such an approval or disapproval will, in turn, mainly be found in legislation. If court decisions bear the risk of endangering governmental policy, the government will react by changing legislation in order to prevent similar court decisions in the future. However, if

---

[45] G Teubner, *Law as an Autopoietic system* (Blackwell,Oxford, 1993), p 5 and "Münchhausen Jurisprudence", (1986) 5 *Rechtshistorisches Journal* 350–56, 351. See also: M van de Kerchove and F Ost, *Legal System Between Order and Disorder* (Oxford University Press, Oxford, 1994), pp 65–72.

[46] *Law as an Autopoietic System*, above n 45, pp 10 and 11.

[47] *Ibid*, p 9.

[48] European Commission, European Council of Ministers, European Court of Justice.

this new legislation does not fit in every respect with the basic rules and principles (Constitution, European Convention on Human Rights) of the legal system, the court, having the power to annul such legislation, might do so. The importance of such phenomena is broader than conferring autonomy on the legal system through its circular closure, they also confer a certain degree of legitimation through the communicative action and argumentation they embody. Even if this legitimation is considered to be only a prima facie one, it reinforces the legal system's autonomy by allowing it to function in daily practice without reference to non-legal sources, values or norms.

(b) Operative Closure and Cognitive Openness

Autopoietic theory has made the useful distinction between "operative closure" and "cognitive openness" of legal systems.[49] The (legal) system, to a certain extent, determines its own elements (the content of the rules), but only to a certain extent. Social facts, values and norms are selected and translated into "legal" facts, values and norms. Reality can only be described by selecting and structuring an immense flow of chaotic elements. For describing and ordering social reality, it is thus necessary for a legal system to select and to order social facts, values and norms. In a way, there is nothing exceptional about this requirement, it is a necessary condition for a legal system to exist. But the basic or raw material comes, to a very large extent, from outside the legal system. As a completely closed system, a legal system simply could not exist. Legal systems are thus "cognitively" open to the external world. However, they remain "autonomous", because they are "operatively" closed: external data are selected and adapted according to an internal logic of the legal system:

"Self-reproduction presupposes that the system is influenced by its environment. Both external and internal factors influence the way a system reproduces itself by extracting and constituting, as it were, new elements from the flow of events, which it then uses by linking them up selectively".[50]

"As soon as legal communications on the fundamental distinction between legal and illegal begin to be differentiated from general social communication, they inevitably become self-referential, and are forced to consider themselves in terms of legal categories . . . The law is forced to describe its components using its own categories. It begins to establish norms for its own operations, structures, processes, boundaries and environments—indeed, for its own identity. When it actually uses these self-descriptions, it has begun to constitute its own components. This leads to the emergence of self-referential circles in relation to legal acts, legal norms, legal process, and legal dogmatics, with the result that the law becomes increasingly 'autonomous'. The law itself determines which presuppositions must be present before one can speak of a legally relevant event, a valid norm, and so forth. Law begins to reproduce itself in

[49] Teubner, *Law as an Autopoietic System*, above n 45, p 65.
[50] *Ibid*, p 21.

the strict sense of the word if its self-referentially organized components are linked in such a way that norms and legal acts produce each other reciprocally and process and dogmatics establish some relationship between these. It is only when the components of the cyclically organized system interact in this way that the legal hypercycle becomes possible".[51]

"Legal autonomy thus refers not only to law's capacity to generate its own order, but also to the self-constitutions of legal actions, the regulation of processes, and the invention of new schemata in legal dogmatics."[52]

Teubner has laid emphasis on the essential role of human agents in the legal system and on the "cognitive openness" of legal systems: their constant interaction and communication with the non-legal world. But, to what extent then can legal systems be said to be "autonomous" if they cannot exist at all without human agents and without an external world "feeding" them?

(c) Types of "Autonomy"

In a very weak sense "autonomy" merely means that a legal rule, or a legal system, can be *identified* as something that is different from morals, religion or other systems of rules and that it is not just a restatement of any set of non-legal rules. Even if the legal system is to a large extent based on such a set, as for example, is Islamic law on the Koran, it changes and adapts these rules from some other perspective, more specifically to some inner logic. This *minimum substantive autonomy* is essential for a (legal) system simply to exist as an identifiable system.

The presence of secondary rules of change and adjudication guarantee the *institutional autonomy* of legal systems. This institutional autonomy has two aspects: a *formal autonomy* (own institutions) and a *procedural autonomy* (own procedures for law-making and for its adjudication). In developed legal systems this institutional autonomy is strengthened by the *professional autonomy* of most people dealing with the creation or the application of the law.

This runs parallel to a *methodological autonomy*, which contains two aspects, namely:

(a) *autonomy of language*: a technical legal language is developed, creating its own concepts and giving a specific meaning to words used in everyday language;
(b) it also encompasses an *autonomy of style*: statutes, judgments, contracts, and the like are drafted in a specific way;
(c) *autonomy of argumentation*: the kinds of reasoning and arguments accepted in law are different from those in other forms of discourse (eg, economic, political or religious discourse).

---

[51] Teubner, *Law as an Autopoietic System*, above n 45, p 33.
[52] *Ibid*, p 34.

An advanced professional and methodological autonomy leads to a *doctrinal autonomy*. The development of its own legal doctrine is an important element for the autonomy of legal systems towards other legal systems. International law or Canon law are more autonomous because they have a legal doctrine of their own. Sub-state communities, like sports clubs, are less autonomous, partly because they lack any legal doctrine of their own.

A minimum degree of substantive and methodological autonomy, together with an institutional autonomy, are common to all legal systems. More advanced legal systems acquire a higher level of autonomy to the extent that they develop each of the elements contributing to their autonomy: content (legal rules derived from other legal rules and principles), language, argumentation, legal profession and legal doctrine.

In such a development, another type of autonomy is brought about: an *autonomy as regards legitimation*. The more sophisticated legal systems are, the more circular they become and the more legitimation of rules and of decisions is possible *within* the legal system, and the legal system as a whole may increasingly succeed in legitimising itself. At least it offers prima facie legitimation, which will only be endangered if there are *strong* non-legal reasons for attacking it (eg, the clearly immoral character of substantive parts of the nazi legal system). Legitimation is more and more worded in *legal* terms and refers to *legal* sources and principles. It becomes more and more circular within a legal discourse. This circularity may limit itself to one and the same legal system, as in the example given above of legislature and judiciary legitimising each other. But it is interesting to note that there is some circularity within the legal discourse across the borders of individual legal systems. Legal systems are legitimised by reference to other legal systems: international law by reference to national law, sub-state law by reference to state law and to international law (eg, recognising the rights of minorities), law of the Member States of the EU by reference to the law of the European Union.

This conclusion leads to a fundamental question: is it the legal system which can be considered "autonomous", or is it rather the "legal discourse"? Or to put it another way, what kind of "system" has really started to live a life of its own, with relative independence from its human agents and the external world? Is it a mechanism of legal structures, procedures and rules which, to a certain extent, is living its own life, or is it a legal discourse, as developed within the legal structures and professions? As the autopoietic legal theorists allege, the components of all social systems, including legal systems, are communications, and not individual beings. Society is not a bio-system but a system of meaning, produced through communications.[53] As regards law, those communications obviously use a legal discourse. But this discourse is to a large extent common to all, or at least several, legal systems. Legal language, legal argumentation and legal doctrine are considerably similar for many legal systems. Moreover, legal systems

---

[53] *Ibid*, pp 29–30, with reference to Luhmann.

happen to be intertwined, both at the level of rules and principles (eg the European Convention on Human Rights and its impact on European state legal systems) and at the level of institutions and procedures (members of national governments constituting together the European Council of Ministers, the European Court of Human Rights having the power to annul state legislation and the oppurtunity and obligation to ask preliminary opinions of the European Court of Justice within the frame of a purely domestic trial, etc). In the end, it becomes very difficult to talk about "autonomy" of legal systems towards each other. When legal systems are producing and maintaining each other, when they strongly influence and partly, or even sometimes completely, determine the content of each others structures and procedures, where then is the autonomy? How could we speak of "autopoietic", autonomous legal systems? Could we not see legal systems in the world today as being just dialects of one common legal language, variants of one common legal discourse? But, if this is correct, we have to analyse the autonomy of law in a way different from that of autopoietic theory.

For the purpose of argument, it is possible and it may be useful to distinguish form from content, ie to make a distinction between the formal structure of legal systems and the content of the rules they produce. But, if one may conceptually conceive of such a distinction, one should be aware of the fact that form and content are actually intertwined and not completely separated from each other. The question of the formal autonomy of legal systems cannot be completely answered without linking it to the question of their substantive autonomy.

3.6.2 Substantive Autonomy

(a) Which Kind of Autonomy?

The content given to the rules in legislation, the interpretation of the law by civil officers, judges and individuals when applying it, or by legal doctrine when describing and structuring the law, are undoubtedly, to a (very) large extent determined by non-legal facts, values and norms. Legal systems are not autonomous in this sense. They receive, and need, an input from outside the system. The substantive autonomy only lies in the fact that the legal system selects and "translates" this external data. It is converted and assimilated in order to fit within the system of legal language and legal principles of the legal system concerned. In fact, this is a kind of formal autonomy, allowing only some marginal change as to content. The essence of the content of the law comes from outside the legal system.

Sometimes, officials who work within the legal system having some power to decide on the application of the law, eg civil officers or judges, have a rather "autopoietic" view of law. They consider law to be cognitively closed from the external world, to be "self-referring", "self-regulating", "self-reflexive", "self-productive", in short, autopoietic, not in a Teubnerian sense, but in a literal one.

This is the kind of kafkaian bureaucracy which to a certain extent runs parallel to the development of advanced legal systems. Here, rules are indeed interpreted as if they would loosen their links with the non-legal world and start their own, new life within the legal system and only according to the mechanism of that system. In fact, legal systems could not function in a reasonable way if they were to solely take from the "outside world" that which they can use and assimilate acording to their own systemic rules. The relation of legal systems with the external world is one of constant communication, not of one-way information. This communication appears most prominently in the interpretation of the law by courts, where the concrete facts of the case, its specific circumstances, some-times changed societal views and other factors, may influence the outcome in a very decisive way. This communication is so intensive, this "cognitive open-nesss" is so prevalent, that any concept of "self-production" of the law by the legal system is necessarily a very fragile one. The legal system "producing" rules just means that the rules are technically adapted to fit into the legal system and so warrant the label "legal". But this is an extremely weak form of "autonomy".

In a way, one could argue that advanced legal systems have acquired a higher degree of substantive autonomy in that they have produced "legal values" which are not derived from non-legal values. A typical example is "procedural" rights, as recognised in Article 6 of the European Convention on Human Rights.[54] These are human rights related to secondary rules of legal systems: minimum guarantees for a fair trial. They refer to values which make no sense except within legal systems. In this way, secondary rules do not only considerably strengthen the institutional autonomy of legal systems but also their substantive autonomy. But are these really "internal values"? Procedural values may have a larger scope than the legal one. In Karl Heinz Ladeur's proceduralist view on

---

[54] Article 6 of the European Convention on Human Rights:

"1. In the determination of his civil rights and obligations or of any criminal charge against him, everyone is entitled to a fair and public hearing within a reasonable time by an independent and impartial tribunal established by law. Judgment shall be pronounced publicly but the press and public may be excluded from all or part of the trial in the interest of morals, public order or national security in a democratic society, where the interests of juveniles or the protection of the private life of the parties so require, or to the extent strictly necessary in the opinion of the court in special circumstances where publicity would prejudice the interests of justice.
2. Everyone charged with a criminal offence shall be presumed innocent until proved guilty according to law.
3. Everyone charged with a criminal offence has the following minimum rights:
   (a) to be informed promptly, in a language which he understands and in detail, of the nature and cause of the accusation against him;
   (b) to have adequate time and facilities for the preparation of his defence;
   (c) to defend himself in person or through legal assistance of his own choosing or, if he has not sufficient means to pay for legal assistance, to be given it free when the interests of justice so require;
   (d) to examine or have examined witnesses against him and to obtain the attendance and examination of witnesses on his behalf under the same conditions as witnesses against him;
   (e) to have the free assistance of an interpreter if he cannot understand or speak the language used in court."

law, very general procedural values are emphasised: keeping open a variety of options; tolerating and making possible a variety of opinions; making a variety of language games mutually accessible and guaranteeing interchangeability among them by breaking up self-reinforcing discourses.[55] All those values have a broad scope, including the ideological and political fields. Thus, procedural values are not by definition "internal" legal values. What is required is to put limits to the arbitrary use and kafkaian working of legal systems. It should prevent, on the one hand, the abuse of law as a legal facade for covering clearly immoral, unjust acts. On the other, it should prevent legal systems from becoming fully autopoietic, from running wild as a system, from losing contact with their societal reasons for existence and sense, from using human beings as simple means for the structural aims of the system.

Can we say that legal systems are "autopoietic" to the extent that they "spontaneously" limit themselves? Of course, from the point of view of the autopoietic theory, we can. But what does this mean?

We could compare this situation to one of a slave, who, as an autopoietic being, is able to adapt to the environment, who is able to remain autonomous in that he or she takes and assimilates a limited number of elements from the chaotic flow of inputs from the external world. As such, the slave takes "autonomously" the decision to behave as a slave and to comply, as a rule, with all the commands of the master, even if they are unpleasant, humiliating, unjust or unreasonable. It will not be possible to use a young child as a slave, because it cannot understand the commands and it cannot decide "autonomously" to abide by them. If one shouts at a baby in an attempt to make it stop crying, it will cry even harder. The same will happen if one beats the child. Threats will have no influence at all. In a way, the child is the "master" and the person responsible for caring for it at any given moment will be its "slave". However, as a system, it will be much more difficult for the baby to survive autonomously than it is for an average adult. Unlike autopoietic systems, it lacks "self-observation", "self-reference", "self-description", "self-reflexivity" and it is rather closed to the external world, with which only very limited comunication is possible for it. The adult, however, is able to communicate much better with the outside world and to act "independently" in accordance with the results of all communications assimilated by him or her. Exactly because (s)he is a full autopoietic system, (s)he can be a slave. It is because (s)he is "autonomous", that (s)he may have, to a large extent, no autonomy at all.

If we can word our conclusion in this paradoxical form, it proves that we are talking about different types of "autonomy". The "autonomy" of human beings or legal systems as autopoietic systems does not refer to the kind of autonomy we have in mind when talking about "autonomous individuals" or "autonomous legal systems".

---

[55] K-H Ladeur, "Prozedurale Rationalität—Steigerung der Legitimationsfähigkeit oder der Leistungsfähigkeit des Rechtssystems?", (1986) 7 *Zeitschrift für Rechtssoziologie* 265–74 at p 273.

It is somewhat awkward to say that the autonomy of a human being enables him to be a slave or that the autonomy of a legal system allows it to be dependent on morals or any other ideology.

Systemic "autonomy" just refers to the identity of the system as such, to its ability to communicate with the external world and to assimilate the information received from it. A high level of communication implies a large influence from outside. The lower the systemic "autonomy", the higher the autonomy as to content: the rules of a card game or of chess are not at all influenced by morals; as regards the content of their rules, these games are much more autonomous than legal systems are. The higher the systemic autonomy, the lower the autonomy as to content. This is the apparent paradox of autopoietic autonomy: the more legal systems are developed and autonomous in a systemic way, the less their autonomy for determining their content.

(b) Degree of Autonomy

In order to analyse the degree of substantive autonomy of legal systems, we have to distinguish between different situations. On the one hand, the link between legal systems differs from their links with all other types of societal system. On the other, the influence from the external world may go deeper than just the level of the primary levels of conduct, and may also partly determine the secondary rules.

(i) Autonomy vis-à-vis Other Legal Systems

As we have argued above, there is a circularity, not only within legal systems, but also amongst legal systems mutually: eg international law is based on state law, but in some cases, state law is derived from supranational law (eg, the European Union or the European Convention on Human Rights). This circularity makes legal systems dependent upon each other. The "collective" gain of autonomy vis-à-vis the economic, political, or other systems and discourses is at the price of a loss of autonomy towards each other. Here, one could also state that the decrease of autonomy vis-à-vis other legal systems increases the autonomy towards the non-legal systems. The primitive legal system of some isolated tribe will be completely autonomous towards all other legal systems, but it will have a very limited autonomy vis-à-vis other societal systems such as morals, religion, the economy etc. Modern legal systems have gained more autonomy in this regard, but lost a great deal of autonomy towards each other. Even at the high point for relatively isolated, centralised nation-states in the nineteenth century, there was a mutual level of legal interdependency. State legal systems cannot exist without at least some official recognition by other States.[56] They need

[56] The legal position as non-state of the South-African "thuisland"–"states", under the Apartheid regime is a good example; being officially recognised by the white South African Government only, these "states" failed to function as a state. They in practice remained decentralised regions within the South African state, but were not real state legal systems on their own.

each other to make, to develop and to enforce international law. Even if international private law has, until recently, always been exclusively national law, it contains rules of reference to other legal systems, thus incorporating "by delegation" the private law of, in principle all, other state legal systems into the domestic legal system.

Non-state legal systems, like national or international sports associations, generally employ some state law to acquire the status of a "legal person" under this state law. When drafting their constitution and rules, they borrow legal concepts from a legal doctrine which is linked to state law. As a corollary, they will also have to take account of fundamental rules and principles of the state legal system(s) in the territory in which they operate, and they will have to comply with basic rights as laid down in international treaties, such as the European Convention on Human Rights, which are enforceable within that same territory.

There is not only an interrelationship between legal systems as regards their very existence and content, but also a community of legal language, style, argumentation, in short a community of legal discourse, running parallel with the development of legal doctrine and of the communication amongst legal systems and amongst lawyers in general. This sometimes very strong community, as, eg with continental European state legal systems, in its turn weakens the autonomy of legal systems towards each other. Language, style and argumentation are not just a matter of form, they hide concepts and world views. For example, distinguishing between "*dominium*", "*possessio*" and "*detentio*" creates another kind of legal reality as regards ownership than when other concepts are used.[57] The kinds of arguments accepted in legal reasoning partly determine the outcome. Based on the same legal rules, the interpretation, and thus the application, of the law may be completely different depending on the acceptability of, eg, a reference to legislative materials, to societal needs, to changed views in society, to a presumed rationality of the legislator etc. In comparative law, it appears that related legal systems sometimes have different rules but similar judicial decisions when the rules are applied to concrete cases. In the first place, this shows to what extent the content of the law is determined through interpretation. Secondly, it proves the importance of a common ideology, based on similar societal circumstances, which, almost imperceptibly, penetrates into law through a common language, style and argumentation. Again, "legal discourse" is the most appropriate term for denoting the whole of legal language and reasoning as embedded in its broad non-legal context. A common legal discourse thus has a decisive influence on the content of the law, on the meaning given to the law in its adjudication.

---

[57] An example of the importance of common language for the content of the law is offered by a few legal concepts, such as "*rechtsverwerking*" (a specific kind of forfeiture right), developed in Dutch legal doctrine and taken on board by doctrine and by courts in the Dutch-speaking part of Belgium. In the French speaking part of this country, this new concept has not been successful, mainly because it proved not to have an appropriate translation in French.

If we take, for instance, the civil law discourses in Belgium, France, Italy and Spain, they will have much more in common with each other, than they have with eg labour law, penal law or tax law within their own legal systems. This does not only show the important degree of communality of legal discourses amongst legal systems, it also points to another element which is important for our analysis: the rather limited unity of legal systems. This will not as such be discussed here. It will suffice to state that different branches of the law should probably be considered to be "autopoietic systems" on their own, or at least, relatively autonomous "auto-productive" systems. It is obvious that there is more "autonomy" of, eg, environmental law vis-à-vis commercial law within one individual legal system than there is between these branches of law within their own legal systems, on the one hand, and the same branches in related legal systems, or in Europe where these fields are subject to regulation by the European Union, on the other. Where then lies the "operative closure" of legal systems?

Ultimately, very little is left of the autonomy of legal systems towards each other: They have a circular interdependence; they have a common legal language, style and argumentation; they borrow rules and concepts from each other. They need to do this in order to strengthen their autonomy towards moral, political or economic discourse (or systems). But, in so doing they have to rely on each other and they lose their autonomy towards other legal systems.

As a conclusion, we have to state that legal systems are not autonomous vis-à-vis each other. They may maintain autonomy towards some legal systems with which they do not have any links at all, but they will never be autonomous towards all, or even a majority of, legal systems.[58]

(ii) Autonomy vis-à-vis Other Societal Systems

In jurisprudence, the autonomy of legal systems with respect to other societal systems has mainly been discussed with regard to the relationship between law and morals. But the influence exerted on law is much broader than that. Some societal systems are normative systems, notably morals, religion, etiquette, customs, usages, ideology. The important social norms will, in every community, be institutionalised through law. In a way, law is an institutionalised manifestation of all kinds of social norms. The law is used to give greater strength, greater authority and greater efficacy to such social norms.

Other societal systems, such as the economy, politics, the arts, sports, information (media), etc, are not normative. However, they offer factual elements which, often in relation with other social norms, lead to social and, eventually,

---

[58] A "contact", and thus at least some loss of autonomy, follows as soon as there is some territorial or personal overlap of legal systems, eg, the territorial overlap in Europe between sub-state law, state law, European law and international law, or the personal overlap between Canon law and state law.

legal norms. Economic data and insights may, together with principles of justice and equality, lead to the development of rules of labour law and social security law. To a certain extent, these non-legal discourses generate their own basic norms: eg, the efficacy rule in economic discourse, the "right of information" in media discourse, the majority rule in political discourse, etc. Such implicit or explicit normative positions inevitably influence the content of law.

Law is only one of many societal systems. In order to function within the society it regulates, law should fit with the other societal systems. A legal system cannot function if it does not observe basic principles of economics, politics, morals, etc. If a legal system really becomes "autonomous" and produces rules which undermine the economic system or the political system or the predominant moral system, it will not last for long.[59] An autonomous production of legal rules is also limited from this point of view. According to the autopoietic theory, legal systems select and adapt the information coming from the outside according to their own systemic criteria. This proves to be only partly true. The selection and adaptation are also, to a certain extent, determined by the other societal systems. Eventually, it is only the technical, legal form which is decided completely autonomously by the legal system.

The same is true for another obvious link between legal systems and other societal systems: the use of *vague concepts* in law. When using, in the drafting of legal rules, concepts like "fairness", "reasonableness", "equity",[60] "abuse", "torts", etc, the law implicitly refers to non-legal normative systems to substantiate the vague concept so as to fill in the actual norm a judge will or would apply to the case. Herein lies a well known link between legal systems and other societal systems, especially morals. Of course, the law still dictates when, and under what conditions, those social and moral rules may be brought into the legal system, but the content of the rules is left completely open. The use of vague concepts cannot be explained on the basis of some laziness or lack of competence in legislative drafting. It is a structural linkage between law and other normative systems, which aims at avoiding both pure gaps in law and overregulation. In the context of great codifications in nineteenth century Europe and of the rise of the welfare state, legislators have often thought that it was possible and desirable to regulate as much as possible through general legislation and leave as little room as possible for individual decisions by civil officers and judges when applying the law. Since then, we have learned the limits and disadvantages of such a top-down approach: it is not possible to foresee

---

[59] An example of legal systems undermining the economic system is the Eastern European countries between the Second World War and the early 1990s. An example of a legal system, which was not observing basic rules of an acceptable, democratic political system, was the South African legal system under Apartheid. An example of an immoral legal system was nazi Germany. Notwithstanding the strong military power which was backing these legal systems, none of them were able to last for more than a few decades.

[60] In the broad sense, not in the technical sense of the common law history and the present day English legal system.

everything nor to adapt every Act each time a change in society would make it appropriate. Moreover, where there was a deep distrust of judges at the time of those codifications, judges today are sometimes considered to be the cornerstone of legal systems, whereas there is greater distrust of legislators. As a result, legislation today will more often use vague concepts, thus delegating to courts the power to "select and adopt" moral or other social rules and to "change" and "translate" them into legal rules. Most prominently, this has been the case in the Dutch Civil Code of 1992, where the rules very often simply refer to "reasonableness and equity".[61] In a way, one could present this as a "trick" by which all social rules may become legal rules when the legal system needs them. There are no non-legal rules: all social rules in the community are potentially legal rules; courts are explicitly empowered to label them "legal" whenever they need them. It is a method, and an efficacious method, of closing a legal system, but at the price of a loss of autonomy. Not only is the content of the rules completely determined by other normative systems, but it becomes impossible for the legal system to control, and keep under control, the impact of other societal systems on that legal system.

The last, and most important, way in which legal systems lack autonomy vis-à-vis other societal systems is with the *interpretation* of law, which follows inevitably from adjudication. Statutory interpretation will not be discussed here.[62] It may suffice to observe the influence of interpretation on the eventual meaning with which law is applied, and the influence of ideology on this interpretation. Bernd Rüthers, for example, has shown to what extent German law enacted before 1933 has been perverted through an interpretation guided by nazi ideology.[63] But such a dramatic influence of ideology on law through judicial interpretation is not limited to such extreme political circumstances. A well-known, and more sympathetic example, is the concept of "abuse of rights", introduced into most continental European legal systems by courts and legal doctrine. It not only refers to moral rules, but also limits the scope of explicitly enacted legal rules on purely moral grounds. Moreover, no secondary rule of the legal systems in question empowered the courts to limit the scope of legal rules by introducing and using such a concept. As human beings, lawyers, and more specifically judges, are not just part of the legal system, they also belong to other societal systems. Sometimes, they change their roles and change their discourse, moving into, eg, a moral discourse. When combining their roles, they smuggle this moral, or other, discourse into the legal system, and suddenly it is a moral system which is determining what the law is, and not the legal system. The concept of "abuse of rights" indeed operates to render that which is "legal" according to the legal system "illegal" on purely moral grounds.

---

[61] To such an extent that the Code has been severely criticised for its vagueness and lack of "legal certainty".

[62] See below 7.4.

[63] B Ruthers, *Die unbegrenzte Auslegung* (JCB Mohr, Tübingen, 1968).

Autopoietic theory accepts that such role-interferences may occur, and that they are even necessary to make intersystemic communication possible.[64] This communication is considered possible because people "speak the 'languages' of various subsystems".[65] But this role-interference and multilinguism may work in two different directions. A judge may act as part of the legal system when selecting non-legal values, norms or other data, but he might also use his position as a judge to introduce such non-legal elements *from a non-legal point of view*. He can switch to, eg a moral discourse, or an economic discourse and just adapt it technically to the extent necessary in order to enable him to label the outcome as "legal". The concept of "abuse of rights" is a typical example of a moral discourse introduced into the legal system and partly *replacing legal discourse*. The legal system has lost control over its content. Other societal systems have broken into the legal system and are changing its function. However, the autopoietic legal system is blind, it does not see what is happening and simply continues labelling as "legal" whatever the judges call "legal", just like a machine putting wine labels on every passing bottle which has the format of a wine bottle, regardless of its content. Limiting law to the structural features of legal systems in order to prove its "autonomy" is comparable to limiting oneself to the analysis of the operation of such a labelling machine when analysing wine and its role in society. Broadening the analysis to the content of the law, on the other hand, makes it impossible to maintain that a legal system is autonomous vis-à-vis other systems.

(iii) Autonomy of Primary and of Secondary Rules

It follows from the autopoietic theory of law, that legal systems should be considered open at the level of primary rules and closed at the level of their secondary rules.

There can be no doubting that the *primary rules* of conduct produced by a legal system are to a (very) large extent influenced by or even borrowed from other societal systems or discourses. There is also a general agreement with the conclusion that, even when rules are borrowed from other normative systems, they are subject to some face-lift or technical adaptation in order for them to fit into legal discourse.

Secondary legal rules, however, seem to be purely legal. They organise structures and procedures through which law may be produced, including both the making and adjudication of the law. At this level, legal systems should be able to maintain their autonomy, not only with regard to form, but also with respect to the content of the rules.

---

[64] Teubner, *Law as an Autopoietic System*, above n 45, p 99.

[65] R Mayntz, "Politische Steuerung und gesellschaftliche Steuerungsprobleme: Anmerkung zu einen theoretischen Paradigma", (1987) 1 *Jahrbuch für Staats- und Verwaltungswissenschaft* 89–110 at p 102.

Unfortunately, this is not the case. Some of the main secondary rules of a legal system are those which determine the "sources" of the law. From several of the examples given earlier, it appeared that external influences on the legal system even altered these sources in a manner which was not regulated by the secondary rules of the system. When judges accepted international law as a source of domestic law, having priority over incompatible rules of the national legal system, they introduced a new source of law and a new hierarchy within these sources, without any "secondary rule" empowering them to do so.

The same holds true for the acceptance and use of "unwritten legal principles" as an independent source of law. The introduction of such principles has been completely determined by ideological asumptions which were not part of the legal system. The general principle of "good faith" for example, has been introduced in several European countries by broadening considerably the scope of a rule which imposes the obligation "to execute a contract in accordance with good faith".[66] Even if the concept of "good faith" could be found in one of the rules embodied in these legal systems, the idea that it could, and should, have an overall application in law is clearly an ideological choice, by which greater weight is assigned to a moral value than the legal system previously gave. In other cases, the moral value could not be found to be assimilated anywhere by the legal system. The most striking example is the previously discussed general principle which prohibits the "abuse" of a right: moral values are introduced as a new source of law, limiting the scope of legal rules as produced by the legal system. This not only affects the content of the primary rules, but also considerably changes the secondary rules: a new source of law is introduced by the judiciary, notwithstanding the absence of secondary rules in the legal system empowering them to do so.

There is yet another way in which elements of the content of law co-determine the structures and procedures by which the legal system is institutionalised. The emergence of procedural rights has strongly influenced these institutions. The case law of the European Court of Human Rights, especially, has considerably changed the structures and proceedings of the national legal systems, which have had to adapt to principles such as the right of defence, the right to be judged by an independent and impartial judge, or the right to be judged within a reasonable time (Article 6 ECHR). This proves that structures and procedures are not value-free, that they cannot be created arbitrarily and completely autonomously by legal systems; non-legal values co-determine the content of these secondary rules.

If values from outside the legal system are able, not only occasionally to influence the content of primary rules of conduct, but also to become an institutionalised source of law on their own, by changing the secondary rules which organise law-making, then it becomes clear that legal systems are not completely autonomous, even at the level of secondary rules. With the external

---

[66] See for further details below 7.5.

world affecting not only the content of the rules produced by the legal system, but also the machinery as such, a legal system can hardly be called "auto-poietic". Legal systems do not completely control and determine their input, nor even the channels through which an input is made possible.

Indirectly, or even directly, the question of the closure or openness of legal systems has been discussed above, closely linked as it is to the question of the autonomy of legal systems. From this discussion, it appeared that legal systems are relatively open systems. In this section, we will attempt to determine more precisely to what extent legal systems should be considered open and closed respectively, in relation to the question of comprehensiveness of legal systems. The latter feature is especially linked with state legal systems, which nowadays, mostly aspire to, and are assumed to be, comprehensive.

By drawing a clear distinction between "is" and "ought", and between law and other normative systems, Hans Kelsen tried to identify legal systems as closed systems. He analysed them from a static,[67] linear and hierarchical perspective, especially from the point of view of the legal legitimation of a concrete application of a legal norm, eg on the occasion of the execution of a judicial decision condemning a person to pay a certain amount of money to another person. For KELSEN, the legal system is closed, as the order contained in the court decision is based on a chain of higher norms, leading ultimately to some hypothetical basic norm that closes the legal system. No external elements influence this legal reasoning.[68] For Kelsen, the legal system is closed, in respect of both primary and secondary rules.

The autopoietic theory analyses legal systems in a dynamic perspective, and emphasises the cognitive openness of legal systems. Legal systems rely on, and need, communication with the external world for the production of new rules. Nevertheless, legal systems are, from this perspective, as closed as the Kelsenian ones. It is not because legal systems are fed by the external world, a fact undisputed by Kelsen, that once the legal rule has been produced as a legal rule, it would not become autonomous. In fact, after becoming legal rules, they start their own life within an *operationally closed* legal system. Both Kelsen and Teubner seem to underestimate considerably the influence of non-legal values

---

[67] Kelsen did himself distinguish between a "static" and a "dynamic" norm system. He called legal systems "dynamic" because "the presupposed basic norm contains nothing but the determination of a norm-creating fact, the authorization of a norm-creating authority or a rule that stipulates how the general and individual norms of the order based on the basic norm ought to be created" (*Pure Theory of Law*, trans Max Knight, University of California Press, Berkeley and Los Angeles, 1967), p 196) Obviously, Kelsen uses the concept of "static" in a very strong sense. For our discussion, however, it seems appropriate to call Kelsen's approach "static", especially when opposed to autopoietic theory or to our own circular and communicative view on law.

[68] Kelsen, *Pure Theory of Law*, above n 67, pp 201–5.

and norms at all levels of legal reasoning, in determining the content of both primary and secondary rules. Kelsen opines that the interpretative choice in law is relatively limited. Whenever there is such a choice, the decision will be based on non-legal values and norms. However, as a rule, the number of such choices seems to be rather limited and, as Kelsen seems to believe, could be limited to a very large extent. All the examples given above and the analysis of statutory interpretation to follow, serve to illustrate how weak the autonomy of law is towards its societal environment, most notably, with regard to its ideological context. Kelsen's attempt to purge the legal system of non-legal ideology, is reminiscent of someone using a sandblaster to clean a person of all impurities. At the end of this thorough cleansing process, nothing will remain of the human body but a skeleton, if even that. It will be pure, but no longer a "person". By reducing legal systems to self-producing, autopoietic mechanisms, Teubner is also forced to reduce legal systems to their skeletal form. Ultimately, the only thing which is really self-producing is the labelling of rules, acts, and the like, as "legal". Kelsen's static skeleton has been replaced by a dynamic labelling machine. They have both succeeded in closing the legal system, but only by reducing it to a limited formal part of its former self. They fail to consider legal systems in their entirety, legal systems as we understand them. In the sense of their analysis, the "system" could indeed be said to be closed, but this "system" covers such a limited part of legal reality, that we could hardly state that "legal systems" are indeed closed systems.

If a legal system is self-productive, is it possible for it to produce any legal norm? Or, in other words, is it possible to assimilate, to translate any non-legal rule into a legal rule? The question of the closure or openness of legal systems has also been posed in a different form: is it possible, on the basis of the legal system in question, to find a legal solution for any problem? In the positivist tradition, lawyers have been anxious to find a positive answer to this question. If the answer were negative, it would entail tremendous problems for any positive theory of law. In practice, judges are expected to give a legal solution to any case brought before them. Article 4 of the Code Napoléon has often been interpreted as implying the comprehensivenes of law. This article made liable to punishment any judge who refused to decide "under the pretext of silence, the obscurity or the incompleteness of the Statute".[69] Following the Kelsenian lines of reasoning, it is necessary for a judge to find legal norms empowering him to decide one way, otherwise his decision would no longer be a legal decision and would thus be void within the legal system. However, in practice, no legal system has rules for every possible form of human conduct. The primary reason for this is that no legal system aims to be comprehensive in every sense. It is true that

---

[69] This article has remained unchanged not only in France, but also in several other European countries where it is still valid. The reasoning it followed arose from the assumption that any contention about silence, obscurity or incompleteness of the law would, according to the wording of Art. 4 of the Code civil, by definition, be just a false "pretext".

following the rise of the modern state and the underlying theories of "sovereignty" there is an implicit claim that state legal systems have an unlimited competence for regulating any kind of behaviour.[70] However, one should not confuse political rhetoric with the principles underlying legal systems. It is true that state legal systems in the last few centuries have claimed the competence to regulate *almost* every kind of human behaviour. For some time a somewhat naïve conception of democracy prevailed, according to which a democratically elected political majority could regulate anything. Today, even that political view is not any longer accepted without limits (human rights, rights of minorities, etc). It should be clear that even the most all-encompassing state legal system already has its strict territorial limits. Courts, in such a legal system, would undoubtedly refuse to decide cases brought before them but having no link whatsoever to the legal system concerned. Not all kinds of human behaviour and interaction can (fully) be regulated by law either: friendship, love, fashion, politeness, and the like, may occasionally have links with legal rules, but *as such* they escape any regulation by law. Furthermore, even within the state territory at least some room will remain for other non-state legal systems, eg as with Canon law in European legal history. Moreover, by recognising fundamental freedoms, modern state legal systems accept areas where the state limits its power of interference, and thus of active regulation.[71] All this means that there is nowadays a weaker claim, which implicitly underlies state legal systems, namely the claim to regulate in principle all domains of private and public life within some well determined territory, but only to some extent, including the demarcation of important areas of non-interference and the acceptance of (in practice unescapable) higher competences of international organisations (the European Union, NATO, the UN, IATA, etc). Combined with the actual conclusion that no legal system ever regulates everything, this can hardly support the thesis of comprehensiveness or closure of state legal systems.

Legal systems can never be complete at the primary level of rules of conduct imposing, in a concrete fashion, some specific form of behaviour. Even if the fiction of a perfect, rational legislator has often been used in the practice of statutory interpretation, every lawyer knows very well that no legislator is perfect, that the possibility of mistakes in the statute cannot be disregarded and that some situation will always arise, unforeseen by the legal system, on which the law is silent or insufficiently precise. Moreover, social reality is constantly changing and the legal system has to adapt to this changed reality. It is actually

---

[70] This statement (ie the *claim*; not that everything would be regulated in fact) seems to be accepted unconditionally by Joseph Raz (*Practical Reason and Norms* (Princeton University Press, Princeton, 1990), pp 150–51) and, with some nuances (see below n 71), also by Atienza and Ruiz Manero (*A Theory of Legal Sentences* (Kluwer Academic Publishers, Dordrecht, 1998), p 105.

[71] Of course, in a Kelsenian sense the system is closed, as there is a (negative) guidance for behaviour: a freedom. However, as Atienza and Ruiz Manero rightly argue, it prohibits the state enacting any *positive* rule of behaviour, and thus weakens the state's implicit claim potentially to regulate everything (*ibid*, p 156).

impossible to do so by constantly changing legislation and amending each detail. Court practice in every legal system shows how this adaptation of the law has, to a large extent, been the responsibility of judges. Even if it was possible, in theory, to make a comprehensive, closed legal system, in practice the above reasons make it impossible to achieve such a result at the primary level of rules of conduct.

In order to avoid this problem, attempts have been made to close the legal system at a secondary level,[72] by introducing some "closing rule". This is a rule at the secondary level determining what shall happen when a situation arises which is not, at the primary level, governed by the legal system. For example, in criminal law most legal systems have a secondary rule permitting all conduct which is not explicitly prohibited by the law. Such a closing rule can be rather easily formulated when demarcating a sphere of non-interference by government, like criminal law, tax law, or administrative law. When regulating private relationships however, it is much more difficult to work out closing rules, and when this is possible, those closing rules only apply to a limited area. An example is, when a contract is ambiguous, it shall be interpreted in favour of the one who made an undertaking and against the creditor (Article 1162 Belgian and French Civil Code). But, at a more general level, it does not seem to be possible to formulate a workable closing rule for the whole private law or for the whole legal system. No legal systems are thus completely closed at this secondary level.

There is, however, a third level at which many legal systems are technically closed. This "technical closure" means that the legal system regulates the gaps in its own system by determining when, how and by whom rules from other normative systems may be used within the legal system. This does not mean that the legal system excludes the use of non-legal rules, it only means that it keeps this use under control by offering general rules which allow the transformation of non-legal rules into legal ones. In modern legal systems, this technical closure at a third level generally takes the form of a power given to the judge to decide a case even when the legal system does not contain rules which apply to it. Sometimes, judges are free to use this power as they like (eg in England, France or Belgium), or the power may be limited as regards the hierarchy of sources the judge is allowed to follow.[73] But even if many legal systems are thus technically closed at this third level, they remain open as regards the question of which rules of conduct belong to the legal system and which ones do not.

Whereas Kelsen believed it was possible to close a legal system at the secondary level, by using closing rules as to the *content* of the law, autopoietic

---

[72] This distinction between primary closure and secondary closure of the legal systems has been made by PW Brouwer, in his article "Openheid van en in rechtsordes", *Rechtsfilosofie en Rechtstheorie* (1979) *Netherlands Journal for Legal Philosophy and Jurisprudence* 128–48.

[73] eg Art 1 Swiss Civil Code: "A défaut d'une disposition légale applicable, le juge prononce selon le droit coutumier et, à défaut d'une coutume, selon les règles qu'il établirait s'il avait à faire acte de législateur." (In absence of an applicable statutory rule, the judge shall decide according to customary law, and, if customs are lacking, according to the rules he would enact if he would have to act as a legislator.)

theory emphasises the third, *structural* level: the power given to a person or body, especially the judge, to "borrow" rules from other normative systems, to "translate", to assimilate them and to incorporate them into the legal system. Again this means that the openness of legal systems, at the level of the content of rules, is recognised, but the legal system is sufficiently flexible to label any non-legal rule "legal" when this seems appropriate. In this way, but only this way, judges are indeed able to give a "legal" solution to any case.

There is, in fact, a fourth level, at which legal systems, by definition, can never be closed. This is the level of the ideological framework of the law, which is, often implicitly, constantly guiding the interpretation of the rules. The exact content of a legal system is not (only) something which is given, but something which is constantly worked out through the interpretation of the law in legal doctrine and in case law. Via this interpretation, non-legal views, values and norms inevitably penetrate the law. As we have seen in the previous chapter, this non-legal influence is not limited to the category of the primary rules of conduct, but it also thoroughly affects the secondary rules, organising structures and procedures for the making and the adaptation of the law. As a consequence, the machinery of the legal system, on which the structural closure at the third level is based, is not a constant factor, but is itself moving under external influence.

In order to give a full acount of what a legal system is, one cannot limit oneself to some static Kelsenian hierarchy of values or to some algebra of legal concepts as in the *Begriffs*jurisprudence. Nor can one limit oneself to the dynamic process of law at the institutional level as the autopoietic theory does. It is also necessary to have, in the same dynamic perspective, a view on the ideological, societal framework of the legal system, which is constantly co-determining the content of the law, both of its primary and of its secondary rules. Legal systems are not only "cognitively" open, but to some extent, also "operationally" open.

3.8 LAW AND CULTURE

3.8.1 General Culture

As law is basically linked to society, to its traditions, to its predominant values, it is, by definition, imbedded in the general culture of that society. This culture is the whole of generally accepted beliefs, values and world views in that society, together with some basic habits and attitudes related to interhuman relations. "Culture" is obviously a vague concept, as it appears from the way it is used and defined in literature;[74] eg "the ordinary social, historical world of sense"[75] or "a generic term for states of mind and ideas".[76] It is, however,

---

[74] See for some criticism: R Cotterrell., "The Concept of Legal Culture", in D Nelken, (ed), *Comparing Legal Cultures* (Dartmouth, Aldershot, 1997), pp 13–31, at pp 15–16.

[75] F Mulhern, *Culture/Metaculture* (Routledge, London and New York, 2000), p xiii.

[76] LM Friedman, "The Concept of Legal Culture: A Reply" in D Nelken (ed), *ibid*, p 35.

broader than "world view" or "ideology" or "habits". It is the combination of all this, in its *mutual interaction*. As Lawrence Friedman puts it, when defining the concept of "legal culture": "these states of mind are affected by events, situations and the like in society as a whole, and they lead in turn to actions that have an impact on the legal system itself.",[77] or Erhard Blankenburg: " 'legal culture' is as much the product of the system as it is its generator".[78]

Legal values and legal habits are part of general culture, but only a limited part. Values and habits can only become legal by some recognition as "legal", by some "legalisation" through institutions which are recognised in society as "legal" bodies with the competence of accepting such values and habits as "legal".

Law thus starts from *general* values, world views, etc. In a second stage, however, law and legal practice *create* some *legal* values, world views, traditions and habits, in other words: a legal culture.

Culture, indeed, is not just a given set of values and norms. It is a constant communicative process in which traditions and customs are assimilated through a collective learning process, on the one hand, but in which, at the same time, virtually all members of that cultural community take some active part in preserving, changing and/or abolishing elements of that culture, eg, by buying, or not buying, some kinds of clothes, literature, music, food, etc, by watching, or not watching, some types of movies, television series, internet sites, etc, by using, or not using, some specific language, etc.

Culture is strongly linked to the identity of a group or a community. Differences with other cultures create or strenghten this identity, be it the identity of the "youth", as compared to elder generations, by the way they dress, the kind of music they listen to, their night life, their eating habits, etc, or the identity of Britons as compared to Germans or other foreign people. Common cultural features, on the other hand, may create a feeling of belonging to a group or community, which is not, or not to the same extent, geographically located: a fan club of a popular singer or movie star, a professional community, foreign people with whom one happens to share the same hobby, students from different countries attending the same postgraduate programme, etc.

3.8.2 Legal Culture

(a) Legal Culture in Society

Legal culture is to a large extent the culture of lawyers as a professional group, the so-called "internal legal culture". To some, rather limited, extent, however,

---

[77] *Ibid*; see also Friedman, *The Legal System: A Social Science Perspective* (Sage, New York, 1975), pp 15–16.

[78] E Blankenburg, "Civil Litigation Rates as Indicators for Legal Cultures" in D Nelken (ed.), *ibid*, p 65.

some legal culture may be identified in society at large, the so-called "external legal culture". It is the widely spread beliefs related to justice and equity, the traditions and habits as to relatively frequently occurring legal relations, such as family relations, or other situations with legal effects, for instance, in the area of criminal law or tort law; it also includes the attitudes of the citizen towards legal rules and legal institutions. Together they create a legal world view in society and some legal awareness, which may in some cases strongly support valid legal rules, or decisions by political, administrative or judicial bodies, but which, in other cases, may also create important problems as to the legitimacy and acceptance of such rules or decisions.

As with every culture, such a legal culture is constantly changing, but slowly. Decision-makers, such as legislative bodies or courts, have to take this into account when changing the law. Many legal rules or policies do not affect this societal legal culture directly. They may be changed "unilaterally" by the (legal) professionals involved in the decision-making process. Fundamental societal values and customs, however, may not simply be changed without the risk of creating important problems, with in the extreme case a revolution or coup d'état, aiming at restoring the previously prevailing legal culture.

(b) Lawyers' Legal Culture

When we talk about "legal culture" we mostly have in mind traditions, values, world views, habits which are prevailing within some legal profession, or amongst lawyers in general (internal legal culture).

Legal education is an important factor in the creation of such a common legal culture, not only as to legal concepts, legal principles, legal techniques, the style of drafting legal texts, and the like, but also as regards the underlying legal, political, social and economic values and world views. All lawyers educated in that legal system inevitably share this legal culture, at least to some (and, in fact, a large) extent. Within each *legal profession* there is, moreover, a socialisation process which reinforces that legal culture, on the one hand, and adds some more specific elements, which are typical for that profession, on the other.

(c) Legal Culture and Legal Harmonisation

In the discussions about legal harmonisation, diverging legal cultures are often seen as an obstacle to any convergence, let alone unification of law. In order to measure the importance and consequences of such cultural differences, however, one first has to determine what kind of legal culture is at stake. It is obvious that the situation is completely different in the case of legal values, which are deeply rooted in society, compared to habits of a group of lawyers. This is not so because the latter would always be easier to change. The strong position of lawyers in society may allow them to block any change rather effectively, certainly if that position is backed by the profession as a whole. The difference lies at the level of the acceptance of the change and its legitimacy in society. Lawyers will end up changing their habits if they are forced by law to do so.[79] Here, diverging legal culture may make harmonisation somewhat more difficult, but it will never be a real obstacle if there is a sufficient political will in favour of such a change. In the case of deeply rooted societal values, such changes will prove much more difficult, if not impossible.

3.9 LAW AND JUSTICE

Robert Alexy rightly argues that every legal system at least pretends to be just and fair.[80] It would be a paradox to enact law with the statement "as from today this unjust rule will be valid". Law may be highly unjust or unfair, but, by definition, it always has the pretension of containing at least a minimum of justice and fairness. Even the Mafia will consider its internal rules to be (very) just and fair: when a disloyal, or simply unsuccessful, member of the group is ordered to be killed, this will never be considered to be unjust by those who ordered it, rather the opposite: "they are the rules of the game".

In the same vein Joseph Raz writes "that it is essential to law that it claims to have legitimate, moral, authority".[81]

Justice, fairness, equity, and the like are as such not essential characteristics for law to be considered "law", contrary to what most natural law scholars have argued. However, a *claim* that the law is fair, just, etc, is endemic to any legal system.

Not all aspects of law are related to morals and justice. There is an overlap between law and morals, but not every moral rule is to be found in a legal form too, and not every legal rule has a moral counterpart. Law has a more limited scope than morals in that it is only concerned with external behaviour, not with thoughts, desires or feelings unless they are linked to such behaviour. On the other hand, it regulates much more than morals. It has the potential to organise society as a whole, and state legal systems generally do so. It *structures* society or some community through *institutions* and *procedural rules* and contains rules of behaviour that aim to realise *collective goals*. Many "technical" rules, as, for instance, traffic regulation, are as such amoral. When there is a moral content, there may be a gradation in the moral character of legal rules. Some have a strong moral content, such as many penal rules or the "good faith" principle laid down in contract law or consumer law. Others have a weaker moral content, such as social security law to the extent that it implies solidarity

---

[79] See eg the changes in attitudes of lawyers in Europe under the influence of the European Union and European human rights law. For a recent analysis of French legal culture(s), also in this respect, see: J Bell, *French Legal Cultures* (Butterworths, London, 2001).

[80] R Alexy, *Begriff und Geltung des Rechts* (Karl Alber, Freiburg/München, 1992), p 62.

[81] J Raz, "On The Nature of Law", (1996) *ARSP* 6 and 16. See also: J Raz, *The Authority of Law* (Clarendon, Oxford, 1979), pp 28–33.

between the poorer or more unlucky citizen and the richer or more lucky ones, or they have only a moral connotation in the context of other legal rules and principles.

It is rather at the level of the making and the adjudication of the law that principles of justice will have a broad application, eg for treating equal cases alike. Fairness of procedure, equality in the scope and adjudication of the law, reasonableness of the content of rules and of court decisions are important conditions for people to accept a legal system, to consider it as "just" even if one does not like some specific rules or the content of a judicial decision by which one has lost a case. In this way a minimal justice is necessary for a legal system to *exist*, as a minimal acceptance is a condition for its functioning and thus its actual existence.[82] This refers to a larger community than the one regulated by this legal system:

> "In contrast with ethical questions, questions of justice are not by their very nature tied to a particular collectivity. Politically enacted law, if it is to be legitimate, must be at least in harmony with moral principles that claim a general validity that extends beyond the limits of any concrete legal community."[83]

Principles of justice, by definition, include a claim to general validity for mankind in time and space. In space, it is especially human rights that claim, and largely succeed, to be valid worldwide. In time, it is the idea of equality among current and future generations that governs the ecological debate.

There is a connection between law and morals, but not a hierarchical relationship. This explains why a legal system does not collapse *as a legal system* because it is unjust; only (sets of) rules or the behaviour of public authorities will be criticised, declared void, and/or sanctioned.

We cannot go further into the complex discussion of the relationship between law and justice or law and morals, as we are only concerned here with defining the law by demarcating its typical characteristics.[84]

---

[82] In the same sense: HLA Hart, *The Concept of Law* (Clarendon Press, Oxford, 1961), pp 189 and 196; M van de Kerchove and F Ost, *Legal System Between Order and Disorder* (trans Iain Stewart, Oxford University Press, Oxford, 1994), p 19.

[83] J Habermas, *The Inclusion of the Other* (Polity Press, Cambridge, 1998), p 245.

[84] Among the immense literature in this field, I would refer to the chapter on "legal systems and morals" in van de Kerchove and Ost, above n 82, pp 124–32 and to Habermas's Postscript in his book *Between Facts and Norms* (Polity Press, Cambridge, 1996), pp 447–62, where he explains why positive law cannot simply be subordinated to morality, shows how popular sovereignty and human rights presuppose each other and makes clear that the principle of democracy has its own roots independent of the moral principle.

4

The Functions of the Law

The concept of "function" covers both the effects which law-makers hope to realise through law (the "aims" of the law) and the actual effects, which may be different from the ones the law-makers aimed at, or which are not linked to any deliberate lawmaking at all and may even remain largely unnoticed.[1]

In traditional jurisprudence attention often has been paid too exclusively to the aims of the law. This is narrowing the analysis to deliberate law-making, thus leaving aside a not unimportant part of the law, but at the same time is it probably overestimating the possible effects of law as a means for social engineering. Summers has rightly called such an approach "naïve instrumentalism".[2]

When taking such a position, moreover, jurists tend to mingle a descriptive analysis with normative points of view. This is especially the case when it is posited that the (main) aim of the law is to realise values such as "justice", "equality", "individual freedom" and the like, thus offering an idealistic picture of law.

Finally, one should distinguish between the aim of concrete legal rules and statutes, on the one hand, and the functions of the *legal system*, on the other. It indeed does not make much sense to talk about "aims" of a legal system, as if such a system would be created purposively, at some specific moment of time, by a community, or part of it, with deliberate purposes, as it is suggested, for example, with the image of the "social contract". All legal systems have, as a whole, developed over a considerable time span. Deliberate law-making may have aimed at varying, and even opposite, goals. The way law is interpreted and applied in practice may be very different from these goals, and, again, even be opposite to them. How then could one determine the "aims" of "the law"? Even when it comes to determining the aims of the legislator as to an Act, problems may easily arise. Political compromises between conflicting interests and opposed goals often end up in statutes with clear rules but with an unclear underlying societal model and purpose.

Here, we are not interested in the aims underlying concrete legal rules, but in the *functions* which are typical for all, or at least most *legal systems*.

---

[1] On the concept of "function" see W Krawietz, *Das positive Recht und seine Funktion* (Duncker & Humblot, Berlin, 1967), pp 39–46.

[2] RS Summers, "Naïve Instrumentalism and the Law" in PMS Hacker and J Raz, *Law, Morality and Society. Essays in Honour of HLA Hart* (Clarendon Press, Oxford, 1977), pp 119–31.

The most obvious function of law follows from the definition of law: *ordering society*. To this basic function a number of other functions are linked, which may be considered to be typical for legal systems, and not just for one or a few of them.

Ordering society means structuring human interaction and human communication. This can be looked at from two different perspectives: from the point of view of society and from the point of view of the individual. In 1973 Lon Fuller wrote a paper on the functions of law for which he has chosen the title "Law as an instrument of social control and law as a facilitation of human interaction".[3] This indicates very well the double perspective from which the functions of law have to be analysed, though they are broader than Fuller's title (and paper) suggest.

Before discussing these two categories of functions it should be noticed that the full range of functions, which legal systems may have, is linked to "political legal orders" only, to those legal orders that are structuring the political debate in a society and have a monopoly of legitimate legal force within some territory, such as state legal systems and, to a lesser extent, international law.[4] The functions of "non-political legal orders", such as sports associations or churches, are more limited.

Here, we will discuss the varying functions of the law in society. We do not pay attention to the functions (of categories) of legal *rules* as far as they are not linked to the societal functions of the law. However, it may be useful to point to two functions of categories of legal rules that are linked to the legal *system* as such. An important amount of secondary rules, mainly those of adjudication, are meant to *maintain* the legal system, to make sure that the set of primary rules of behaviour is by and large functioning in social practice. The secondary rules of change, in their turn, guarantee the possible *transformation* of the legal system, its constant, or at least regular, adaptation to the changing environment.[5]

4.1 STRUCTURING SOCIETY

From a societal perspective we may distinguish two main functions of law: (a) structuring political power, and (b) creating and keeping social cohesion.

---

[3] Published in: L Legaz y Lacambra (ed), *Die Funktionen des Rechts*, ARSP Beiheft 8 (Frans Steiner Verlag, Wiesbaden, 1974), pp 99–105. In this paper Fuller mainly argues that traditional jurisprudence has largely neglected the function of facilitating human interaction and focused too exclusively on the function of social control.

[4] See above, 3.4.

[5] Bobbio calls these two functions "second order control" and sees them as typical for "complex normative systems" (N Bobbio, "Nouvelles réflexions sur les normes primaires et secondaires" in C Perelman (ed) *La règle de droit* (Bruylant, Brussels, 1971), p 118).

4.1.1 Political Power

Over the last few centuries there has been a strong link between law, state and politics, to such an extent, that it has led to several confusions, such as limiting law to state legal orders or equating legal systems with political systems.[6] Anyway, it is hardly deniable that one of the main functions of law is structuring political power and decision-making: "Political power can develop only through a legal code".[7] In modern state legal systems this is clearly visible in constitutions. Not only are they the basis for the legal system, their main content is about organising political power: which institutions will exert what political power? Who will elect or appoint their members? Who has the right to political participation (the right to vote and the right to be elected)? Which procedures have to be followed? Who will control the way political power is exerted by those institutions and how? Which basic rights belong to the citizen and, therefore, limit the power of political bodies?

The importance of law for politics is still increasing. In the past, political disputes were often solved with military force. Today, it is rather courts than armies that are used for it, and most notably constitutional courts and, in Europe, the European Court on Human Rights.[8]

Law is not only structuring political power, it is, especially in current societies, also to a very large extent *legitimating* it. Political decisions are considered to be legitimated when they have been enacted through a legally correct procedure, by a political body that has been appointed or chosen through a legally correct procedure. In open, pluralist societies, this is for most political decisions the only generally acceptable form of legitimation. Thus, law has a function of legitimating political power, whilst, on the other hand, law relies on this political power for its own legitimation.

---

[6] Most prominently in comparative law, by distinguishing, in the second half of the twentieth century, a "socialist legal family" when categorising legal systems in the area of *private* law (see, for a critical comment on this, M Van Hoecke and M Warrington, "Legal Cultures, Legal Paradigms and Legal Doctrine: Towards a New Model for Comparative Law", (1998)47 *International and Comparative Law Quarterly* 495–536, at p 499).

[7] J Habermas, *Between Facts and Norms* (Polity Press, Cambridge, 1996), p 134. "Normatively substantive messages can circulate throughout society only in the language of law. Without their translation into the complex legal code that is equally open to lifeworld and system, these messages would fall on deaf ears in media-steered spheres of action. Law thus functions as the 'transformer' that first guarantees that the socially integrating network of communication stretched across society as a whole holds together" (*ibid*, p 56).

[8] A clear example is offered by the many trials which followed the American presidential elections in 2000 and which, eventually, made the *judges* choose the president, on the basis of their (politically inspired) interpretation of *legal* rules, against a (narrow) majority of the population.

4.1.2 Social Cohesion

Jürgen Habermas has criticised Max Weber for his one-sided emphasis on the law's function of organising political power,[9] thereby neglecting law's important role in achieving *social integration*. Following Parsons, Habermas argues that in primitive societies social integration was achieved through ordinary language and face-to-face interaction, including rites and religious cults, at the level of relatively small "societal communities". In modern times law took over this function of social integration in the "civil society" at a more abstract and anonymous level. Interaction frameworks and contexts are now juridically structured and offer general rules and procedures for claims and conflicts, which previously had to be managed on the basis of habit, loyalty or trust. The juridification of potentially all social relationships has, moreover, universalised democratic citizenship, with rights of political participation. This participation is exercised both in a network of voluntary associations protected by basic rights and in the forms of communication within a political public sphere produced through the mass media.[10]

Thus law offers a framework within which citizens may reach understanding on norms and values, realise collective goals, bargain between interest positions and solve conflicts. All this plays an important role in bringing about or keeping social cohesion or integration.[11]

The public political debate is not only part of the political decision-making process and an essential element for its legitimation. It, moreover, plays an important role in bringing about social cohesion. It is the forum where the content of common norms and values is determined, where priorities among collective goals are discussed, where competing interest positions are bargained. Law is the means through which all this is put into practice and structured into a coherent whole. In modern democratic societies the constant communication among people, the public political debate inside and, mainly, outside the political bodies, most notably via the mass media, is of paramount importance for effectuating these functions of the law.

Moreover, law has also an important symbolic[12] value.[13] It may, eg, play a role in creating a feeling of national, or regional, or European identity. Once

---

[9] J Habermas, *Between Facts and Norms* (Polity Press, Cambridge, 1996), pp 66–73

[10] J Habermas, *Between Facts and Norms* (Polity Press, Cambridge, 1996), pp 73–76

[11] This function of law is especially relevant from a sociological perspective. It is interesting to note that in scholarly legal writing this point is never raised.

[12] Here, we are not discussing the phenomenon of enacting rules that are *meant* to remain symbolic. Sometimes, indeed, politicians try to satisfy pressure groups or other categories of citizen, by enacting a legislation that meets their wishes, whereas in practice nothing changes. See on this "symbolic legislation": M van de Kerchove and F Ost, *Legal System Between Order and Disorder* (Oxford University Pres, Oxford, 1994), p 122; M van de Kerchove and F Ost, *Jalons pour une théorie critique du droit* (Publications des Facultés universitaires Saint-Louis, Brussels, 1987), pp 344–51.

[13] WJ Witteveen, P van Seters and G van Roermund (eds), *Wat maakt de wet symbolisch?* (WEJ Tjeenk Willink, Zwolle, 1991), p 253.

some values are laid down in legislation they will easily be considered to represent the world view of a large majority in society, even if this is not the case (eg, because a large majority may have no specific view on it at all). This symbolic role of law, in its turn, strenghthen social cohesion.

Achieving social cohesion implies the function of *consolidation* of the social system and of the legal system. Law tends to protect and to maintain the social order it is regulating.[14]

4.2 FACILITATING THE INDIVIDUAL'S LIFE

Through rules and institutions law is structuring society and, by this, simplifying life for the people living in that society.

(Legal) rules reduce the complexity of constantly taking decisions in life. Rules make life easier. They offer a framework of decisions, which are already choices amongst differing reasons. We do not have to decide ourselves, again and again, eg, whether it is better to drive on the left side or on the right side of the road. It has been decided for us.

But there is more. It does not only help us by orientating our behaviour and limiting the choices we have to make. It also helps us to predict the choices and the behaviour of other people. This means that we may, for instance, trust all other vehicles to drive on the same side of the road.

Rule determined behaviour is not determined by the isolated rule as such, but also by the social context and the interaction with other actors. Law creates "shared reciprocal expectations" (Fuller)[15] or "stabilised expectations of behaviour" (Habermas)[16] or "congruently generalized behavioral expectations" (Luhmann)[17]. Fuller rightly posited that law not only serves to facilitate human interaction, "but that it derives *from* interaction".[18] Law is not just something that is there as a "fact", it is made and adapted in a day-to-day practice by officials and by the addressees of the law. It is the official law *as interpreted and applied* in practice that determines the kind of behaviour one may expect. In Europe, for example, it would be naive to consider the signs with speed limits on motorways to be a sound basis for predicting other drivers' behaviour. The

---

[14] I Szabo, "Les fonctions sociales du droit", in L Legaz y Lacambra (ed), *Die Funktionen des Rechts*, ARSP Beiheft 8 (Frans Steiner Verlag, Wiesbaden, 1974), pp 63–84, esp. at p 77.

[15] L Fuller, "Law as an instrument of social control and law as a facilitation of human interaction" in L Legaz y Lacambra (ed), *Die Funktionen des Rechts*, ARSP Beiheft 8 (Frans Steiner Verlag, Wiesbaden, 1974), pp 99–105, at p 101.

[16] J Habermas, *Between Facts and Norms* (Polity Press, Cambridge, 1996), eg at pp 122 and 144 (table 2). Fuller defines "custom" as "stabilized expectancies that arise from past interactions" (*ibid*, p 103).

[17] N Luhmann, "The Unity of the Legal System" in G Teubner (ed), *Autopoietic Law: a New Approach to Law and Society* (Walter de Gruyter, Berlin and New York, 1988), pp 27–28.

[18] L Fuller, "Law as an instrument of social control and law as a facilitation of human interaction" in L Legaz y Lacambra (ed), *Die Funktionen des Rechts*, ARSP Beiheft 8 (Frans Steiner Verlag, Wiesbaden, 1974), pp 99–105, at p 103.

"real law" is made in interaction between the citizen and the law officials. When it is generally known that speed control on motorways is not a priority for the police, and that, moreover, with a speed limit of 120 km an hour, automatic registration is put into operation as from 136 km an hour only, the behaviour of the average driver will adapt to it. "Stabilised expectations of behaviour" are thus rather based on the result of this interaction than on the statutory text or the "official law" only.

Once there is such a stabilisation of expectations, be it in conformity with the written law or not, we can talk about *"legal certainty"*. This should not be seen as a kind of absolute certainty but rather as a stabilising framework for behaviour. It should be obvious that the kind of absolute legal certainty, which many theories have proposed, that could follow from a strict application of well-determined (legislative) rules, is an illusion. It is impossible, and even undesirable (see below chapter 7), to govern law completely from above and to cut it loose from any moral or practical input in the adjudication process to a sufficient extent for creating such a kind of absolute certainty.[19] At the most one may achieve a relative legal certainty within "a legal culture of uncertainty",[20] that constantly has to adapt, at all levels, and not only at the legislative one, to a changing environment and changing circumstances. Depending on the field of law, "legal certainty" may be a stronger or a weaker concept. In tax law or criminal law, for instance, there will be stronger requirements as to legal certainty, in order to protect the citizen from arbitrariness, but this includes the actual practices of public administration and not only a strict application of statutory provisions, at least when such practices are advantagous for the citizen.[21]

When legal rules are generally followed and the decisions of law officials (police, administration, courts) largely accepted in society, it creates some generalised "respect for the law", which reinforces its being followed and increases legal certainty. Thus, it facilitates the individual's life as he may, with confidence, rely on the expected behaviour of others.

Law facilitates the individual's life not only by reducing social complexity through a stabilisation of reciprocal expectations of behaviour. In fact, only by this is chaos prevented. It is simply a necessary condition for life as such. This reduction of complexity prevents our social environment becoming chaotic, which would make any kind of meaningful life impossible. But law does more than preventing chaos, it also creates positive conditions for facilitating human interaction, human communication and the development of the individual. It

[19] See, in the same sense HP Olsen and S Toddington, *Law in its Own Right* (Hart Publishing, Oxford, 1999,) pp 35–41 and 115, criticising Gustav Radbruch's Autonomy Thesis (autonomy of law from morality). See further on Radbruch's views SL Paulson, "Lon L. Fuller, Gustav Radbruch, and the 'positivist' theses", (1994) *Law and Philosophy* 313–59, esp. at pp 328–41.
[20] K-H Ladeur, "Perspectives on a Post-Modern Theory of Law: A Critique of Niklas Luhmann, 'The Unity of the Legal System' " in G Teubner (ed), *Autopoietic Law: A New Approach to Law and Society* (Walter de Gruyter, Berlin and New York, 1988), pp 242–82, at p 273.
[21] See, in this sense, a decision of the Belgian Supreme Court (Hof van Cassatie/Cour de cassation) in a tax case: Cass. 13 February 1997, *Rechtskundig Weekblad*, 1997–98, 400–1.

offers a stable environment for strategic actions of individuals, who want to organise their lives as they prefer. If we want to set up a business, we may want to buy property. In order to achieve this, we first have to know from whom we could acquire that property[22] and how. Thus, we need property law (land law) and contract law. Without any form of property law or contract law, nothing could be done.

This function of allowing and facilitating strategic actions is fulfilled through six more specific functions: (a) law creates spheres of individual autonomy, by granting a minimum of individual liberties, both privately ("private autonomy") and politically ("public autonomy"); (b) it prevents undesired behaviour of others and promotes desired behaviour; (c) it co-ordinates human behaviour, (d) it facilitates private arrangements among people; (e) it allocates the available resources; (f) it brings about some redistribution of goods and services; and (g) it solves conflicts between citizens.

4.2.1 Creating Spheres of Autonomy

All legal systems, even those determined and controlled by the most dictatorial political regime, leave some sphere of autonomy to the citizen, at least for private interaction. Some freedom of contract, for instance, is endemic to all legal systems.

Modern democratic legal systems also establish an important sphere of public autonomy: human rights that guarantee a participation in public life, including a direct or indirect participation in the political debate. By this, such rights guarantee not only the structuring of political power and the advancement of social cohesion, they also facilitate the individual's life. The individual disposes of areas of freedom, which can be used, or not, as one likes. One can be a candidate to elections or not, one may use one's right to vote, or not,[23] one may be a member of many associations or of none, one may use the freedom of religion or not. A free press is probably primarily important for public debate and opinion formation, and most people will never want to use it themselves, but if they wish to do so they can.

Spheres of autonomy may be used to isolate oneself from others, such as the right to privacy, and create "islands" where individuals may organise their life without any intrusion from the outside world. In most cases, however, "individual freedom" is a condition or an opportunity for interaction with others: privately (freedom of contract, confidentiality of mail) or publicly (freedom of

---

[22] In the early years after the collapse of the communist regimes in central and eastern Europe at the end of twentieth century, the impossibility of determining the "real" owner of property has been an important obstacle to foreign investments and the setting up of commercial activities.

[23] Even in countries where there is an obligation to take part in the parliamentary elections (such as in Belgium) it is always possible to hand in a blank or invalid ballot paper.

association), within a context of strategic action (freedom of contract) or of communicative action (freedom of speech).

4.2.2 Bringing About Desirable Behaviour

The most common image average citizens associate with law is criminal law, which forbids many kinds of socially deviant behaviour under the threat of punishments. This prohibition of deviant behaviour certainly is primarily achieved by penal law, but not exclusively. Tort law too aims at avoiding undesirable behaviour that could prejudice others. Sometimes taxes are used as a means to convince people to avoid less desirable activities or to use products that damage health or the environment. In fact, all branches of law incorporate rules intended to influence people's behaviour. By steering people's behaviour in general, each individual may find his or her social environment considerably improved: a safer environment, thanks to an effective criminal law and policy, traffic regulation and safety conditions for means of transport, etc; a more healthy environment, thanks to environmental law and taxes on polluting activities (cars, smoking, industries); a pleasanter environment, thanks to the regulation on town and country planning, and on access to professions such as architect; and so on. All this considerably facilitates the individual's life. As law brings about desirable behaviour amongst *others* it improves the individual's good life.

4.2.3 Coordinating Human Behaviour

The co-ordination of the behaviour of individuals is advisable, or even necessary, in two types of cases.

When people act individually in the same field, it is desirable to organise individual strategic actions in such a way that they are not unnecessarily hindered by each other. An example is traffic regulation. Most rules in this area aim at facilitating the use of the road by as many users as possible through *co-ordination*, eg, by indicating which side of the road has to be used in each direction, who will have priority at a crossing, where it is allowed to park and under what conditions, etc. Many legal rules fulfil this kind of co-ordinating function. Another example is the organisation of the competences of courts for lawsuits.

Especially in non-statal legal systems, another kind of co-ordinating function of the law is clearly obvious. When, eg, starting a sports club, some people wish to engage in some type(s) of sport, not individually but together. In most cases sports cannot be played in isolation. Some sports activities are typically team sports (football, hockey, basketball), for others one needs an opponent (tennis, chess, boxing), and this is also the case for any individual sport if one wants to compete. In order to achieve this goal (candidate) sports(wo)men have to create or to adhere to a group with this common aim. For this association they need a structure and rules that will determine who will have access to the association, what the rules of the game are and/or by whom they will be determined and changed and how. They will appoint a board, a trainer, a director, etc. At the opposite of the traffic situation, co-ordination here is not meant to facilitate individual strategic action, but *collective* group action. Co-ordination then is essential to make such action possible at all. As the members of the sports club are, by definition, interested in achieving good performances, they will be willing to accept limits to their individual opportunities, including the authority of the trainer, the manager, the board, and the like to decide what is in the best interests of the club.

State legal systems fulfil this type of co-ordinating function only to a limited extent. In most cases a smaller or larger minority (and, on occasion, even a majority) will disagree with the goals the government wants to reach and for which legal rules have been enacted. However, as far as the political majority is concerned, such rules may act as a co-ordinating framework for collective action.[24]

4.2.4 Facilitating Private Arrangements

Only part of the law is aimed at directing behaviour in some specific, desirable way. Often law just co-ordinates collective or individual action (see above) or offers means with which people may make *private arrangements* with others, as they like, or with only limited restraints. In such cases the law offers the necessary legal *tools* for such arrangements, such as types of contract. Regularly the law also offers some *model* for these arrangements, which means that statutory rules will automatically apply to the extent that no other rules were stipulated by the involved parties. If they are satisfied with the model very little will have to be done, for instance just indicating which appartment will be rented and how much will have to be paid each month. Everything else will then be governed by the, as such not compulsory, statutory rules.

Such private arrangements may serve both individual strategic actions (eg buying a very cheap priced good one needs) and collective actions (eg setting up a form of future co-operation such as a company).

4.2.5 Allocating Resources

Mainly through rules of property and competence, law determines who is allowed to use available resources and within which limits. Together with a

---

[24] See on the co-ordinating function of law "for those who subscribe to the purposes of the organization": C Gans, "The Normativity of Law and its Co-ordinative Function", (1981) 16 *Israel Law Review* 333–49 (the quotation is to be found at p 348).

minimal freedom of a sufficiently large number of individuals, it is a prerequiste for any arrangement among them. The making of a contract is impossible without, first, the legal ability (freedom and competence) to enter a contract and, secondly, the right to dispose of the resources (money, goods, services) that are transferred through that contract. It has to be decided which property will be public (within a smaller community, eg a family, or within a larger one, such as a village or a state) and which one will be of private use. As economic analysis of law has shown, most rules in most legal systems tend to make this choice according to the principle of optimum efficacy. When bargaining costs are low, private property is more appropriate; when they are high, because of the large number of people involved, public property is more efficient.[25] For similar reasons, it may also be desirable to limit the competences of the private owner, eg when the damaging effects of some use of the property, such as environmental pollution, are not private but public.[26]

4.2.6 Redistributing Goods and Services

The law not only determines the "starting position" of the individuals by allocating the available resources, it also offers the framework through which they may themselves reallocate those resources, and, moreover, law itself redistributes goods and services.

When people die we need rules that tell us to whom his properties, claims and debts should go: the community, the family or those he indicated (eg in a will), or whether (some of) his rights and obligations simply disappear with him. In all societies at least some rights are transferred to others after the death of the rightholder. This means a redistribution of goods.

In primitive societies there may be rules such as the obligation for adult male members of the clan to work from time to time for the chieftain. This entails a redistribution of services.

In modern societies there is a much more complex redistribution of goods and services through taxes, social security allowances, and the like, on the one hand, and a large provision of services by public authorities (education, public transport, roads, military protection, etc).

The function of redistribution of goods and services thus seems to be typical for all legal systems.[27]

---

[25] R Cooter and T Ulen, *Law & Economics*, 3rd edn (Addison-Wesley, Reading MA, 2000), p 160.

[26] *Ibid*, 150–59.

[27] It is especially Joseph Raz who rightly has pointed to this largely unnoticed social function of law (J Raz, *The Authority of Law* (Clarendon Press, Oxford, 1979), pp 171–72).

4.2.7 Solving Conflicts

Solving conflicts is both part of the way law is structuring society and its function of facilitating life for the individual citizen. Even when done by courts, solving conflicts is part of the organisation of political power. Court decisions also play a role in achieving social cohesion. From the point of view of the individual, on the other hand, the availability of bodies that can solve conflicts and the existence of procedural rules that structure the way this can be done, are important boundary conditions for using the law and the rights and competences it awards. Without effective control over the implementation of law, including sanctioning, many legal rules would be largely disregarded. But this as such is not the problem of the individual, but the problem of the authorities. For the individual it is important to have at his disposal an institution that can *authoritatively determine the rights and duties* of the conflicting parties. By this, the organisation of the settlement of conflicts is a necessary condition for law to fulfil the other functions that aim at facilitating the individual's life.

5

The Concept of a Legal Norm

Legal systems contain different types of "norms" or "rules" or "legal sentences". The basic type of norm is the prescriptive rule of behaviour, which says what one should do, should not do, or may do in certain circumstances. As already discussed above, it is typical for legal systems that this type of primary rules of behaviour are backed by a whole set of secondary rules. Those secondary rules create the framework for the primary rules, especially as regards their coming into being, their change and abolition and the way conflicts may, or should, be solved. Secondary rules not only also contain rules of behaviour, addressed to officials in the legal system, but, moreover, encompass an important amount of other kinds of rules, such as power-conferring rules, which do not, as such, contain any guideline for behaviour, but only indicate who will be in charge or will have the power for making some kind of legal act (eg, the power to make a contract or a will, the power to decide a case). Legislation also offers many definitions of legal institutions, concepts, and the like, and other kinds of "descriptive" or rather performative stipulations, called "qualifying dispositions" or "constitutive rules": they establish, for instance, the courts and Parliament, they determine what the consequences are when a legal act has been declared void, etc. One should clearly distinguish between a "norm" and a "legislative disposition". Not every article in a statute or a code contains a norm. Moreover, as will be discussed later,[1] one should also make the distinction between a norm and its formulation. First, normative dispositions are often worded in apparently descriptive sentences. Secondly, one single sentence may, in some cases, contain more than one norm, whereas in other cases one has to combine several provisions for reconstructing all the parts of one single norm.

In this chapter we will concentrate on the "norm" as rule of behaviour, or, as Honoré has called them, "directly normative rules".[2] The other types of legal rules will only partly and occasionally be discussed, when it seems useful for our general line of reasoning.[3] Here, we will not enter into the problems of the terminology of the norms either. Here, the words "norm" and "rule" are used as

---

[1] See below chapter 7.

[2] AM Honoré, "Real Laws" in PMS Hacker and J Raz, *Law, Morality and Society* (Clarendon Press, Oxford, 1977), pp 99–118, at p 112.

[3] For a thorough discussion of the different kinds of legal sentences we may refer to the excellent work of M Atienza and JR Manero, *A Theory of Legal Sentences* (Kluwer Academic, Dordrecht, 1998), p 192.

synonyms, for stylistic reasons, even if, on other occasions "rule" may be used in a broader sense, including legal dispositions without direct normative scope.[4]

5.1 NORMS AS REASONS FOR HUMAN ACTION

Norms may be seen from different points of view. As we will argue later on, a norm should always be seen in the context of a communication between its norm-sender and its norm-receiver(s). Many one-sided, and thus defective, theories of law have been built upon an overemphasis on the norm-sender, or the norm-receiver, or the norm-text.

If we are here emphasising norms as reasons for human action, it is not with the intention of narrowing the concept of legal norms to this only, but rather to provide a starting point for the analysis of this concept. Pioneering work on norms as reasons for action has been done by Joseph Raz in his book *Practical Reason and Norms.*[5]

Raz makes a distinction between reasons which prevail because they are stronger than other reasons, on the one hand, and reasons which simply exclude other reasons, on the other. In the first case, there is a conflict between, as he calls it, first-order reasons. This conflict is resolved by the relative strength of the conflicting reasons.[6] In the second case, the conflict is of a different type. Raz gives the example of a soldier who is ordered by his commanding officer to appropriate and use a van belonging to a tradesman. His friend urges him to disobey the order pointing to weighty reasons for doing so. The soldier does not deny that his friend may have a case. But, he claims, it does not matter whether he is right or not. Orders are orders and should be obeyed even if wrong, even if no harm will come from disobeying them. As a subordinate it is not for you to decide what is best. The order is a reason for doing what you were ordered to do, regardless of the balance of reasons. However, one may depart from this general rule if, for example, one were ordered to commit an atrocity.[7]

The order of the commanding officer is, for the soldier, a second order reason, which actually excludes the balancing of the reasons, weighed by the commanding officer. Raz calls "exclusionary reasons" second order reasons to refrain from acting for some reason. Conflicts between first-order reasons and second-order exclusionary reasons are resolved, not by the strength of the competing reasons, but by a general principle of practical reasoning which

---

[4] For a general overview of the different meanings of "norm", see: GH von Wright, *Norm and Action. A Logical Inquiry* (Routledge & Kegan Paul, London, 1963), pp 1–16. It is interesting to note that, at the opposite of what I think to be the usual meaning of the words in legal parlance, "norm", with von Wright, bears a broader meaning than "rule": "norm" is used as a general concept, which includes "rules", "prescriptions" and "directives" (p 15).

[5] 1st edn (Hutchinson, London, 1975); 2nd edn (Princeton University Press, Princeton, 1990).

[6] *Ibid*, p 36

[7] *Ibid*.

determines that exclusionary reasons always prevail when in conflict with first-order reasons. Exclusionary reasons may vary in scope and exclude all or only some of the first-order reasons. They may also conflict with and be overridden by another second-order reason.[8]

According to Raz, the main problem of understanding rules is to see what sort of reasons rules are, and how they differ from other reasons.[9] In order to make this analysis, Raz makes a distinction between "mandatory norms", "permissive norms" and "power-conferring norms".[10]

Mandatory norms are those norms which are more commonly called "prescriptive".[11] They include a very wide range of rules and principles regulating human conduct. It seems that mandatory norms, in Raz's view, include all kinds of norms which are not "permissions" or "power-conferring norms". Raz argues that all mandatory norms are both first-order reasons and second-order exclusionary reasons. From the point of view of the person who follows such a rule, it means a *belief* in it being an exclusionary reason. He may be wrong, the rule may eg be invalid or not correctly interpreted, but for him it is an exclusionary reason. On the other hand, a norm is valid if, and only if, it ought to be followed. Thus it follows that a rule is valid only if it is a valid exclusionary reason.

Norms are reasons for actions but have, in their turn, to be justified. But we need not know what these reasons are in order to apply the norm correctly to the majority of cases, precisely because these norms are exclusionary reasons which do not need to be balanced with first-order reasons. Therefore, norms are regarded as complete reasons in their own right and not just as part of a chain of reasons.[12]

Permissions indicate the absence of constraints. A strong permission is a permission based on exclusionary reasons: it is based on reasons and not merely on their absence (as is the case for weak permissions).[13]

---

[8] *Ibid.*

[9] *Ibid*, p 51.

[10] This distinction is very similar to the main distinction made by WN Hohfeld when analysing the concept of "right": rights/duties (mandatory norms), privileges (permissive norms), and powers (power-conferring rules) (see below 5.5).

[11] Raz, above n 5, p 49.

[12] *Ibid*, p 79.

[13] It has been argued that there are no "permissive rules", as weak permissions are only the absence of rules (allowing explicitly what otherwise is not regulated does not add anything to normative reality), whereas strong permissions, together with the mandatory norm to which they are an exception, may be reformulated as mandatory norms with a more limited scope, in which the exception has already been left out (see, eg, Echave-Urquijo-Guibourg and Ross, as commented on by Atienza and Ruiz Manero (*A Theory of Legal Sentences* (Kluwer Academic, Dordrecht, 1998), pp 90–94). However, what is true for strong permissions, namely that the mandatory norm to which they are an exception may be reformulated, so that the "permissive rule" could become superfluous, is not true for the weak permissions. Strong permissions are much more concrete than weak ones. If a sign says that traffic is not allowed in this park, except bicycles, the permission is obviously very specific. Weak permissions, by definition, cannot be very concrete, as there is some non-regulated field, in which a countless amount of concrete actions can be conceived that are all allowed, because they are not, directly or indirectly, legally prohibited. Moreover, a third category should be distinguished, a kind of "strong weak permission". An example is "freedom of speech". It is a strong

Exclusionary permissions differ from exclusionary reasons in that they do not entail that one ought to disregard the excluded reasons. They merely entitle one to do so. Exclusionary permissions are strong permissions. They are not merely the result of the absence of reasons to the contrary. They always require a justification.[14] Permissive norms have the same structure as mandatory norms. A statement of a permissive norm states that certain norm subjects have an exclusionary permission to perform the norm act when the conditions of application are satisfied. They differ from mandatory norms only in the deontic operator: the exclusionary permission operator replaces that of the exclusionary "ought" coupled with a first-order "ought" which figures in statements of mandatory norms.[15]

A *normative power* is an ability to affect exclusionary reasons which apply to one's own or to other people's actions. An act is the exercise of a normative power if, and only if, it is recognised as effecting a normative change. It is, amongst other possible justifications, an act of a type such that it is reasonable to expect that, if recognised as effecting a normative change, acts of this type will be generally performed only if the persons concerned want to serve this normative change. Power-conferring norms resemble permissive norms and differ from mandatory norms in having a normative force without being themselves complete reasons for action.[16]

Everybody will agree with Raz that rules often function as a reason, and generally as a decisive reason, for a person to act in some way and not in another one. More problematic is the thesis according to which rules constitute reasons of a *different kind,* compared to other reasons. Why should rules a priori, or even generally, *exclude* all other reasons? Are they not simply balanced with other reasons? When, for example, in 1991 the Belgian King refused to enact the Abortion Act, voted by Parliament, it was obviously *moral reasons* which functioned as exclusionary reasons, putting aside all other reasons, including all legal rules.

Of course, this is a rather exceptional case. In daily life we are confronted with many situations in which rules indeed determine our behaviour, excluding all other reasons favourable for any other kind of behaviour, just because of their status as a rule. When we enter, for example, a private car park we are, normally, not going to park our car in a space with a "staff only" sign. But even in such a case we still might decide to park our car in a prohibited space, because we are in a hurry, because there are no other parking spaces available, and

permission because it is explicitly worded in the law, but it has in common with weak permissions that it does not regulate a specific conduct, but a whole field in which a countless number of actions can be conceived of that are allowed because of the explicit "weak" permission. Not a specific behaviour but a, rather abstract, *type of behaviour* is explicitly allowed. It creates an explicit field of liberty for the citizen, with a duty of non-interference for all other people, including public authorities.

[14] Raz, above n 5, pp 89–90.
[15] *Ibid,* pp 89–97.
[16] *Ibid,* pp 97–106.

because we do not need the parking space for more than a few minutes. Here also, the rule does not seem to function as an exclusionary reason, as the rule, and the presumed reasons for that rule, are clearly balanced with other reasons, as, for instance, those mentioned in the example.

It is obvious that the rule implies at least a change in the reasons for choosing one parking space rather than another. When two equivalent spaces are available, but one of them is reserved, any person acting rationally will use the space which is not reserved. But the same will occur when it is very hot and there are a sunny space and a shady one available. Every rational being will park his car in the shady parking space. The strong heating of the car after having been parked in the sun for a few hours is an annoying effect one will try to avoid, just as one will try to avoid problems, discussions and sanctions which could occur because of parking in a reserved space.

Are rules then not even a different kind of reason, let alone a reason which would exclude all other reasons? It depends from which perspective the rule is looked at.

Of course, the authority of the rule enacting person or body should be recognised by the person who is expected to take it into consideration as a reason for his actions. Let us take the example of a woman who, after having searched for a parking space for some time, has at last found one, but a man comes to her, and says, without further legitimation, that this space is reserved. She will not be inclined to accept that this man has a power to enact or to adjudicate a rule containing a parking prohibition. She still might consider the obvious wish of the man, that she would not use this parking space, as a weak, or even strong, reason for deciding whether she would leave or move her car. But she would not see it as the application of a legal rule.[17] When this man legitimated himself as a police officer, however, she would probably not even ask why this space is reserved, for whom, etc, but simply abide by his directive and look for some other parking space. As a rule, here, the authoritatively enacted norm will indeed function as a reason, excluding other reasons.

Does this mean that the rule will, a priori, exclude any other possible reason? Of course not. If the woman, for example, needed the urgent help of a physician and the parking space was in front of a hospital or of the physician's house, she would invoke this reason for disregarding the parking prohibition. In most cases she would even succeed in convincing the police officer.

In fact, the wording "exclusionary reason" suggests more than what seems to be meant by Raz.[18] The fact that there is a legal rule imposing some type of

---

[17] She might see it as an application of a rule of courtesy, but this rule would, with the opposite result, also apply to the man in his attitude towards the woman.

[18] In his Postscript to the second edition of *Practical Reasons and Norms* in 1990, Raz writes "The very claim that there are reasons of the kind I called exclusionary was met with skepticism on the part of many readers" (*ibid*, p 178). He admits that he contributed himself to some confusions (p 184) and that on some points his argument was defective (p 198). The comments he makes in this Postscript are helpful for eliminating some misunderstandings, but the exact scope of the concept "exclusionary reason" still remains somewhat unclear.

behaviour does not exclude the very *reasoning* about the appropriateness of that behaviour.[19] It does not exclude that, all things considered, the rule will not be followed, because there are (very) strong reasons for disregarding the rule in this particular situation. Legal rules are only prima facie exclusionary reasons.

Legal rules are the result of a decision, a decision which is based on reasons. The reasons which were in favour of deciding to enact the rule have been balanced with other reasons, which could have led to the repudiation of the proposed rule or to a different content. It is this weighing and balancing which has authoritatively reached a decision and has been laid down in the rule. Influenced by Raz's writings, Hart has taken over the concept of "rules as exclusionary reasons for action", but speaks about "peremptory reasons for action".[20] As MacCormick has noted, these reasons "are peremptory exactly in that they close further debate on a question—whatever may remain open to question, at a certain point the law settles its answer to issues raised before it".[21]

It is the weighing and balancing of the reasons, which were the subject of *that* debate, that is closed. Of course, new, very peculiar factual reasons may occur on the occasion of the application of that rule. The rule does not exclude these new reasons from being taken into account. It simply excludes that the debate on the balanced reasons is opened again each time the rule is meant to be applied. As already pointed out above, (legal) rules reduce the complexity of constantly making decisions in life. They offer a framework of decisions, which are already choices amongst differing reasons. Moreover, they also help us to predict the choices and the behaviour of other people through a generalised expectation of behaviour.

Rules, thus, facilitate actions in two ways. First, they offer the citizen ready-made decisions, exempting him from balancing a number of reasons. Only if he has a strong reason for not following the rule, will he have to reconsider the choice. Secondly, they create a generalised expectation of behaviour on behalf of the other citizens, and give people something to hold on to to decide how to behave.

In this sense, rules are peremptory or "exclusionary" reasons for action, not because they would eliminate people's reasoning about the desirability of following the rule in a specific situation, but because they eliminate the *necessity* of doing so. Modern law "removes tasks of social integration from actors who are already overburdened in their efforts, at reaching understandings".[22]

Until now we took for granted that legal rules influence human behaviour. Actually, primary rules of behaviour are, by definition, meant to do so. Otherwise they would not make sense. Law, of course, contains many rules,

---

[19] Postscript to the second edition of *Practical Reasons and Norms* in 1990, p 184.

[20] HLA Hart, *Essays in Jurisprudence and Philosophy* (Clarendon Press, Oxford, 1983).

[21] N MacCormick, "The Concept of Law and 'The Concept of Law' ", (1994) 14 *Oxford Journal of Legal Studies* 1–23, at p 11.

[22] J Habermas, *Between Facts and Norms* (trans William Rehg) (Polity Press, Cambridge, 1996), p 38.

which as such do not aim at directing human behaviour although, indirectly, they may influence it.[23] They belong to the secondary rules, which are left aside in the discussion here. But also the direct influence of primary rules on people's behaviour should not be overestimated. The desired behaviour will not follow: when the rule is unknown to the involved person, when it is misinterpreted (by himself, or by officials or others who instruct him), when by inadvertence or for emotional reasons the rule is ignored, or when in the person's (risk) calculation the disadvantages of following the rule are more important than its advantages. The more rules a legal system contains, the higher the risk that some, or many, of them will not be followed. This is the paradox of the developed welfare state: the more rules, the less it is likely that all, or most, of those concerned will know them, the higher the risk that those rules will conflict with each other and lead to interpretation problems and/or a forced ignoring of one of them, and the more difficult and expensive it will be to control and effectively sanction the undesired behaviour. All this creates a weakening of the authority of law in general and makes it even more difficult to enforce the rules and to direct human behaviour, even in more essential matters.

Power-conferring rules are reasons for action, not in the sense that they would be sufficient conditions for action, as rules of behaviour generally are, but in a weaker sense: they create the (necessary) framework within which people *may decide how to behave.* They are necessary, but not sufficient, conditions for action. The power to conclude contracts or to be in charge of a management, for instance, are the basis for deciding about one's actions and in that sense reasons for it, although they do not determine what precise kind of action will be taken.

For officials, however, power-conferring rules play a more important role: secondary rules of that type very clearly determine behaviour of officials on whom such power has been conferred. The reason is that such powers are generally not conferred with the freedom to use them or not, but with a *duty* to use those powers to the best of one's abilities, in the light of a determined aim. A judge, for instance, has the duty to decide a case within a reasonable time and according to the law. His power to do so is not a sheer opportunity, as the power to conclude contracts generally is, rather it is the essence of his function and determines the kinds of action he is *bound* to take.

Therefore, one cannot state that power-conferring rules are always doubly conditional, as Atienza and Ruiz Manero argue, in that they say how we should behave *if* certain conditions are fulfilled and *if* we want to bring about a certain result.[24] This is only correct when there is a *freedom* to bring about a certain

---

[23] Eg performative rules in a constitution enacting that there is one Supreme Court, or that "the colours of the official flag will be red, yellow and black", or that "the country is divided in ten provinces" will have an indirect influence to the extent that people accept the "existence" of that Supreme Court, national flag, and provinces and, for instance, use that type of flag at special occasions. However, this is only an indirect effect of such constitutional provisions, which do not contain "rules" in the strict sense.

[24] M Atienza and J Ruiz Manero, *A Theory of Legal Sentences* (Kluwer Academic, Dordrecht, 1998), p 66.

result or not. Secondary rules, conferring powers to create, abolish or change law, generally contain such a freedom, but those related to the adjudication of the law do not, or offer only a rather limited freedom to choose, at least at the level to decide whether to take an action or not. Once a case has been brought to court, the judge does not have any freedom to decide the case or not: it is his duty to use his powers to decide the case. In practice, the judge will almost always have some freedom as to the content of his decision, but not at the level of "the results he would like to bring about himself", as those results are determined by the law he has to apply. The judge has only some, more or less limited, freedom as to the *interpretation* of that law.

Powers conferred upon officials—but sometimes also upon private persons (eg in a company)—seem, thus, to be combined with, explicit or implicit, principles containing positive guidelines for behaviour. Very generally speaking, in the public area they are all so combined: a legislator or a government are presumed to take all useful actions in the interest of the population, within the limits of their powers. In the private area too they often are (parents, for instance, are presumed to take all useful actions in the interest of their children), but not always (eg, the power to accept or to refuse an inheritance may be used completely freely). Depending on the kind of public authority, the freedom to take an action or not and to decide about its content may be more limited or less: a constitutional law-giver will have very limited constraints, whereas local authorities will have many more. It is a matter of gradation, but all powers conferred upon officials imply a duty to take at least some kind of positive action, and not just a duty to abstain from some kinds of action (eg, because they fall outside one's powers, or because they infringe on human rights).

5.2 NORM-SENDER AND NORM-RECEIVER

In language, and in communication in general, words, sentences, signs, etc, are a way of communicating a message from a sender to a receiver. One should distinguish between the message as such, the forms used for communicating the message, the person(s) who send the message, and the person(s) who receive it[25].

A message does not make sense, or at least can hardly be understood or be correctly interpreted, if it is not linked to this communication process between sender and receiver. If we accept this for messages in general, we have to admit that the necessity to take into account the sender and the receiver is still more obvious for norms.

Norms are means, used by some norm-sender to regulate some society. As regards primary rules of conduct, the norm-sender aims at regulating and guiding the behaviour of some group of norm-receivers. If the norm-sender wants to make sure that conduct in society will adapt to his aim, the norm-message

---

[25] This will be more extensively discussed below in chapter 7.

should be transmitted adequately to the norm-receivers concerned. If, on the other hand, norm-receivers want to interpret and apply the norm correctly, they should take into account the aims of the norm-receiver.

The whole problem of interpretation of the law is, inter alia, linked to the question to what extent the aims of the norm-sender, the will of the legislator, should determine the interpretation and application of the law. This problem will be discussed later. Here, we can already argue that many theories of law cannot give a correct account of the law because they overemphasise one of the elements in the relationship of "norm-sender – norm – norm-receiver".

The *command theory* of law, for example, sees the law as the pure will of the sovereign. Most notably, John Austin[26] saw *every* legal rule, and not just the common type of rule, as a command of the sovereign addressed to the citizen. This order is, for Austin, closely linked to a *sanction*, defined as threat of a harm. In this conception it is the will of the sovereign which exclusively determines the content of the rule or "command". In interpreting a norm one will necessarily focus on this will only, leaving aside the wording of the norm-text and the practical problems a concrete application may entail.

The *Realist Movements* reduce the whole law to the point of view of the norm-receivers. In American realism one focuses on the judges as norm-receivers, in Scandinavian Realism rather on the citizens. The most celebrate quotation is "The prophecies of what courts will do in fact, and nothing more pretentious, are what I mean by the law." of Oliver Wendell Holmes,[27] but probably the most typical, or rather extreme, exponent of this overemphasis of the judges as norm-receivers is Jerome Frank. According to Frank, people need certainties in their life, including legal certainties. This leads them to the creation of all kinds of myths, including the myth of a complete and closed legal system, that would offer an answer to every legal question, and the myth that judges do not create law, but apply only pre-existing rules.[28] In reality, however, according to Frank, law is a set of variable, only within some limits predictable, decisions. The so-called "legal rules" and "legal principles" are nothing else but mythical constructions, that act as stimuli, which influence judicial behaviour, but not more than other stimuli such as the ideology of the judge, his sympathies and antipathies, his political convictions, etc. In this approach, legal rules completely lose their *normative* content.

Along the same lines of reasoning, Scandinavian Realist Theories have also deconstructed legal concepts such as "legal norm", "right", "duty", or the "will of the legislator" as mystifications of a non-existent reality. Axel Hägerström criticises Kelsen, who founds the law basically in the "will of the state", and defines it not as a psychological will but as "the expression of the unity of the

---

[26] J Austin, *The Province of Jurisprudence Determined* (Weidenfeld and Nicolson, London, 1954 (first published J Murray, London, 1832)).

[27] OW Holmes., "The Path of the Law", (1897) *Harvard Law Review* 475–78, at p 463.

[28] J Frank, *Law and the Modern Mind* (New York, 1930), p 41.

organisation defined as legal order".[29] For Hägerström this is a definition of unreal concepts by other concepts that lack any link with reality.[30] Moreover, this is circular reasoning: norms are only considered to be "legal norms" when they can be attributed to a "state will", but, says Hägerström, the concept of "will of the state" does not refer to an empirical reality, but is a legal concept which is included in the concept of "legal norm". As a consequence, the "will of the state" can only be defined by the "legal norm", and vice versa. When referring to the "will of the people", as is the more traditional approach to law, Hägerström argues that there is no real "general" or "collective" will, but only some metaphysically posited meta-individual will, presented or conceived as the "will of the people".[31] He also criticises the confusion between "command" and "duty". A command only expresses the wishes of the commander and does not entail any "duty" as such. This "duty" is nothing but the subjective feeling of the citizen that he ought to follow that command or rule.[32] As a result of social influences and pressure associations are created in the mind of people between laws and feelings of duty, which give the false impression that some kind of "objective duty" would exist as linked to those laws. From this, Hägerström concludes that law has basically a socio-psychological foundation. Legal awareness, fear of anarchy, some tradition of following "the valid law", regular sanctioning by public authorities of deviant behaviour, and the like create in society a kind of "superstition" that this law really exists. This approach of Scandinavian Realism also empties the law of any normative content and any deliberate social ordering.

Black letter theories of law reduce the norm to its text, isolated from both norm-sender and norm-receiver. They consider that a text can be "clear" and that any interpretation of such a text of which the meaning is "obvious" is a distortion of the "real" meaning of the norm laid down in that text. Hence, such an interpretation is prohibited: *Interpretatio cessat in claris.* For determining the meaning of this norm, both the will of the norm-sender and the interpretation by the norm-receiver or the specific circumstances of the case are considered to be irrelevant.

Further on in this book I will argue that only a dialectic, communicative approach may solve this problem, in which norm-sender, norm-receiver and norm-text mutually presuppose each other and co-determine the meaning of the norm. Here, I wish simply to conclude that a norm has at least *something* to do

---

[29] H Kelsen, *Hauptprobleme der Staatslehre entwickelt aus der Lehre vom Rechtssatze* (Tübingen, 1911), pp 183 and 699.

[30] A Hägerström, *Der römische Obligationsbegriff im Lichte der allgemeinen römischen Rechtsanschauung*, vol I (1927), p 12.

[31] A Hägerström, *Inquiries into the Nature of Laws and Morals* (Almquist & Wiksell, Uppsala, 1953), p 22.

[32] This analysis of "duty" as a "metaphysical concept" has been further elaborated by Vilhelm Lundstedt (see his *Die Unwissenschaftlichkeit der Rechtswissenschaft*, vol I (1932), esp. at pp 56 et seq.

with some norm-sender and with some norm-receiver, and that both are of some relevance for analysing, interpreting and applying norms.

Having admitted this, we now have to determine who in practice should be considered to be the norm-"sender" and who to be norm-"receiver", when confronted with some norm in a specific legal system.

5.2.1 The Norm-Sender

In modern legal systems, the bulk of legal rules is issued by a legislator, who has been determined by the legal system itself. Generally, this legislator may easily be defined and recognised as the norm-sender for the rules he has enacted.

But, the question remains, whether the individual or body that enacted a law should always be considered to be the "norm-sender"; to be the legislator whose will is relevant for the interpretation and application of the norm.

For example, the German historical school in the nineteenth century considered Parliament or other "legislators" to be only a mouthpiece of the "*Volksgeist*", an embodiment of the views of the law and the sense of justice in society. The real norm-sender in this view is "the people", the community of the citizens.[33] Parliament is considered to be only a technical intermediary.

On the other hand, there are a lot of cases where the formal norm-sender, the official legislator, can hardly be said to have expressed aims in the law, as he may not even have known the content of the law he has enacted. For example, in Belgium each year hundreds or even thousands of Royal Decrees (*Koninklijk Besluit, Arrêté Royal*) are enacted, implementing the more general statutes enacted by Parliament. These decrees are formally enacted by the King. It is, however, very doubtful whether the King has read any of these decrees and in most cases whether he is even aware of the content of the decree he has signed.

To a lesser extent the same problem may arise in other cases. For example, in Parliament, when rather technical matters have been prepared and discussed in a parliamentary commission and afterwards simply approved by the whole Parliament, most of its members will not be fully aware of the content or the scope of the Act.

Does this imply that it does not make sense to talk of "the aims of the norm-sender" or "the will of the legislator", as this "legislator" obviously did not have a precise idea about the content of the law, let alone have any "aim" or "will"? Is this a decisive argument requiring us to abandon the concept of "norm-sender" and to study norms isolated from any "norm-sender"? The answer is no.

In all cases the *formal* legislator should be considered to be the "norm-sender", precisely because he is so defined by the legal system itself, and, as a rule, generally accepted to dispose of such legislative powers.

---

[33] FC von Savigny, *Vom Beruf unsrer Zeit für Gesetzgebung und Rechtswissenschaft* (Freiburg im Breisgau, 1892, 1st edn, 1814), p 5 et seq.

An analoguous situation is where someone has signed a contract without reading it and without being aware of a large part of its content. He is still a party to the contract, a party whose will is relevant when interpreting the contract.

The legislator may to a large, and even to a very large, extent rely on opinions in society ("*Volksgeist*"), on proposals of pressure groups, on preparatory work by a small (parliamentary) commission, by civil officers, by specialists within the political party or parties of the majority, etc. If the legislator formally enacts the law without being (completely) aware of its content and scope, it just means that within certain limits (be they sometimes very large limits) the legislator relies on prepatory work done by people he trusts and from whom he accepts (a priori) the draft of a law. Together with the draft text the formal legislator also, inevitably, adopts the aims, the will of its author(s). By giving the formal authoritative mark to a law, eg by signing a royal decree, a king or other legislator decides that a norm is enacted and should be applied according to the conscious will of the legislator or, to the extent that he has no conscious will as regards the Act, according to the "delegated" will of the draftsmen of the Act.

As Joseph Raz worded it:

> "Law making does not imply knowingly making the law one intended, but knowingly making a law one could have known one is making."[34]

One should indeed distinguish between the *formal legislator* and the *substantive "legislator"*. The formal law-giver is completely determined and defined by the secondary rules of the legal system. The actual authority of this formal legislator depends upon the degree to which the secondary rules empowering this legislator are generally accepted by the community to which it is expected to apply.

Much confusion has been caused by the use of the concept of the "*will of the legislator*". For example, when analysing legislative materials, lawyers often try to find out whose will is relevant for determining the "will of the legislator". When, for instance, a rather specialised matter has been discussed in parliament, statements made by members of the parliamentary commission, who were more acquainted with the field and who discussed the draft more thoroughly, will be considered to have more weight than statements made by other Members of Parliament. The "will of the legislator" is here, more or less, equated with the will of some members of this legislative body. When (part of) the substantive legislator is part of the body which constitutes the formal legislator, the problem that a "parliament" cannot have a "will" as such seems to be solved in an acceptable way along this line of reasoning.

In some cases, and even in an important number of them, however, the formal legislator is completely disconnected from the substantive legislator(s). This is, for instance, the case with, at least most of, the above mentioned Royal

---

[34] J Raz, "On the Nature of Law", (1996) *ARSP* 1–25, at p 22.

Decrees. If the concept of the "will of the legislator" is understood in a psychological sense, then one is faced with a difficult choice: either (a) one has to conclude that the formal legislator did not have any actual will with regard to the Act under consideration, so that there is no "will of the legislator" and the Act does not have any meaning, or (b) one has to take into account the will of the substantive legislator(s), with as a consequence that, indirectly, a normative power is recognised on behalf of people who do not have any such power according to the secondary rules of the legal system, or (c) one has to determine some fictitious "will" of the formal legislator, which leaves it completely to the interpreting norm-receiver to determine its content: the will of the norm-applier is presented as if it were the "will of the legislator".

In legal practice and in legal doctrine the way out of this problem has often been seen in discarding the "will of the legislator" to be discovered behind the statutory text and to keep to this text only. However, this is rather an ostrich attitude: the problem is not solved, but one just tries not to see the problem, by putting one's head in the sand of the statutory text.

A way out of the problem is to see the work of the substantive legislator as a kind of implicit delegation by the formal legislator(s), as has been suggested above. But one could also put it in a somewhat different way. Every legislative act is presumed to be the result of a political debate and of a, limited or extensive, communication with other actors, outside the legislative body: the administration, pressure groups, lobbies, the judiciary, legal doctrine, technical experts, or even, via the media, the whole community.[35] The legislative draft and, eventually, the enacted text are the result of such a communication process, which may sometimes be very intensive and broad. The enacted legislative text puts an authoritative end to this debate and to the information input. The legislative act is a synthesis of this communication process. This synthesis can only be correctly understood in the context of the communicational elements on which it is based. In this sense, the "will of the legislator" has nothing to do with some psychological will of (members of) the formal legislator. If this concept of the "will of the legislator" is used, it can only mean some objective result of a preparatory communication process as it has resulted in some final text. The text can only be understood in the light of this preparatory process, but the exact scope of this communication process may only rightly be understood in the light of the final text, as formally enacted by the formal legislator.

We may conclude that the formal legislator always has to be considered to be the norm-sender, even if he is not at all aware of the context of the enacted norm. The formal legislator *as such* does not determine the meaning and scope of the norm, but only the status of the norm as valid rule within the legal

---

[35] A, limited, route of communication between legislators and the community also takes place via the elections. Changes in legislation are sometimes directly, and often indirectly, influenced by changes in the electoral behaviour or by expected changes at the next elections, or by an attempt to avoid such changes.

system. The *meaning* of the norm is determined in a much broader context, but this is another discussion to which we will return later on.

5.2.2 The Norm-Receiver

Are legal norms addressed to the citizens, to the judges, to both, or to neither of them? This is a question which has entailed a lot of discussion, especially in German jurisprudence. Nowadays this question may seem rather odd. The discussion, however, is still interesting in that it focuses on an important aspect of the legal norm: the distinction between the content of a norm and its linguistic formulation. The problem of the wording and of the meaning of norms will be discussed later, within the frame of the methodology of law. Here, we simply conclude that the abovementioned discussion of the norm-receivers is to a large extent due to the confusion between the norm and the wording of the norm.

A first theory considers the judge, by exclusion of the citizen, to be the only norm-receiver, because, amongst others, legal norms are often worded so as to address only judges.[36] This is especially so in penal law: most penal codes do not actually explicitly forbid stealing, murdering, raping, etc, they rather contain rules stipulating that those who have stolen (murdered, etc) have to be punished as follows (. . .). At first sight, this might be interpreted as being a norm addressed only to the judge, imposing on him some duty to punish criminals, and not some rule of conduct imposed on the citizens. Very few people will nowadays agree with this view. It is obvious that penal provisions are in the first place meant to be primary rules of conduct, forbidding some behaviour, defined as "criminal". But, on the other hand, these penal provisions, as they are worded, also contain a secondary rule addressed to the judge, empowering him to punish, but also imposing on him the duty to punish.

The theory which considers the judge to be the only norm-receiver also relies on a few other arguments:

(a) citizens do not know the content of the law;[37]
(b) when the law is violated, sanctions may only be applied by a judge;[38]
(c) the abstract rule is addressed to the judge, who, in turn, makes the rule more concrete and gives some order to one or more parties at the trial.[39]

---

[36] See eg J Binder, *Rechtsnorm und Rechtspflicht* (Erlangen, 1911), p 11; ME Mayer, *Rechtsnormen und Kulturnormen* (Breslau, 1903), pp 7–8; A Ross, *On Law and Justice* (University of California Press, Berkeley and Los Angeles, 1958), p 33.

[37] ME Mayer, above n 36, pp 6–9; EE Hirsch, "Die Steuerung menschlichen Verhaltens" in M Gruter and M Rehbinder (eds), *Der Beitrag der Biologie zu Fragen von Recht und Ethik* (Duncker & Humblot, Berlin, 1983), pp 285–87.

[38] R von Jhering, *Der Zweck in Recht*, vol 1 (Leipzig, 1884), pp 333–38.

[39] ME Mayer, above n 36, p 45. This seems also to be the position taken by Kelsen (see his *General Theory of Norms* (Clarendon Press, Oxford, 1991), pp 52–55).

The first argument is a pragmatic argument, which has hardly any influence on the theoretical analysis of norms and of their relation with norm-sender and norm-receiver. Moreover, judges also, like all lawyers, often "do not know the content of the law". They have to look it up. The difference with the ordinary citizens is not that judges know all the legal rules and the citizens none of them. There is only a gradual, not a categorical difference. And in some technical matters, which the citizen is well acquainted with, eg because of professional reasons, the citizen may know a number of specific legal rules, the judge being even not aware of their existence. But, as a lawyer, the judge has a better general knowledge of the law and has the skills for finding his way around the legal sources to a much greater extent than the average citizen.

The two other arguments rely on the command theory of law, that interprets all laws in terms of commands, addressed by a norm-sender to a norm-receiver.[40] We will not discuss this theory in depth, and instead limit ourselves to the conclusion that the command theory reduces all norms to only one type: mandatory primary rules of conduct, obliging or forbidding some behaviour under specific circumstances.

Moreover, these primary rules are not considered to be addressed to the persons concerned, but to the judges in charge of the adjudication of these rules. Thus, the large majority of people following rules without any judicial decision would, within this view, not follow "legal rules". It is obvious that such a theory does not give a correct account of the law.

When one admits that law organises human conduct in society, one should also admit that at a certain moment in time some norm-sender, "legislator", introduces new rules or changes existing rules in view of changes of conduct in society. Judges and other legal institutions are only *means* helping to implement the rules, correcting deviant behaviour and solving other problems related to the interpretation and adjudication of the law. They can hardly be considered to be the main reason for a legal system to exist.

Other theories have proclaimed that no addressee is needed as a condition for the conception of a "norm", because in its conceptual clarity a norm could only be conceived as an "unpersonal ought".[41] Here, an abstract, purely theoretical approach is obviously neglecting an essential part of the law: a means for ordering society, which necessarily includes influencing people's behaviour through rules.[42]

---

[40] See eg J Austin, *The Province of Jurisprudence Determined*, n 26 above, and the *Uses of the Study of Jurisprudence* (Weidenfeld and Nicolson, London, 1955 (first published J Marray, London, 1863)), pp 17, 254–57, 358–61.

[41] Eg: E Mezger, "Die subjektiven Unrechtselemente" in a special issue (*Sonderband*) of (1923) 89 *Der Gerichtssaal* 245.

[42] Hans Kelsen, for his part, concentrates on this behaviour, probably as a reaction against those purely theoretical approaches: "To say that a norm is 'directed' to a person simply means that it is the *behaviour* of a person, human behaviour, which is obligatory. . . . The term 'norm-addressee' is simply a way of saying that the behaviour decreed to be obligatory in the norm is human behaviour, the behaviour of a human being" (*General Theory of Norms* (Clarendon Press, Oxford, 1991), p 8, see also pp 89–91.

5.2.3 The "Norm-Sender" of Non-Statutory Norms

Although even in England there is a growing importance attached to laws enacted by official bodies, which are gradually replacing large parts of the judicially elaborated common law, important norms within this legal system, which have been introduced and refined by courts in the course of history, are still valid.

In less developed legal systems, such as international law or the law of primitive societies, customary law plays an important role.

And even in the most developed legal systems, norms sometimes have an atypical origin, such as "unwritten general legal principles" as they have regularly been accepted by courts in continental Europe over the last decades.

In all these cases, trying to determine a "norm-sender" faces us with severe problems. The only identifiable "norm-sender" would be the judge(s), who worded the norm for the first time. But, for most lawyers it will not be this court which will be considered to have "invented", "issued", "enacted" the norm. Generally, it will be assumed that the judge only stated, concluded, derived, worded a pre-existing norm, which was in one way or another already part of the legal system. In some cases this means that the wording of some legal norm is a necessary result of making the legal system fit with its underlying moral framework and/or with currently generally accepted ideology in the society or community to which the legal system applies. This means that, in the end, the "norm-sender" is "tradition" or "currently prevailing ideology". Here, it becomes impossible to link such norms to some identifiable formal "norm-sender", the substantive norm-sender being some rather vague historical or sociological data.

Such "norm-senderless" norms are not a deficiency of less developed or imperfect legal systems, they are endemic to any legal system of a political community. They show such legal systems to be necessarily a balance between social engineering and tradition. A legal system which was to remain a fixed system of traditional rules would become less and less adapted to the society it was presumed to order. It would inevitably lead to some revolution, making partly or completely *tabula rasa* with the old legal system. An example is the Russian Revolution of 1917. If, on the other hand, the rulers in a society were to use the law for changing society thoroughly, including traditions which the bulk of the citizens considered to be part of their cultural identity, this would also lead to a revolution. Examples are the revolution in Romania against the dictatorship of Ceausescu in the 1990s, or the Islamic Revolution in Iran against the Shah in the 1980s.

Tradition and currently prevailing ideology have been developed throughout a longstanding communication process in which all previous and current members of society participated (be it simply by their attitude of acceptance/refusal of the rule). It escapes any ruling by some legislator. It belongs to the paradigmatical framework of the law *within* which the legislator, the judge, or anybody, has to act. Legal systems cannot govern their historical and ideological framework, they are, on the contrary, partly dominated by it.

Therefore, it would not make sense to try to identify some "norm-sender" for legal rules or legal principles which are directly derived from the legal system's historical or ideological framework by an official of the system who does not, on his own behalf, have the power to enact such a rule. In practice, of course, such a switch from legal discourse to a non-legal one, within legal reasoning, may be criticised. One might also argue that reference to "tradition" or to "prevailing ideology" is nothing but a rhetoric disguise for a judge's own ideology. We are not entering into that discussion here. If suffices to assume that, at least on some occasions, reference is made to tradition or to prevailing ideology, and that at least in some cases such a reference is made correctly.

5.3 INTERNAL AND EXTERNAL ASPECT OF THE NORM

In order to understand the nature of norms one has to analyse the difference between a mere regular pattern of conduct on the one hand, and the application of norms on the other.

From the outside, in both cases the observable behaviour is identical. All or most members of a community behave in certain circumstances in the same way: they have breakfast in the morning, they walk on their two legs (and not on one leg, or on their hands, etc), they drive their car on the same side of the street, when playing football only the two men in the goals use their hands for taking the ball, they are dressed in a similar way (eg they all have shoes), etc.

For a Martian they all seem to be aspects of the same type of human behaviour. He is not able to distinguish between rule-governed behaviour and mere habit.

To understand this behaviour, the Martian needs to have a view on the reasons for that behaviour. As we saw above (5.1), norms are important reasons for human conduct. But they are not the only ones. Knowing and understanding the norm that governs behaviour will help us to understand human conduct. Looking at human conduct may help us to understand the (way in which the) norm (is applied), but it cannot suffice. Pure empirical observation of human behaviour may never lead to any information about the content of norms.

On the other hand, however, our Martian being aware of the existence of some "sources of law", neither will it suffice to look at and decode Acts, statutes, treaties, etc, to make conclusions about human behaviour. Soon he would realise that the written law can not always be relied on for predicting human conduct. Some legal rules are generally applied, other ones less often or rarely, and some are almost completely neglected.

To understand rule-governed conduct one thus has to know the rules, but not just the rules. Human behaviour is not only determined by some *knowledge* of (legal) rules, but also by some *attitude* towards these rules. Besides the external element, the rule as such, there is some necessary internal element, which makes people behave according to the rule.[43]

Let us take an example. Bigamy is in most legal systems prohibited by the law (both in criminal law and in civil law). In Europe this rule seems to be very generally applied. Violations are very exceptional. But only marriage with two men or two women is forbidden. Unmarried people can live together in the same way, without any legal obstacle. Nevertheless, such a situation is as exceptional as bigamy, although there is no rule prohibiting it. Legal rules are thus a reason to behave in a certain way, but neither a sufficient reason nor the only reason. A monogamous way of life thus also has other reasons: moral convictions, financial and sexual limits, social pressure, etc. The legal rule, prohibiting bigamy, as such may thus be of very little influence on monogamous behaviour.

In order to be applied as a legal rule, this rule should (a) be *known* by the norm-receiver, and (b) the norm-receiver should *feel compelled* to act according to this rule. This feeling of being bound by a rule forms the core of the internal aspect of the legal norm. It is this internal aspect that makes it possible to distinguish between rule-governed conduct on the one hand, and more general patterns of conduct (eg having breakfast in the morning) on the other hand. It is only in this case that the legal rule is a reason for a person to act in the way he does.

The acceptance of the legal system as a whole, ie the recognition of its set of secondary rules, is a necessary, but not a sufficient, condition for feeling compelled by each of the legal system's primary rules. Here, we are discussing the acceptance of the individual rules only, but the "internal aspect" also applies to the set of secondary rules, but to this set as a whole rather than to each of these secondary rules individually.

Within that feeling of being bound by a legal rule, one can moreover distinguish several degrees,[44] as already discussed above (3.5):

(a) *"complete acceptance"* (the rules have been internalised to such an extent that no control or threat of sanctions to follow these rules is needed);

(b) *"conditional acceptance"* (the rules are followed if they are considered to be equitable and properly implemented from the point of view of equal treatment);

(c) *"forced acceptance"* (the rules will only be followed if there is adequate control and if appropriate sanctions are applied).

---

[43] This distinction has been introduced by Hart: HLA Hart, *The Concept of Law* (Clarendon Press, Oxford, 1961), pp 55–56 and 86–88. See also JW Harris., *Law and Legal Science* (Oxford, 1979), pp 56–57; N MacCormick, *HLA Hart*, Series "Jurists: Profiles in Legal Theory" (W Twining (ed)) (Edward Arnold, London, 1981), p 33–40; N MacCormick, *Legal Reasoning and Legal Theory* (Clarendon Press, Oxford, 1978), pp 275–92.

[44] Neil MacCormick has made a similar distinction with five degrees of acceptance: "full, moderate, reluctant, minimal, and prudentially" ("The Concept of Law and 'The Concept of Law'", (1994) 14 *Oxford Journal of Legal Studies* 1–23, at pp 17–19). He is rather considering the acceptance of the whole of a legal system's (primary) rules, but the core of his argument is the same: acceptance is not a matter of all or nothing, but a matter of degree.

If a large majority of the population accepts the rules in one of those three ways, the rule will be efficacious. In each case, a person will feel bound by the rule. The internal perspective may be different, as for some people the feeling of being bound is based on personal convictions, whereas for others it is based on fear of sanctions. There is some degree within this internal perspective. But in all cases this internal element, necessary for following a rule, is present.

This internal perspective, of course, only makes sense for those to whom the rule applies. All others will only have an external perspective: "completely external" in the case of the Martian, "informed external" in the case, eg, of the legal scholar writing a book on some law subject, or "committed external" in the case of, eg, an advocate advising her client how she should behave according to the law.

Acceptance is, to a large extent, socially determined and strongly based on social interaction and communication. This appears most clearly in the case of a conditional acceptance. The interaction among the norm-receivers and the actors of the legal system, together with the information on this interaction (eg on the question whether offenders are sanctioned) are essential for determining the degree of individual acceptance.

5.4 THE STRUCTURE OF NORMS

5.4.1 The Basic Structure of a Norm

The basic structure of a legal norm is the hypothetical or conditional utterance *"when a fact X has occured, then person P1 should, as a necessary consequence, do Y to person P2"*.[45] This structure is analogous to the one of a descriptive utterance, by which a causal relationship is reported: *"when a fact X occurs, it will, as a necessary consequence, entail Y"*. The only difference between both kinds of utterances is the deontic operator "should" in the legal norm, whereas the causal relation utterance contains the descriptive element "will entail."

Hans Kelsen used this distinction as a main starting point for his analysis of law. He called the normative counterpart of the causal relationship the imputation relationship (*Zurechnung*). To him, this was also a basic distinction within sciences: on the one hand descriptive sciences (eg physics), study causal relationships, and on the other hand normative sciences (eg legal doctrine, ethics), use imputation as their method.[46]

The distinction, however, is not to be found at the level of the *relationship*, as Kelsen thought. Between causal relationship and imputation relationship there

---

[45] In this sentence "fact" has a very broad meaning and encompasses eg situations, or a large number of facts. "Person P1" and "person P2" may mean one or several persons or even a very large number of people.

[46] See, eg, H Kelsen, *General Theory of Norms* (Clarendon Press, Oxford, 1991), pp 22–25.

is a difference as regards the kind of consequence, but not as regards the kind of relationship. The basic logical structure is in both cases "when . . . , then . . .", ie a causal relationship between cause and consequence.[47] There is only a difference at the level of the *consequences*. With causal relationships the consequence is a natural regularity, independent of any human will, whereas the imputation relationship relies on human will: a person or a group of persons (eg a law-giver) wants something to happen; this entails and presupposes the possibility of deviant behaviour by those on whom a rule has been imposed.

A norm does not make sense (a) when it is completely impossible to behave the way that is imposed by this norm, or (b) when it is completely impossible to have deviant behaviour (eg a norm requiring people to breathe). A norm only makes sense when someone may decide to comply with the norm or not.

Von Wright makes a distinction between the causal consequences of an act and the result which follows from the definition of that act. In the act of "closing a window", this closing is not a (causal, extrinsic) "consequence" of the act but the intrinsic logical result. The change brought about by the act follows directly from the *definition* of this act, whereas the cold one would catch because of the window having been opened is a causal consequence of the act.[48] This distinction would suggest that Kelsen was right in clearly distinguishing "causation", or rather "imputation", in law from the (real) "causation" in positive sciences. When a "law" in natural sciences is determined, it always refers to external elements that bring about some result (or, in von Wright's terminology, "consequence"), whereas a "law" in a legal system itself creates the consequences (or, in von Wright's terminology, "result") of the conditions it has also determined itself. Thus, in a "natural" law the relationship between condition and effect is extrinsic and "causal", whereas in law it is an intrinsic *logical* tie. In a way this is true: law creates its own "legal reality" at the opposite of the sciences (or at least to a much higher extent). However, from the point of view of those who have to follow or to apply the norm, the "conditions" are as external to the "consequences" as in the case, eg, of sheltering from a thundery shower in order to avoid both its certain consequences (becoming wet because of the rain) and the uncertain ones (being killed by a lightning strike). In both cases, one will behave so as to avoid unwanted (external) consequences. The legal consequences of breaking a rule will be put into practice by a judge, a policeman, a civil officer, and the like, for whom the legal conditions are, of course, *external* elements to be found in statutes or judicial decisions.

Moreover, both the conditions and the legal consequences the legal norm determines will always be *interpreted* in the light of *external* elements, such as the specific characteristics of the case, the aim of the legislator, problematic consequences of a literal, strict application of the norm, etc.

---

[47] J Klanderman, *Ratio, Wetenschap en Recht* (Zwolle, 1986), pp 86–87.
[48] GH von Wright, *Norm and Action* (Routledge & Kegan Paul, London, 1963), pp 39–40.

Thus there is only a purely logical tie as long as one limits oneself to the norm in isolation from any application. Once the norm comes to life a purely internal logical approach becomes too narrow, if not impossible.

The structure of a legal norm must not be confused with the linguistic wording of the norm. Often there is a large difference between the two.[49]

One should also distinguish between a norm and a normative statement, which is a statement about a norm. Norms cannot be "true" or "false", as they are not describing but prescribing reality. They can only be "valid" or "invalid" within a given normative system. Normative statements, on the other hand, are true if they make a correct statement about a norm. They are false if the statement is not correct.

Normative statements may be direct or indirect. They are direct if they include only statements with either a normative operator (eg "ought to") or a normative predicate (eg "has a duty"). Otherwise they are indirect normative statements.[50] For example: "*On 1 January, 2002, monetary regulation has changed radically within the countries of the European Union that introduced the euro*" is an indirect normative statement.[51]

True normative statements are either pure, or applicative, or both. A normative statement is pure if the existence of certain norms suffices to make it true. It is an applicative statement if there is a norm and a fact which together are sufficient to make it true. Whether a statement is pure or applicative depends upon the content of the legal system.[52] Raz gives the example of a statement of the type "*The inhabitants of Oxford ought to do A*". This statement is pure if there is a law to the effect that the inhabitants of Oxford ought to do A. It is an applicative statement if there is a law that the inhabitants of all the towns with a population of over 100,000 ought to do A, and if Oxford has a population of over 100,000.[53]

The set of all the pure normative statements referring to one legal system completely describes that system. Formulating these normative statements is the task of legal doctrine. Thus, this discipline can be seen as an *empirical* science[54]

---

[49] See below 7.3.2.

[50] J Raz, *The Concept of a Legal System*, 2nd edn (Clarendon Press, Oxford, 1980), p 49.

[51] Von Wright calls propositions that state the existence of a norm, as such indirect normative statements do, "*norm-propositions*" (above n. 48, p 106). I have a slight preference for Raz's terminology, as any norm-proposition is inevitably at the same time a normative statement, but rather worded in a more distant, indirect way. Saying that the euro has been introduced in 2002 is, indirectly, positing that as from 2002 one *has* (or at least is allowed) to pay in euros in those countries. Using the distinction between "direct" and "indirect" normative statements therefore seems to be somewhat more elegant and clear.

[52] Raz, above n 50, p 49. According to Raz a normative statement is both pure and applicative if there are two independent sets of conditions each sufficient for its truth, and if in virtue of one it is pure and in virtue of the second it is applicative (*ibid*).

[53] *Ibid.*

[54] One may, of course, also see legal doctrine as a *hermeneutic* science, but, just as history for instance, it is at least partially an empirical science and it is *possible* to see it as being basically an empirical science, depending on how broad "empirical" is defined. Here, "empirical" is opposed to Kelsen's normative conception of legal doctrine.

that is concerned with questions of truth about the existence of norms and of their exact meaning. At the opposite of what Kelsen posited, legal doctrine is not a "normative science" but a science about norms. If norms cannot be true or false, normative statements can. From this perspective, norms are facts, their existence or non-existence can be detected, argued for and proven, at least to the same extent as "facts" in other social sciences.

5.4.2 The Elements of a Norm

Each norm[55] contains three structural elements:

(a) a positive or negative act-situation (doing or not doing x);
(b) an ought or may deontic operator;
(c) the conditions under which the deontic operator applies to the positive or negative act-situation.

When taking together the act-situation and the deontic operator one comes up with four possible modalities of legal norm:

(a) a *positive directive* (an order): one ought to do something, eg "Spouses have the duty to live together" (Article 213 Belgian Civil Code);
(b) a *negative directive* (a prohibition): one ought not to do something (it is forbidden to do it), eg "It is forbidden to address personally petitions to the Parliament" (Article 43 Belgian Constitution);
(c) a *positive non directive* (absence of order): one is allowed not to do something, eg "The usufructuary offers surety . . . ; however, the father and mother who have the statutory usufruct of the goods of their children, . . . , do not have to offer surety" (Article 601 Belgian Civil Code);
(d) a *negative non directive* (absence of prohibition): one is allowed to do something, eg "The occupier may at any time take and destroy the wild rabbits on his land" (Article 7 Belgian Hunting Act 28.2.1882).

In ordinary language no distinction is made between an absence of order and an absence of prohibition. Both are referred to as "permission".

These four modalities form a logical square (see Figure 5.1). A "duty" and a "permission not to do" are opposite, contradictory relations. When one has a duty to do something he is obviously not allowed not to do it, and, if there is a permission not to do, there cannot be a duty to do. Between a "prohibition" and a "permission to do" there is a similar relationship. When one has a permission to do something, this behaviour cannot be prohibited, and vice versa.

---

[55] "Norm" is used here in its standardised meaning, linked to primary rules of behaviour. I leave aside questions such as whether power-conferring rules are "norms" or not. For this kind of discussions and for a more thorough analysis of legal sentences in general I refer to the excellent work of Manuel Atienza and Juan Ruiz Manero, *A Theory of Legal Sentences* (Kluwer Academic Publishers, Dordrecht, 1998), in which an overall theory of legal norms and legal sentences is offered.

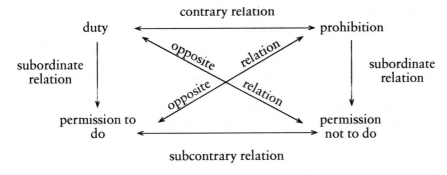

Figure 5.1: Four modalities of legal norm

"Duty" and "prohibition" are contrary concepts. It is logically not possible that a duty and a prohibition apply to the same person as regards the same behaviour. If such a case arises, it is called an antinomy. But it is possible that there is neither a duty, nor a prohibition. The behaviour may be explicitly allowed (strong permission) or merely allowed because it is not governed by any rule at all (weak permission).[56]

On the other hand it is possible to have both a permission to do and a permission not to do, whereas it is not possible to have neither of them. A duty implies the permission to do (but not vice versa). Lack of permission to do implies lack of duty to do this (not vice versa). A similar subordinate relation exists between a "prohibition" and a "permission not to do".

Lastly, a norm should also stipulate the conditions under which it applies. Each legal norm is hypothetical[57]. A legal norm always has to meet specific conditions

---

[56] See for the distinction between weak and strong permissions: GH von Wright, *Norm and Action* (Routledge & Kegan Paul, London, 1963), pp 85–90; A Soeteman, "Weak and strong permission in the law" in Å Frändberg and M Van Hoecke (eds), *The Structure of Law*, Series Skriften från Juridiska Fakulteten i Uppsala (Iustus Förlag, Uppsala, 1987), pp 21–35. Arend Soeteman is probably right when he argues that the distinction between weak and strong permission is rather a matter of degree than a dichotomy (above, p 29). See also: M Atienza and J Ruiz Manero, *A Theory of Legal Sentences* (Kluwer Academic Publishers, Dordrecht, 1998), pp 90–115, where it is argued that differences in meaning of a "permission" are determined by the context rather than by the distinction between "strong" and "weak" permission as such . . . . Here, however, we cannot enter into those discussions.

[57] "Hypothetical" is used here in the broad sense that at least some conditions should be met in order to make the norm applicable. However, even in the narrow sense in which von Wright defines "hypothetical" (as opposed to "categorical") one may doubt whether there are any legal norms that would not have to be categorised as "hypothetical": "We shall call a norm hypothetical if its condition of application is the condition which must be satisfied if there is going to be an opportunity for doing the thing which is its content, *and some further condition*" (von Wright, above n 56, p 74). In my opinion there are always at least some negative "further conditions", unless the norm is reformulated so as to include all those further conditions. But, in this way, the problem is reduced to a matter of wording and it becomes possible to formulate, artificially, all norms as categorical ones. This is not very helpful for the analysis of the concept of norm. Hans Kelsen argued that all (general) norms are hypothetical already because "all norms are valid merely conditionally" (*General Theory of Norms*, above n 46, p 21).

before it applies to a concrete situation. There are no absolute norms. The prohibition to kill, which seems prima facie to be absolute, only applies to human beings[58] to whom the legal system as such applies (on grounds of nationality, or because the killing has been committed in a certain territory). Moreover, the prohibition to kill is not valid under all circumstances, as eg in the case of self-defence, in case of war, or in case of execution of a criminal.

Summarising, one can state that *a legal norm stipulates the legal consequences which ought to occur when specific conditions are met.*

5.4.3 The Characteristics of Legal Norms

Apart from the substantive, prescriptive elements discussed above, legal norms have two other notable general characteristics: (a) they are not standing alone, but serve specific ends within the broader context of the legal system and (b) they have formal characteristics.

(a) Legal Norms as Means for Ends

Be it in a primitive or in a developed legal system, legal norms are never purely arbitrary commands. They may be adequate or not, but they are always meant to serve specific purposes, which are part of a broader, more or less coherent, world view. As well worded by Robert Summers, legal rules:

> "are designed directly or indirectly to serve substantive policy or to serve fundamental political values, or private preferences, or equity (or one or more of these types of ends at the same time);"

and they are, moreover

> "based directly or indirectly either on an empirical generalization implying a causal relation between means and ends, or on a theory about how law can organize and facilitate some end such as the election and accountability of political leaders, or on a general moral or social principle, or on a conception of the essential form or the otherwise appropriate form of an institution, process, method, or the like."[59]

Without discussing this further here, I would like to emphasise the context dependency of norms: they have not only to be viewed from the perspective of the norm-sender–norm-receiver relationship, but also in the light of the concrete ends for which they are means, and all this, in its turn, has to be located in the context of the legal system as a whole and of its underlying world view(s). Practical problems that may arise in finding those underlying ends, theories and world views do not mean that they would be absent. Sometimes they will have

---

[58] Although there might be other rules prohibiting the killing of (some) animals.
[59] RS Summers, "How Law is Formal and Why It Matters", (1997) 82 *Cornell Law Review* 1165–229, at p 1175.

to be partly (re)construed by the interpreter, who, by doing so, will make the legal rule fit both with the legal system to which it belongs and with the community to which it has to be applied, including its dominant values and world views.

Legal norms may also serve as means for ends from the point of view of the norm-addressee in all cases where the norm offers opportunities that *may* be used or not. One may use contract law in order to reach some end, such as disposing of an attractive dwelling; one may use freedom of association for founding a wine-tasting club or a political party; one may use legislative choices within matrimonial law for securing the future of the spouse who does not have their own income, and so on. This, of course, is not a characteristic of the norm as such, but of the *functions* of the law, as discussed above. Law serves two types of ends, collective ones and individual ones. In many theories, law is seen too exclusively as a means for societal ends only, thus neglecting the role law plays in offering means for the individual ends of citizen.[60] Anyway, in both cases, law is a means for reaching individual or collective ends and should, as a consequence, be seen from that perspective.

(b) The Formality of Legal Norms

In primitive legal systems, legal norms may have only a very weak formal character, limited to some degree of generality and definiteness in its wording and to some "recognised authoritative encapsulatory form" as Summers calls it.[61] In more developed legal systems, the formal characteristics of legal rules are broader. Following Summers, we may distinguish five types of "formality" that can be found in any developed legal system, and most prominently in state legal systems.

(i) Essential Form

By "essential form" is meant those characteristics which are essential for a legal rule to be considered to be a "rule": it must be *prescriptive* (in the broad sense as discussed above), sufficiently *general*, *complete* and *definite*.[62] Of course, as a definitional minimum to fall under the concept of "rule" each of these characteristics has to be present to some degree, but not in the full sense.

"*Generality*" means "applicable to a category of factual situations" even if in practice only a very few cases or even just one case happen to fall under the rule.

---

[60] Hans Kelsen is one of those who seem to have underestimated this double function of the law when clearly excluding any, causal, means-end relationship from the law in which only imputation relations would exist (*General Theory of Norms*, above n 46, pp 9–12). This position is linked to Kelsen's rather narrow view on norms as "ought sentences", in which commanding norms are the "typical" norms and the other types (permissive, derogating and empowering norms) are defined as a kind of (absence of) command (see, eg, *ibid*, p 96).

[61] Summers, above n 59.

[62] *Ibid.*

"Generality" may pertain to the *subjects* of the rule or to the number of *occasions* for which it is given. The latter form of generality distinguishes a rule from an isolated prescription or command.[63] In law, "generality" is also required at the level of the number of possible subjects: the rule should be abstract and not individualised. This does not exclude that a rule, on occasion, would apply to one single person, eg, because only one person happens to fulfil the conditions for the application of the norm, or because the rule, by definition, can apply to one person only at one moment of time (eg, the rights and duties of the Prime Minister or of the President of the Supreme Court). It just requires that at the moment of the enactment of a rule it is possible that the rule will apply to a whole *category* of people, such as "all future Prime Ministers".

"*Completeness*" just means that the conditions, the legal consequences and the deontic operator have to be present in order to call a sentence, or a set of sentences, a "legal norm".

"*Definiteness*" does not exclude a vague wording of the rule, it only requires the norm to be sufficiently precise to be applicable at all, possibly to act as a guiding rule for behaviour.

(ii) Structural Form

The definitional elements that create the "essential form" also determine the structure of the norm, including the conditions that should be fulfilled for the legal norm to apply, the deontic operator and the legal consequences the norm determines. Moreover, the *degree* of generality, completeness and definiteness will also influence the *structure* of the norm. A very generally worded legal norm, that is quite complete, but not very definite, for instance, will be called a "legal principle". More concrete regulation, on the other hand, will show a lower degree of generality, but a more definite and precise wording.

(iii) Expressional Form

The mode of expression of a rule, according to Summers, encompasses:

(1) the extent of its explicitness;
(2) the extent it is set forth in writing;
(3) the extent it is set forth in a technical or other specialised vocabulary; and
(4) the extent it is formulated with compactness and organisational rigor.[64]

Unwritten, rather implicit, rules are typical for less developed legal systems in which customary law is still strongly linked with religion, but they are also to be found in developed legal systems, eg in the form of "unwritten general principles of law".

---

[63] Von Wright, above n 56, p 83.
[64] Summers, above n 59, p 1179.

The two other elements of expressional form listed by Summers are linked to the professionalisation of law. It refers to a methodological specialisation, including a specialised legal vocabulary, style and structure. However, highly professionalised legal systems may also have rules that are worded in a vocabulary that is only to a very limited extent technical, for instance because the law-maker wants the rules to be easily understood, and thus followed, by a large group of people (eg traffic regulation, abortion rules, rent law, human rights). This will also tend to be the case with contractual or regulatory rules drafted by non-lawyers. Some of such rules may be very "technical", but not in the sense of legal-technical, but in the sense of a specialised domain that is regulated from the perspective of other techniques, such as the minimum technical requirements for the safety of products. This is another kind of "technicality" that is typical for an important proportion of the rules in developed legal systems (eg environmental law, banking law). When combined with a high degree of legal technicality it may make the legal rules very definite and complete, but also highly unaccessible for non-specialists, who then should have a minimal knowledge of both fields: law and the technical field the law aims to regulate.

(iv) Encapsulatory Form

By "encapsulatory form" Summers refers to the kind of "legal source" (constitution, statute, customary law, judge made law, etc) or "recognized legal form or mould" in which the legal rules are set forth, the mode in which the law manifests itself.[65] This form is closely linked to the previous one, the expressional form, especially its aspect of being presented in writing, but it pertains rather to what lawyers call "legal sources" than to the way the rule is presented to the external world. This aspect of formality thus has to be distinguished from the form of expression, although there are some parallels, but not for 100 per cent, as there are, for instance, unwritten constitutions (eg in the United Kingdom) and customary law, in its turn, may be recorded, as happened to a large extent in Europe in the Middle Ages and the Renaissance.

(v) Organisational Form

Some legal rules have a formal *content* in that they organise the legal system with rules of procedure, of competence, of evidence or other secondary rules. Here, we want to limit ourselves to the kinds of formality listed above, as this kind of "form" overlaps with what is discussed elsewhere in this book. From the point of view of studying law's formal aspects, as Summers does, it makes sense to add this kind of "substantive" form. Here, however, the perspective is different, so that it should suffice to just mention it, for the sake of completeness.

---

[65] *Ibid*, 1179.

5.5 THE CONCEPT OF "RIGHT"

5.5.1 Types of "Rights"

Norms award rights and duties. Norms differ by the kind of "rights" (and correlative duties) they confer. An analysis of the concept of right is a necessary part of the analysis of norm, as the content of a norm is basically determined by the kind of right it confers.

Analytical jurisprudence has made a major contribution to the analysis of this concept. Most famous is the work of Wesley Newcomb Hohfeld (1879–1918).[66] Norms may award different types of right: a "claim", a "power", a "privilege", an "immunity", a "liberty". Three of them may be considered to be really different, and equally important, conceptions of "right": claim, liberty and power.

A *claim* entitles someone to ask someone else to give something or to do or not to do something (eg an invoice). The correlative of a claim is a duty (in a strict sense) for the other person(s).

A *liberty* recognises the freedom of the right-holder to behave as he likes, within an, as such, non-regulated field (eg freedom of speech). If this freedom is an exception on a more general prohibition, it is called a "*privilege*" (eg the freedom to beat, or even to kill, someone in case of self-defence). The correlative of liberty (and privilege) is the absence of rights against the liberty right-holder. This means that there is no "legal" correlative, as there merely is an absence of legal relations and regulations. This case is similar to the abovementioned one of permission. If liberty derives only from a weak permission there is no legal regulation at all. If liberty is granted by a strong permission, as is the case here, it defines some "regulation-free territory" in favour of the liberty right-owner.

A *power* is a legally recognised or conferred capacity of creating, divesting or altering rights and duties (in their broad sense) (eg the power of a trustee). The power to influence ones own legal position is a "capacity".[67] The power to influence the legal position of other people is a "competence".[68] When comparing it to liberty, one could say that the latter encompasses all acts without direct legal consequences, whereas power entails a freedom to influence rights and duties. They form the legal and the non-legal side of freedom (in the sense of legally relevant consequences).

The correlative of "power" is "*liability*": a person is liable to accept the exercise of power by someone who has this power to influence his legal position.

Hohfeld especially tried to analyse the different types of "right" by opposing them to each other within the frame of a logical square.[69]

---

[66] WN Hohfeld, *Fundamental Legal Conceptions as applied in judicial reasoning* (Greenwood Press, Westport, 1978) (reprint) (first published in (1913) 23 *Yale Law Journal* 16)

[67] Capacity can be full or limited.

[68] Competence can be discretionary or goal determined.

[69] Although Hohfeld himself did not really use the logical square as a scheme. He limited himself to bringing together different pairs.

As regards the rights which are not directly aimed at influencing other rights, ie the field of (juristic) facts one can construct the scheme shown in Figure 5.2. "Claim–no-claim" and "duty–liberty" are opposites. They are contradictory and exclude each other. One cannot have a claim and no-claim at the same time. If someone has a duty he is not free as regards the acts for which he is under duty.

"Claim–duty" are contrary concepts. One cannot be eg a creditor and a debtor for one and the same debt. But it is possible that there is no debt and that one has neither a claim nor a duty.

"Liberty–no-claim" are subcontrary concepts. One either is free to do something or has no-claim whatsoever as regards the same act, or both. One can have at the same time a freedom to do and no-claim, but one has at least one of both. A claim implies a liberty and a duty implies that one has no claim. Conversely, if one has no liberty one cannot have a claim and if one has no no-claim (which means one has a claim) one cannot have the correlative duty.

As regards the rights which are influencing rights, ie the field of legal acts (*acte juridique, Rechtshandlung*) one can construct the scheme shown in Figure 5.3,

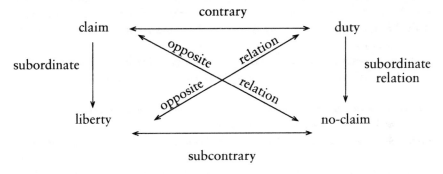

Figure 5.2: Types of right—juristic facts

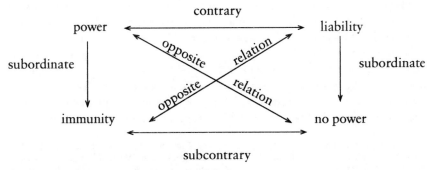

Figure 5.3: Types of right—legal acts

with the same relations between the concepts. Here two (negative) concepts have been added—"immunity" and "no-power".

Immunity is one's freedom from the legal power of another as regards some legal relation (eg tax exemptions).

No-power, or "disability" as Hohfeld calls it, just means the absence of power.

5.5.2 Types of Legal Relations

In some cases, rights are clearly relations between two, or more, determined people. When I buy a car, I have a claim towards the seller to deliver that car, and he has a claim towards me to pay the price for it. A *ius in personam* is typically a claim, but any kind of claim, such as the claim of the tenant to non-interference by the landlord in the property he has let to him. More generally speaking it may be a claim to give something, to do something, or to abstain from doing it.

In other cases the situation is more complex and has prompted discussions in jurisprudence.[70] Does property, for instance, imply a legal relationship with everybody else (all having a duty of non-interference) or a legal relationship with the thing owned (it is *my* property, the thing belongs to me, I have full power over it), or both?

When it comes to the concrete enforcement of any kind of rights, it is obvious that there will be a conflict, and at least in that sense a legal relationship, between concrete persons, not between a person and a thing, nor between a concrete person on the one hand and an abstract generality of people on the other. But here we are confronted with the concretisation of a right towards one offender of one's right, eg a thief, whereas nobody would deny that the property rights in the stolen good are valid *erga omnes*, including those who are not aware of the existence of those property rights and/or for whom it never will have any practical relevance whatsoever. But in all cases, there is the *potential* of becoming practically relevant and creating some specific concrete legal relationship.

Moreover, a right *in rem*, such as property, has a wider scope than claims (of non-interference) towards others. It also entails the right to sell, to hire or to let, and the like. This does not necessarily mean the power, ie the "capacity", to do it oneself, but in all such cases of legal incapacity someone else will have the power to act as a trustee on behalf of the right-holder. Here, again, one should not confuse the possession of a right with taking concrete legal steps within the frame of its exertion. Taking this into account, we may argue that even a one-year-old child has the "power" to sell his property, or, more generally speaking,

---

[70] See, eg J Raz, *The Concept of a Legal System*, 2nd edn (Clarendon Press, Oxford, 1980), pp 180–81, with criticism on Hohfeld and references to Honoré; DN MacCormick, "Rights in Legislation" in PMS Hacker and J Raz, *Law, Morality and Society. Essays in Honour of HLA Hart* (Clarendon Press, Oxford, 1977), pp 189–209, esp. at pp 205–07.

that the concrete legal capacities of a right-holder do not affect the content of the rights, only their exertion. This means that, in this sense, every owner of a good has some power concerning it being sold, hired, etc.

The rights of an owner are, of course, not limited to transferring rights in his property to other people. The most important reason why people buy something is to have the opportunity to use it, and to use it as they like, in other words a *liberty* fully and freely to dispose of the good, the *ius fruendi, utendi et abutendi*. But liberty as such does not imply any relationship with other people. It, of course, implies the claim of non-interference and the reciprocal duty of everybody else to honour the rights of the owner concerning his property. However, when no such interference comes into play, the owner still has "rights" over the good, which are much broader than simply denying other people the right to use it. Here, it makes sense to talk about a legal relationship between a right-holder and a thing, a *ius in rem*. This, of course, is another kind of relationship than, for example, a contractual relationship, in which two legal persons create or change some rights. It is also different from typical liberty rights, such as freedom of speech, of religion, and the like. Such freedoms also create an area of liberty to act as one likes, outside any legal relationship with other people (except the abstract claim of non-interference), but without any direct link to specific goods, in contradistinction to property rights.

Summarising, we can state that "property" contains a bundle of rights, including a claim (of non-interference), a liberty (to use) and a power (to transfer the property rights partly or fully). When we have a closer look at the kinds of legal relationship it creates, it appears that the claim of non-interference towards all other people and the power to transfer rights are only "passive" legal relationships, with the *potential* of one day becoming real ones. In many cases they remain dormant. When, for instance, I buy a screwdriver it is not very likely that other people will try to interfere with my property rights or that I will transfer rights in it to anybody else. The liberty to use my property, in our example the screwdriver, however, will always be an active relationship with that thing. Even if I never use it, or if I throw it away, because I consider it to be of bad quality, it always means an active use of my *liberty*, as I may freely decide to use it or not, to store it somewhere or to throw it away.[71]

Thus, we may conclude that a *ius in rem* entails an active legal relationship with the thing(s) concerned and a dormant relationship with potentially everybody else, whereas a *ius in personam* entails an active legal relationship with one or more determined persons.

---

[71] When throwing away the good I own, of course, it also means the use of my power to abolish my property rights.

6

The Concept of a Legal System

6.1 A "BASIC NORM" OR A "RULE OF RECOGNITION" AS CLOSING RULE FOR A LEGAL SYSTEM?

We briefly discussed above (in 3.3.1) Hart's "rule of recognition" and Kelsen's "*Grundnorm*" in the context of the formal institutionalisation of law. We argued that such closing rules cannot be part of the legal system, and thus not "law", and, moreover, that they are not rules or norms but facts. Here, we will discuss some more aspects of this "closing rule approach".

The need for a closing rule has different origins: (a) a positivist *legitimation* of legal systems, (b) the *identification* of a (valid) legal system, both from a normative point of view (b1) and from a scientific point of view (b2), (c) *unification* of the legal system, (d) separation of law and morals, and (e) separation of norms and facts.

Most notably Hans Kelsen believed that he succeeded in reaching all these aims through one single closing rule, the *basic norm*.[1] However, Kelsen wrestled a lot with the status of this *Grundnorm* and, eventually, had to accept that it was but a fictitious a priori, accepted by legal scholars.[2]

Hart had more limited ambitions with his "rule of recognition", which concentrated rather on the identification of the legal system and its acceptance in legal practice through "a complex, but normally concordant, practice of the courts, officials, and private persons in identifying the law".[3]

Not only Hart, but Kelsen also ultimately had to rely on the *social effectiveness* of a legal system in order to identify it as an independant, valid legal system.

In practice, there are not many problems with the identification of legal systems. The question is even hardly ever raised outside some occasional discussions in legal theory. In many legal systems the legitimation of that system as such is not perceived as a problem either. The unity and coherence of legal systems more often will be considered to be problematic, but none of the practical problems is solved by any type of closing rule. And the same goes for the

---

[1] H Kelsen, *Pure Theory of Law* (University of California Press, Berkeley and Los Angeles, 1967), pp 203–4 and 211–14 as for (a), 8 and 201 as for (b), 195 and 205–8 as for (c), 66–67, 201 and 219–20 as for (d) and 193–95 as for (e).

[2] Compare H Kelsen, *General Theory of Norms* (Clarendon Press, Oxford, 1991), p 256 with his *Pure Theory of Law*, above n 1, at pp 198–99, where the basic norm is considered to be "not a positive but a presupposed norm".

[3] HLA Hart, *The Concept of Law*, 2nd edn (Clarendon Press, Oxford, 1994), p 110.

separation between law and morals: as already discussed above, "closing rules" do not really separate legal systems from the external world, but rather allow the importation of moral rules into the law on an ad hoc basis. If, both for Kelsen and for Hart, legal systems ultimately rely on social effectiveness for their identification, these *normative* systems are founded on a *fact*: social acceptance.

Why then did so many legal theorists feel the need to work out or to discuss the idea of a closing rule for the identification and positivist legitimation of law?

A first reason is an erroneous linear approach to the legitimation of law, with an impossible *regressus ad infinitum*, which, then, has to be stopped by an artificial "basic norm". My position, as already developed above, is a *circular communicational approach*.

Kelsen's approach is static, historical and linear. He has to go back to the first constitution from which each following constitution, and, hence, any current legal rule or judicial decision may be directly derived.[4] For him, the current acceptance of that historical Constitution creates the basic norm, which simply states "that one is bound to accept any legal rule or decision derived from it in a legally valid way".[5]

This approach assumes that legal systems are closed and coherent wholes, that law is made by official law-makers and more or less mechanically applied by those in charge of the adjudication of law. As argued above, law is not a set of pre-existing rules, but a normative machinery which is constantly developed and refined *in legal practice*. It is never fully coherent, and coherence is to a large extent added through daily practice in case law and in legal doctrine. Validity or social acceptance are hardly ever linked to some historical constitution, it is the *current working of the legal machinery* which makes a legal system be accepted or not. Once the legal institutions and the way they work, in other words the secondary norms of the legal system, are by and large accepted, the legal system is identifiable and valid, independently of the effectiveness of the primary rules of behaviour, but also independently of any "basic norm" or "rule of recognition". The validity of a legal system is not determined on the basis of a static set of norms, which should be directly derivable from some first Constitution and its underlying "basic norm", but rather in the light of a dynamic interaction amongst legal institutions (and, more and more, amongst legal systems (see 3.6.2)), as they are sociologically accepted in current society.

Another misunderstanding is the confusion between "validity of a legal system" and political, ideological or moral discussions about the main officials in a legal system (eg a government) or about single rules or sets of rules of behaviour in that system.

---

[4] Kelsen, above n 1, p 200.
[5] "Coercive acts ought to be performed under the conditions and in the manner which the historically first constitution, and the norms created according to it, prescribe." (*ibid*, 201.)

A legal system is different from the political regime it is linked with. Large parts of the law are not at all affected by ideology or morals, and still govern human living together to an important extent. Traffic regulation, for instance, is not very likely to be influenced by a change of political regime.[6]

A legal system is also different from its set of rules of behaviour. It may be accepted as a system, and without any discussion, even by those who severely criticise some of its rules (which is a very common situation). The legal system of the USA remains accepted by all Europeans, even if many of its states apply the death penalty frequently, although the death penalty is generally considered in Europe to be uncivilised, immoral and in conflict with basic human rights.

Within a legal system it is the circular interaction between the different types and levels of legal institutions which legitimates the legal system as a whole, by recognising each other, and each other's "products" (legislation, judicial decisions, etc) as being "legally valid". And all this is backed by a mutual recognition of legal systems and their "products".

From all this it follows that the *identification* of a legal system as being and producing "valid positive law" is different from a moral, political or other ideological *legitimation* of "the law".

In the first case, we talk about "validity" in the sense of an existing *empirical reality*, and, to some extent, also in the sense of a *weak form of legitimation*: we "accept" the legal system, perhaps only because there is no alternative and we need legal officials to enforce a contract, to marry, to apply for a visa, etc.

In the second case, we talk about a *strong form of legitimation*, not of the legal system as a whole but of *parts of it*: the political regime, the working of the police forces, abortion regulation, discrimination against women, or against immigrants, or against people with a statistically atypical behaviour, such as homosexuals, etc. Here, if somebody considers that "one ought to follow the legal rules", because they are morally just, it means a full, strong legitimation, which is different from the "legitimation" of a police officer in an undemocratic country, who asks a foreigner to show his passport (and who, in most cases, willingly will do so), or the "acceptance" of a job by a woman who considers it unfair that she will be paid less for the job than her male colleagues, or the "acceptance" of a judicial decision enacted by a judge one considers to be incompetent, etc.

This strong form of legitimation is not required for the legal system as a whole. It would, moreover, be impossible to judge every rule of a legal system

---

[6] This confusion between political system and legal system, based on a too narrow and rigid conception of "legal system" is, for instance, apparent in the following questions asked by Joseph Raz in the context of the problem of the *continuity* of legal systems: "A sucessful *coup d'état* or the establishment of a new state may give rise to various problems: Are previous laws still in force? Do persons who previously held high office still hold it or should they be renominated? Can the new regime or state claim taxes and debts owed to the old one? Can a person who commited an offence before the change be prosecuted after it has occured?" (J Raz, *The Authority of Law* (Clarendon Press, Oxford, 1979), p 83. Some such questions will, of course, arise after such radical political changes have occurred, but they will remain relatively marginal.

from one single ideological perspective. At the most a legal system may be judged *negatively* against a set of basic values, such as the European Convention on Human Rights.

For the weak form of minimal legitimation we need for recognising a legal system to be "valid", no "basic norm" is required, just a sufficiently large social acceptance of the legal institutions—in Hart's words "a rule of recognition". But is it a "rule"? This depends, of course, on how one defines a "rule". However, even with a broad definition, it seems difficult to consider the *acceptance* of a normative whole, the *belief* in the validity of a legal system to be a "norm" or a "rule" itself. It is nothing more than a socio-psychological fact.

It is assumed that it could be considered to be a rule because it could be worded as the acceptance of the normative statement "whatever is issued by this legal system according to its own procedures should be abided by". But even this normative character of such an acceptance of the law is doubtful. It is probably more realistic to word it as "it seems wise, or it seems preferable, to act according to what the officials tell us". As we are faced with a weak form of legitimation, even a forced acceptance of a legal system may suffice to create or to maintain an empirically valid legal system. People do not need a strong normative position as "one ought to abide by the law", they may simply accept it willy nilly.

In any event, no matter how one tries to construct a "rule of recognition", it will never be a norm but at the most the *acceptance* of a norm, or rather the acceptance of a *normative statement*, but probably only the *actual acceptance of the validity of a legal system as an empirical fact*, without necessary normative connotation (except, of course, the recognition of the existence of an internal normative logic within that legal system).

For the strong form of legitimation of parts of a legal system, it does not make sense to talk about some single "basic norm" either. Depending on the kind of rules, principles, institutions, procedures, etc, under discussion, other (sets of) values, from diverging non-legal normative sources may come into play: morals, religion, economic policy, or other world views. Whatever the closing rule may be that one accepts for the validity of the legal system, it never will suffice as such for offering a strong legitimation for specific legal rules or legal decisions. It is neither a necessary nor a sufficient condition. Not sufficient, as it will have to be backed by considerations that are external to law (morals, politics, economics, etc). Not necessary, as legal and political practice show how easily formal legal reasons are discarded when some result is strongly wanted from a moral or political point of view.[7]

---

[7] See, for instance, the example of the interpretation of the Belgian Constitution as to the validity of statutes enacted by the government, instead of Parliament, during the Second World War, below 7.7.3. Another example is the creative interpretation of the same constitution, so as to allow a constitutionally valid enactment of the Belgian Abortion Act 1991, notwithstanding the King's refusal to sign that Act (M Van Hoecke, "Ideologische Grenzen der Gesetzesinterpretation. Der König der Belgier und das Abtreibungsgesetz", (1991) 22 *Rechtstheorie* 215–20).

6.2 THE STRUCTURE OF A LEGAL SYSTEM

6.2.1 What Kind of System?

Is law a "system" or is it just presented and perceived as a well structured whole? Joxerramon Bengoetxea has rightly argued that the conception of law as a system operates as a *regulative ideal* in the different stages of legal practice and legal science.[8] It is only partly present in legislation. To a large extent systematisation is achieved in daily practice. It is a goal lawyers try to achieve through interpretation in judicial decisions and in scholarly legal writing.

As discussed above in chapter 2 on defining law, structures are, indeed, rather *models* that are used for understanding reality, than given "facts" that could simply be "found" in reality. The same goes for law. The whole history and main activity of legal science has been structuring legal data into a coherent whole. In nineteenth-century Europe this structuring activity found its apogee in codes that systematised large fields of the law.[9] Through this interaction between legal science and legal practice clearly structured conceptual models became positive law. Legal doctrine was transformed into positive law. Theory became part of reality.

In jurisprudence rather opposite pictures of law have been presented as to its degree of systematisation. For Systems Theory and Autopoietic Theory, the "system" is the core of the legal phenomenon. For the Pure Theory of Law, every legal system is clearly identifiable as such, through the all-founding basic norm, and well structured through norms and bodies of higher and lower ranking. Legal Realists, on the other hand, deny the existence of "legal rules", which would "exist" in some "legal system". As there are no "rules" they can hardly be structured into a "legal system". These theories are the result of an overemphasis on theory in one case, or on practice in the other, and by doing so they are neglecting the impact of the discarded element.

One may take the concept of *system in a very strong sense*, conceived as a closed system, which is complete and consistent and for which it can always be determined whether something is part of this system or not. In such a case it is not difficult to "prove" that law is not a "legal system".[10] Each of those characteristics is problematic as far as law is concerned. However, an open, incomplete and not fully consistent normative whole may still be called a "system". *System in the weak sense* only requires some *structure*, some relationship among

---

[8] J Bengoetxea, "Legal System as a Regulative Ideal" in H-J Koch and U Neumann, *Legal System and Practical Reason*, ARSP Beiheft 53 (Franz Steiner Verlag, Stuttgart, 1994), pp 65–80.

[9] The two main codes being the French *Code civil* (1804) and the German *Bürgerliches Gesetzbuch* (1896, in force as from 1 January 1900).

[10] See on this strong conception of (legal) system: Bengoetxea, above n 8, pp 66–67, and M van de Kerchove and F Ost, *Legal System Between Order and Disorder* (trans Iain Stewart, Oxford University Press, Oxford, 1994), pp 35–55.

the elements of the system, which makes it possible to identify it as something that exists on its own and can be distinguished both from a number of unordered elements and from other systems. As van de Kerchove and Ost have pointed out this entails four questions to be answered: (a) what are the elements of the system? (b) how are they ordered? (c) what is the relation between the system and its environment? and (d) what is the system's characteristic evolution?[11] Depending on the kind of system one is studying (eg a mathematical system, the human body, a social system) the answers to these questions may vary quite considerably, but there will be a typical answer that characterises that system "as a system".

Here, we will discuss mainly question (b). Question (c) has already been discussed above (in 3.6) on the autonomy of law. Questions (a) and (d) will be dealt with in connection with question (b) "how are the elements of a legal system ordered?"

6.2.2 What is Structured and How?

(a) The Machinery of Law

Let us start with the question on the typical evolution of legal systems. By definition, law is dynamic, not static. It contains an important number of rules which regulate *changes* in the law. Law governs its own changes. This is not only one of its main characteristics according to the autopoietic theory of law, even Kelsen stated that law "regulates its own creation".[12] It does it through what Hart called "secondary rules of change". It is these secondary rules of change, together with the secondary rules of adjudication, that form the *machinery of the law*. Technically speaking, the content of the primary rules of behaviour may be anything, without affecting the legal *system*. If we talk about the typical structure of legal systems, it is the *relationship* between primary rules and secondary rules, on the one hand, and among secondary rules, on the other, that we should focus on. As Lawrence Friedman has put it, we should perceive "a legal order not as a catalogue of rules or norms, but as an operating unit".[13]

In developed (state) legal systems we are faced with a complex hierarchy of (primary) rules of conduct: international rules (with or without direct effect), constitutional rules, statutory rules, rules enacted by the executive power, etc, combined with territorial hierarchies and divisions of power (village, town, province,

---

[11] M van de Kerchove and F Ost, *Legal System Between Order and Disorder* (trans Iain Stewart, Oxford University Press, Oxford, 1994), pp 10–12.

[12] Kelsen, above n 1, eg at p 209.

[13] L Friedman, "Law as a System: Some Comments" in T Eckhoff, L Friedman and J Uusitalo (eds), *Vernunft une Erfahrung im Rechtsdenken der Gegenwart / Reason and Experience in Contemporary Legal Thought*, Rechtstheorie Beiheft 10 (Duncker & Humblot, Berlin, 1986), pp 311–15, at p 311.

region, etc). There will be some obvious analogies when we compare a number of (state) legal systems: a limited number of (very) general rules on top and very detailed regulation at the lowest level of the hierarchy. General rules tend to be valid for a large territory, whereas local regulation is typically very concrete. History and comparative law also created rather similar models with a comparable or even identical terminology in state legal systems worldwide. However, all this does not mean that such structures are typical for law in general. A primitive legal system may know no hierarchy at all among its primary rules of conduct. These rules may all be perceived as customary rules of equal ranking. In such legal systems the *structure* is to be found at the level of the secondary rules and of their relationship with the primary rules. So, we may conclude that the hierarchy among primary rules of behaviour is *not* typical for the structure of legal systems, albeit that it is a common characteristic of *developed* legal systems.

It is in these developed (state) legal systems that several kinds of structures may be "discovered" or construed a posteriori: a *logical* structure of concepts and rules,[14] or a hierarchy of principles and their underlying *values*,[15] a formal hierarchy of *sources of law*, determining the hierarchy of the norms or decisions they contain,[16] a mainly didactical division of the legal system into subsystems or *branches of law* (public law/private law, labour law, administrative law, environmental law, etc) and further subdivisions, including "legal institutions" such as "divorce", "sureties", "mortgage". All those analyses of the structure of legal systems largely depend on the concrete content of the studied legal order. Therefore, they will not be discussed further here.

In giving an overview of the currently valid law of (a branch of) a legal system one has to take a static position, one has to offer a "snapshot" of that system. When looking at the machinery of law, however, one is forced to look at it from a dynamic point of view. *Understanding* law means, amongst other things, having a historical perspective on the coming into being, the change and the abolition of legal concepts, rules and institutions. One needs not just a picture of law, but a "movie" on legal development.

---

[14] Eg J Ray, *Structure logique du Code civil* (Félix Alcan, Paris, 1926), p 296; A-J Arnaud, *Essai d'analyse structurale du Code civil français* (L.G.D.J., Paris, 1973), p 182; GF Puchta, *Cursus der Institutionen*, 10th edn, vol 1 (Leipzig, 1893) (1st edn, 1841): "Es ist nun die Aufgabe der Wissenschaft, die Rechtssätze in ihrem systematischen Zusammenhang, als einander bedingende und voneinander abstammende, zu erkennen, um die Genealogie der einzelnen bis zu ihrem Prinzip hinaus verfolgen und ebenso von der Prinzipien bis zu ihren äussersten Sprossen herabsteigen zu können." (*ibid*, p 36). With this theory of the Genealogy of Concepts was Puchta the main representant of the German school of the *Begriffsjurisprudenz*, which was precisely emphasising this inner logic of concepts and rules as being the skeleton of the legal system.

[15] Eg CW Canaris, *Systemdenken und Systembegriff in der Jurisprudenz entwickelt am Beispiel des deutschen Privatrechts* (Duncker & Humblot, Berlin, 1969), p 46 et seq, and esp. at p 51.

[16] To be found in any textbook on law, but most prominently represented in legal theory by the *Stufenbau* Theory developed by Adolf Merkl and adopted by Hans Kelsen (AJ Merkl, "Prolegomena einer Theorie des rechtlichen Stufenbaues" in H Klecatsky, R Marcic and H Schambeck (eds), *Die Wiener Rechtstheoretische Schule. Schriften von Hans Kelsen, Adolf Merkl, Alfred Verdross*, vol 2 (Europa Verlag, Vienna), pp 1311–62.

Another distinction, that is relevant for the question of which elements are part of the structure of a legal system, is the one between "formal" structure and "substantive" structure. Most theories have emphasised one of them.[17] From what has been said above, one could infer that it is the formal structure which prevails, as we should concentrate on secondary rules rather than on primary rules of behaviour. However, by this one would erroneously assume that secondary rules are purely formal. Rules of procedure, for instance, have many formal aspects, but at the same time they may contain fundamental substantive elements. An important number of the rules laid down in the European Convention on Human Rights, for instance, protect *procedural* values, such as the right to defence, trial by independent judges and within a reasonable time, the right to appeal, etc. Thus, secondary rules are both formal and substantive. Moreover, as van de Kerchove and Ost have noted "these two modes of structuration of law are not only compatible but also complementary and partially interdependent".[18] Again, we are faced with a characteristic of circularity. Even if secondary rules of change determine the content of the primary rules of behaviour, they may, in their turn, be bound by such rules. The competence a legislative body possesses to enact legal rules is never arbitrary, even if at first sight this authority remains within the limits of its competence and follows the required procedures scrupulously. It has to take into account higher ranked legal rules and principles, such as a constitutional equality principle or the prohibition of slavery laid down in an international treaty.[19]

(b) Hierarchy, Anarchy or Circularity?

Van de Kerchove and Ost also criticise both the (purely) linear, hierarchic (eg Kelsen) and the (purely) anarchic[20] (eg Luhmann) approaches to law. They consider the first one to give a more or less true picture only of nineteenth-century public law and the second one of contemporary public international law.[21] Following writers such as Hofstadter and Morin they introduce the concepts of "tangled hierarchy" and "strange loops", which they consider useful for giving a better picture of law. They point to the interaction between different levels "in which the top level reaches back down towards the bottom level and influences it, while at the same time being itself determined by the bottom level".[22] This is precisely the phenomenon, that has been described above, in the context of the

---

[17] See for an overview of some of such theories: van de Kerchove and Ost, above n 10, pp 35–65.

[18] van de Kerchove and Ost, above n 10, p 37. They develop this idea on pp 57–60.

[19] Eg Art 4 of the European Convention on Human Rights, also laid down in Art 4 of the UN Declaration on Human Rights of 1948.

[20] Van de Kerchove and Ost denote Luhmann's approach as "circular". I avoid the use of this concept here, as I am using it myself with a different meaning, and it should be clear that my approach is different from the autopoietic one, as appeared from my critical analysis of this theory above, in 3.6 on the autonomy of law.

[21] Van de Kerchove and Ost, above n 10, p 68.

[22] *Ibid*, p 69.

discussion on the autonomy of law, of the current relationship between legislator and judiciary and between the European Union and its Member States and that I called "circular".[23]

It could be doubted whether there are any legal systems that could be considered to be purely hierarchic or purely "anarchic" as even van de Kerchove and Ost seem to suggest. If we accept, as also these authors do, that the validity of any legal authority is ultimately based, at least partly, on its *acceptance* by those subjected to it, we are already faced with an element of circularity. This should allow us to conclude that no legal system is completely "hierarchic" nor fully "anarchic", but always circular to some extent. It is true that public law in a strongly centralised state will be more hierarchic, whereas contract law in states with a liberal economy will tend to be rather anarchic. The extent to which legal systems, or parts of them, will be closer to one of those models thus entirely depends on the content and context of the law. A minimum of circularity, on the other hand, may be considered to be typical for any legal system—circularity in the sense of a mutual interdependence and interaction between persons and bodies within that legal system as regards the *production* and *legitimation* of law.

(c) Circularity: Game or Communication?

In developing the idea of circularity, or, as they call it, "tangled hierarchies", van de Kerchove and Ost use the model of the "game", including both "game" and "play" as is the case with the French word "*jeu*" in the original French edition. Partly quoting Crozier and Friedberg, they write:

> "The game, essential instrument of organized action, reconciles freedom and constraint. The players remain free, but, if they want to win, they must adopt a rational strategy in accordance with the nature of the game and conform to the game's rules. This instrument of analysis has the advantage, Crozier and Friedberg believe, of making it possible to supersede both the strategic perspective, which is confined to the actor's subjective point of view, and the systemic perspective, which is limited to the system's determinism. In a game, the rules condition the actors' strategy, but in return are also conditioned by it."[24]

By using the image of the game, van de Kerchove and Ost rightly point to the interdependence and interaction between legal system and legal subject, hence between the logic of the system, on the one hand, and the logic of solving concrete problems or of the individual's strategic actions, on the other:

> "A game is neither the effect of anonymous programming nor the product of a sovereign will. As a space of creativity, it measures the effect of the subject's intentionality, which is largely unpredictable, on the rigidity of a convention; as a regulated field, it

---

[23] I prefer to use this word rather than the somewhat puzzling, and perhaps superfluous, concepts of "tangled hierarchy" and "strange loops".

[24] *Ibid*, p 109.

expresses the will's re-orientation in response to a largely uncontrollable collective structure."[25]

The model of the game may be useful to show the deficiencies of some one-sided approaches to be found in jurisprudential literature, it still seems to be too limited to give a full picture of the problem. A game refers to a *closed* normative system, with a limited number of rules and of players, and that are well defined. In a game the action and interaction of players will never change the rules of the game.[26] In contradistinction to law, a game[27] offers a framework for *strategic action* only. Law, on the other hand, also creates an important space for *communicative action*, both in the sense of "normatively regulated action", through which members of a social group orient their action to *common values*[28] and in the sense in which HABERMAS defines the concept of "communicative action":

> "the concept of *communicative action* refers to the interaction of at least two subjects capable of speech and action who establish interpersonal relations (whether by verbal or by extra-verbal means). The actors seek to reach an understanding about the action situation and their plans of action in order to coordinate their actions by way of agreement."[29]

When setting up an enterprise with partners, or when actively taking part in politics and in elections, there may be a good deal of strategic action involved on behalf of each participant in that endeavour, but it cannot *completely* be reduced to that. The idea of reaching a common goal, which is very clearly underlying both the idea of contract, in the private area, and of democracy, in the public domain, transcends purely individual strategic action. It requires communication and coordination of action. This is not only true for the individuals who may at first sight just want to use the means offered by the legal system in order to reach their own ends, it is also true for the bodies that have the power of creating or adjudicating the law. They cannot act as competing institutions that could freely act strategically towards diverging goals. They have to

---

[25] Van de Kerchove and Ost, above n 10, p 109.

[26] Of course, players may agree to change the rules, but, by doing so, they are creating a new game, eg playing chess with the aim of getting rid as quickly as possible of all one's pieces; taking the other's piece is compulsory, whenever possible; the one who succeeds in forcing the opponent to take all his pieces wins the game; otherwise all standard rules of chess apply. This is a funny game, which does not take much time, but it is not chess, even if at first sight everything seems to be the same, with the exception of just one changed rule: the duty to take pieces, which otherwise is only a permission.

[27] Even if one takes it in the broader sense of the French "*jeu*", there is no common goal *outside* the play or the game. It is playing which is as such the goal of the playing activity, whereas law is not the goal of law. If other types of action are involved in a play it would rather be *dramaturgical action*, in which "the actor evokes in his public a certain image, an impression of himself, by more or less purposefully disclosing his subjectivity . . . and steer their interactions through regulating mutual access to their own subjectivities." (J Habermas, *The Theory of Communicative Action*, vol.1, *Reason and the Rationalization of Society* (tran T McCarthy, Polity Press, Cambridge, 1984), p 86).

[28] *Ibid*, p 85.

[29] *Ibid*, p 86.

"build" and to develop the legal system through communicative action, both with each other and with society in general, including the citizen, the press, and legal doctrine. The communicative action through which the different persons and bodies are interacting within a legal system creates "a collective, uninterrupted, and multidirectional process of circulation of meaning"[30] and goes, by this, beyond a purely bilateral communication or any form of game or play. As all this is closely linked to language and to interpretation we will come back to this point below in chapter 7 on the methodology of law. I just want to add that it is in this collective, uninterrupted circulation of meaning that the "legal system" functions as an important regulative ideal and, by this partly creates its systemic structure.

(d) The Building Blocks of Legal Systems

It would seem obvious to have started this chapter with the question of what the building blocks are which are the elements of the typical structure of a legal system. However, this is probably the most difficult question to answer. As already argued above, primary rules of behaviour are the most visible, and of course essential, elements of any legal system, but they do not determine the structure of legal systems in general. Secondary rules of change and adjudication are as essential to legal systems as their primary rules, but they are partly determined by the content of those primary rules. The circular relationship between primary and secondary rules, between form and substance, between the making of the law and the adjudication of the law, make it very difficult to identify well determined building blocks and their mutual relationship.

Candidates for being such basic building blocks are "legal rules", "legal concepts", "legal principles", "legal sentences",[31] "legal institutions", or a combination of some or all of them.[32] However, they all suffer from problems of vagueness: as will be discussed below, "legal rules" are not identical to the legislative text in which they are laid down and, thus, are partly the result of an

---

[30] Interestingly enough this is what Van de Kerchove and Ost write when discussing Dworkin's metaphor of the chain novel and defining the legal production of meaning (above n. 10, p 97). So we probably agree as to the analysis of the legal phenomenon, but we might disagree as to the appropriateness of *"jeu"* (game + play) as a model for explaining it, mainly because we do not seem to associate this concept with the same reality.

[31] C Alchourron and E Bulygin, *Normative Systems* (Vienna and New York, 1971), p 50. For these authors these are the *necessary* building blocks without which no system can exist (*ibid*, p 69; see also: E Bulygin, "Legal Dogmatics and the Systematization of Law" in Eckhoff, Friedman and Uusitalo, above n 13, pp 193–210, at p 199). Also for Manuel Atienza and Juan Ruiz Manero legal sentences are "the most elementary units of law" (*A Theory of Legal Sentences* (Kluwer Academic Publishers, Dordrecht, 1998), p xi).

[32] Such a broad approach in which legal norms, legal institutions and legal activities are included can, eg, be found in: W Krawietz., "Recht und moderne Systemtheorie" in Eckhoff, Friedman and Uusitalo, above n 13, pp 281–309, at p 291. See also JW Harris, *Law and Legal Science. An Inquiry into the Concepts Legal Rule and Legal System* (Clarendon Press, Oxford, 1979), esp. at pp 24–25 (for an overview of varying theories) and the conclusion at pp 165 to 171, with the revealing subtitle "An overall view of law".

interpretation of that text; "legal concepts" refer to rules and, generally, present in a nutshell a whole bundle of rights, duties, liberties, competences, and so on; "legal principles" are broadly worded fundamental rules that are interpreted and partly filled in whilst applying them to concrete cases (or even to a very large extent in case of "unwritten general principles of law"); "legal institutions", lastly, are simply sets of principles, rules and concepts, and they are subsystems rather than building blocks.

The problem perhaps again arises from an underlying assumption of linearity, clear hierarchy and relative simplicity of legal systems. When we accept that law is better represented by a complex whole of interwoven circularities, with "tangled hierarchies" and "strange loops", it is a concept of *network* that we have to use instead of that of (pure) hierarchy. Such a network may interconnect a very large number of elements, which together form a complex whole that is neither anarchic nor hierarchic. We may compare it to the model of "neural network" used for analysing the working of the human brain, but also fruitfully applied in the area of artificial intelligence. Especially for application in the area of law, this model has proven to be much more adapted to (legal) reasoning than traditional linear, hierarchical models of deduction used by (formal) logic. Instead of the binary choice between "true" and "false", the neural network model offers a *scale of degree of probability*. As a result, the structure of a system should not be viewed, in the light of such a model, as a hierarchy, in which the higher elements determine the (truth of) the lower ones, but as a network of relationships that produce meanings with a higher or lower probability of "truth".

According to Gunther Teubner "legal acts" are the elements that are *produced* by the legal system, but, at the same time they are the basis for legal changes, which then, in their turn, produce new legal acts, and so on.[33]

Generally speaking, however, for autopoietic theory, including Teubner, the basic element of any social system is *communication*. Here, communication is opposed to the human being, who in traditional theories is considered to be the basic element of any social system, or, as far as law is concerned, communication is opposed to legal norms, legal subjects or legal actors.[34] Autopoietic theory does not deny the importance of those human beings, it merely moves the perspective from a group of individuals to a *social system* built with *communications* among human beings. It is also through communication that the social system is reproducing itself: "Legal acts are those communicative events that change legal structures".[35]

In this approach "communication" bears a broader meaning than in common language. It means "a synthesis of information, communication and compre-

---

[33] G Teubner, "Evolution of Autopoietic Law" in G Teubner (ed), *Autopoietic Law: a New Approach to Law and Society* (Walter de Gruyter, Berlin and New York, 1988), p 221.

[34] G Teubner, "Introduction to Autopoietic Law" in Teubner, above n 33, p 3; N Luhmann, "The Unity of the Legal System" in Teubner, above n 33, pp 16–17.

[35] G Teubner, "Introduction to Autopoietic Law" in Teubner, above n 33, p 4.

hension, and not merely the action of communication as such".[36] Thus, according to Luhmann, "the social system consists of meaningful communications—only of communications, and of all communications",[37] and "the legal system, too, consists only of communicative actions which engender legal consequences".[38] By this, the *meaning* given to any legally relevant element (norms, institutions, facts, activities, etc) becomes of paramount importance for the question on systematicity in law. It remains unclear how, according to auto-poietic theory, this meaning is produced. Of course, autopoietists tell us that it is the legal system itself that produces those meanings within its own operatively closed, but cognitively open, world. But what does this mean? And the same goes for the autopoietic definition of "meaning", such as: "form of a surplus of references to further possibilities".[39] We will enter the discussion on the meaning of "meaning" more thoroughly in the chapter on methodology of law.[40] Here, it may suffice to conclude that the autopoietic approach suggests that the "system" of law is not given but *produced* on a daily basis in legal practice. According to Luhmann the *unity* of the legal system is created by "autopoietic reproduction of elements by elements on the basis of circular, recursive norma-tivity",[41] the *structure* of the legal system consists of conditional programmes which establish an "if a, then b" relationship between the condition and the con-ferment of norm quality.[42] In other words: the secondary rules that identify something as having a normative value within the legal system form its structure. This, I think, does not add much to the debate. In fact, one may also argue, as Ladeur did, that in autopoietic theory the "system" cannot be said to consist of elements: "The system is in a paradoxical way made of . . . systems!", as there is "an infinite succession of 'computation of computation' which characterises the systemic recursivity of a program reading the results of its own lecture".[43]

In any event, we should reach a provisional conclusion as to the basic elements which should be considered to be the building blocks of legal systems. It

---

[36] Luhmann, above n 33, p 17.

[37] *Ibid*, p 18.

[38] *Ibid*, p 19.

[39] N Luhmann, *Soziale Systeme. Grundriss einer allgemeinen Theorie* (Suhrkamp, Frankfurt am Main, 1984), p 93.

[40] Obviously, the conception of "meaning" is one of the weakest points in the autopoietic theory, at least with Luhmann (see K-H Ladeur, "Perspectives on a Post-Modern Theory of Law" in Teubner, above n 33, pp 266–69), even if Luhmann tried to offer a rather lenghty analysis of "mean-ing" ("Meaning as Sociology's Basic Concept" in N Luhmann, *Essays on Self-Reference* (Columbia University Press, New York, 1990), pp 21–79). By completely disconnecting "meaning" from any concept of "subject" (*ibid*, p 23) it is very difficult, if not impossible to link such a theory with any kind of legal reality.

It is interesting to note that also for Kelsen (and probably for many more legal theorists) the con-cept of "meaning" has been a pitfall (see further, below 7.2.1, and R Moore, *Legal Norms and Legal Science. A Critical Study of Kelsen's Pure Theory of Law* (The University Press of Hawaii, Honolulu, 1978), pp 104–9).

[41] Luhmann, above n 34, p 23.

[42] *Ibid*, p 24.

[43] Ladeur, above n 40, p 262.

appears that the theories on law's systematicity are determining those basic elements rather than the other way around. This confirms to what extent the "legal system" is not some given fact, but the product of a theory. Therefore, it does not make much sense to attack any theory because its author chose the wrong building block. We can emphasise primary rules of behaviour as basic elements, if we want to point to the substantive structure of a legal system; we can emphasise the secondary rules, if we want to investigate the dynamic structure of the legal machinery; we may emphasise "communications" (in the autopoietic sense) as basic elements, if we want to analyse the pure systemic functioning of law, independent from any concrete legal reality; we may emphasise "legal arguments" as basic elements, if we want to present law mainly as the product of an argumentation on the meaning of the law, and so on. From their perspective, all these approaches may successfully argue in favour of the "basic elements" of law they have unveiled. Intuitively, however, we may assume that each of those approaches is one-sided and cannot give a full picture of law. We need at the very least a combination of some of them. But what kind of system will come out of that combination? Some very complex superposition of structures that do not fit well, or even not fit at all, with each other. The drawing of a "system", a "structure" which by definition is meant to reduce complexity, would fail to reach that end. We cannot look at law, or at anything else, from all possible points of view at the same time. That means that, inevitably, the chosen point of view will to a large extent determine the "systems theory", whereas the chosen theory will to a large extent determine the "basic elements" of law that are relevant for *that* type of structure.

(e) Coherence

What could be added to this that would be valid for any kind of legal system? Probably not much, except that there should be a fairly large degree of *coherence* among the legal rules. As Aleksander Peczenik has observed: "even a well-known anti-coherentist, Joseph Raz, has admitted 'that the application of each of the distinct values ought to be consistently pursued, and this generates pockets of coherence'."[44]

Coherence means, in the first place, *consistency* or absence of contradictions. There should be no incompatible rules, and if so, they should be very exceptional and the system should offer a solution for solving such antinomies, eg through interpretation.

Secondly, "coherence" refers to some structural links, to some internal *cohesion* among the elements of the legal system. It would, for instance, not make much sense to develop a detailed regulation on private property without making

---

[44] A Peczenik., "A Coherence Theory of Juristic Knowledge" in A Aarnio, *et al.*, *On Coherence Theory of Law* (Juristförlaget, Lund, 1998), pp 9–15, at p 14, with reference to: J Raz, *Ethics in the Public Domain. Essays in the Morality of Law and Politics* (Clarendon Press, Oxford, 1994), p 315.

theft punishable. This means that legal rules have to support each other, at least to some extent. This is not only true for the relationship among primary rules of conduct, but also for the relationship between primary rules and secondary rules. It would not make much sense to create a set of rules on contract law without giving at least some persons and/or bodies the competence to make, to change and to dissolve a contract or without giving anybody, eg a judge, the power to decide about it in case of conflict. And, of course, secondary rules should fit with each other. For instance, the procedural rules have to fit more or less perfectly with the rules creating legislative or judicial institutions and awarding them some competences.

At last, there should be some *external cohesion*. Law should fit with society, with its underlying culture and shared values. Not necessarily in a perfect way, but at least to some extent and even to a relatively large extent, because of the requirement of minimal acceptance of the legal system by those to whom it is meant to apply.[45]

Whereas consistency is a negative all or nothing condition for any legal system (no contradictions), the broader concept of "coherence" refers, positively, to an ideal of perfect fit of all elements with each other, that in practice will be reached to a certain degree, but never perfectly.[46]

6.3 FORM AND SUBSTANCE: THE STRUCTURE OF LEGAL SYSTEMS AND CONCEPTIONS OF DEMOCRACY

In legal systems, especially those which are structuring political orders such as, most prominently, state legal systems, the *structure* of the legal system is to an important extent determined by the underlying conception of democracy or of any other kind of view on political decision-making.

Let us compare the structure of the legal systems of twentieth century Germany: the current *Bundesrepublik*, the former German Democratic Republic, the Third *Reich*, the Weimar republic and the *Kaiserreich*. Differences between those legal systems can hardly be explained by different traditions or religious backgrounds, as would be the case when comparing it, for example, to the legal systems of the USA, of the former Soviet Union or of the Taliban regime in Afghanistan. Differences between the legal systems in Germany in the twentieth century could be explained by economic changes or changes in legal culture, but only to a limited extent, as the much less radical changes in other countries, such as France or the United Kingdom, over that period show. It cannot be denied that the dominant ideological and political views are the main explanation for the dramatic changes this country has seen

[45] See above 3.3.2 on sociological institutionalisation and 3.5 on law and coercion.
[46] L Wintgens, "On Coherence and Consistency", in: W Krawietz, RS Summers, O Weinberger and GH von Wright (eds), *The Reasonable as Rational? On Legal Argumentation and Justification. Festschrift for Aulis Aarnio* (Duncker & Humblot, Berlin, 2000), pp 539–50, at pp 540–41.

during the twentieth century. The most visible, but superficial, divergences are to be found at the level of terminology (eg, *Reich*/Republic; *Reichsgericht*/ *Bundesgerichtshof*). Less visible are the differences in structuring the rule-making powers. At first sight, indeed, those structures may seem to be rather comparable: Parliaments drafting general rules, an executive power implementing them through its administration, and courts solving disputes. Overall, even procedural rules do not show radical differences. However, what has been typical for the least democratic regimes in twentieth century Germany was a *parallel circuit* of political and legal decision making through a very high concentration of power within a monopolistic political party (the National-Socialist Party (NSDAP) in nazi Germany, the Socialist Party (SED) in the GDR), thus creating a "dual State".[47] Through an unlimited power to make, to change and to adjudicate the law (or not) the leaders of those political parties could completely disturb the traditional legal system at all levels. On the one hand there was a "classic" legal system that could remain relatively unchanged over time; on the other hand, the scope and applicability of that system was limited by the ideology and interest of the ruling party. In the GDR, for example, the scope of private law was narrowed to a large extent, because whole areas, such as housing or labour relations, became "public law". In nazi Germany whole categories of citizen, such as most notably Jews, were excluded from almost any right that could be derived from the legal system. In practice, moreover, non-legal sources interfered directly with the adjudication of the law, *contra legem*, such as the political programme of the NSDAP[48] or Hitler's book *Mein Kampf* in nazi Germany,[49] or, to a lesser extent, the interest of the party or the political wishes of the Soviet Union in the GDR. In both cases the structure of the legal system at first sight seems to have remained unchanged, but is in reality subjected to another hierarchy in which the will of the political leaders is the final, overruling legal source. In nazi Germany it even went further than two competing hierarchies. It became largely anarchic to the extent that lower ranked officials and military men could take any arbitrary decision, referring to "the will of the *Führer*", without any effective control or sanctioning of such abuses.

In current democratic states, including present-day Germany, on the other hand, the *structure* of the political and legal system is to a large extent determined by *substantive* democratic principles. The rule of law requires a separation of powers, to some extent at least between the legislator and the executive, and totally between these two branches of state power and sources of law-making, on the one hand, and courts on the other. The basic principles determining the structure of the legal system are, as a rule, laid down in a written constitution that cannot easily be changed. Law-making is primarily carried out by legislative bodies

---

[47] See, as to nazi Germany, E Fraenkel, *The Dual State. A Contribution to the Theory of Dictatorship* (Oxford University Press, Oxford, 1941).

[48] Eg Hanseatisches Sondergericht 9 January 1940, *Der Deutsche Rechtspfleger*, 1940, 876.

[49] Eg Reichsgericht 7 January 1938, *Entscheidungen des Reichsgerichts in Zivilsachen*, 1938, 157.

that are elected on the basis of free elections that take place on a regular basis. Courts will check whether rules issued by lower ranking bodies are compatible with those enacted by higher ranked ones and will, the case arising, annul or narrow the scope of the incompatible lower rule. A minimal pluralism combined with the equality principle entails some free space for private law-making through contracts, wills, constitutions of associations, and the like. It is revealing that the criticism on the "democratic deficit" of the European Union is directly linked to the *structure* of the European legal system with, it is posited, too many law-making powers with the executive (European Commission, Council of Ministers) and the judiciary (European Court of Justice) and too little with the only directly elected legislative body, the European Parliament.

Thus, when analysing the structure of legal systems we have to take into account this intertwinement of form and substance. The structure of legal systems cannot be studied in isolation from its content.

Moreover, when studying modern (state) legal systems we also have to take into account underlying conceptions of democracy or competing conceptions that are part of the public political debate within the society to which the legal system applies.

An example is the discussion about the future democratic shape of the European Union, although the underlying theories are not always clear and coherent, partly because many different discussions are mingled (cultural identity, economic development, democratic legitimation, etc) and partly because the discussion has hardly begun and the theoretical positions are not yet clearly elaborated .

A better example, for our analysis, is the (mainly) American discussion between *"Liberals"* and *"Republicans"* and the third alternative, *"deliberative politics"*, as proposed by Jürgen Habermas.

The discussion between Liberals and Republicans can also be worded in terms of an opposition between "individualists" and "communitarians" or between "basic rights" and "procedural rights", or "substantivists" versus "formalists", or, in more traditional jurisprudential terms, "natural lawyers" versus "positivists".

An important feature of Western legal thinking over the last two or three centuries is the emphasis on *human rights*, the idea that some rights are innate to any human being and not "awarded" by some political body, however democratically legitimated it may be, let alone that they could be withdrawn by such a democratic majority. It is the conviction of the Liberals that one should prevent political bodies, including democratic majorities, from abusing their power and from infringing such basic rights of individuals or minority groups. This approach is deeply rooted in our tradition of natural law theories, which has taken different shapes since the Middle Ages, but has culminated in Human Rights Declarations at the end of the eighteenth century as a result of the rationalist natural law approach of modern times. Meanwhile it became part of positive law on a worldwide scale, in constitutions and international treaties.

"Republicans" have problems with this natural law flavour of rights. They consider rights to be ultimately "nothing but determinations of prevailing political will".[50] What is important for democracy, according to the Republicans, is the creation of a "public sphere", "within which persons can achieve freedom in the sense of self-government by the exercise of reason in public dialogue".[51] Once this condition fulfilled, republicanism becomes a typical positivist theory of law:

> "In a republican view, a community's objective, common good substantially consists in the success of its political endeavor to define, establish, effectuate, and sustain the set of rights (less tendentiously, laws) best suited to the conditions and mores of that community."[52]

According to this view there are no absolute rights. They may change according to the "conditions and *mores*" of the community. The outcome is democratically legitimated if the public debate and everyone's possible paricipation in it are guaranteed. This can be achieved through procedural rules that guarantee such a public dialogue.

Thus, for Liberals a legal system is primarily a structure of *rights*, whereas for Republicans it is rather a system of *procedures* for establishing such rights. For Liberals it is the *content* of the law that counts, rather than its form. For Republicans it is the best possible form, the procedures structuring the public dialogue and collective decision-making, which are the best guarantee for the best possible *content* of the law. For Liberals there are a number of (more or less) eternal fundamental rights, that exist independently of any political or legal system, whereas for Republicans law and rights change according to place and time. Of course, Republicans cannot escape the acceptance of "absolute" or "undebatable" rights and principles, such as the *equality* of all human beings and, hence, their undeniable right to participate in the public political debate. We will not discuss this further here, but, as appears from the reciprocal criticism, both theories have to face weak points.

Being part of the Western legal tradition, it indeed is very difficult to deny the existence of basic rights and to leave it to political majorities to determine their existence and scope, as daily political practices all over the world seem to confirm. On the other hand, Republicanism has a point too, by emphasising the importance of the public debate and the necessity to guarantee an open, free and equal dialogue, which can mainly be achieved through procedural rules.

On the basis of this conclusion, Habermas proposes his theory on *"deliberative politics"* as a way out of the inconveniences of both theories.[53] He tries to

---

[50] F Michelman, "Conceptions of Democracy in American Constitutional Argument: Voting Rights", (1989) 41 *Florida Law Review* 446

[51] F Michelman "Political Truth and the Rule of Law", (1988) 8 *Tel Aviv University Studies in Law* 284.

[52] Michelman, above n 50, p 446.

[53] See, for this debate] Habermas, *The Inclusion of the Other. Studies in Political Theory* (Polity Press, Cambridge, 1999) (1st German edn, 1996), Pt V "What is Meant by 'Deliberative Politics'?", pp. 237–64.

offer a synthesis of form and substance, of rights and procedures, of individualism and collectivism.

Like the Republicans, Habermas refuses to see the citizen as atomised individuals, cut off from a community, as bearers of individual rights which they could freely use, as money in an economic market. He agrees that the individual should be conceived as part of a community. However, unlike the Republicans, Habermas regards the political system "neither as the peak nor the center, nor even as the structuring model of society, but as just *one* action among others".[54] Moreover, he has a pluralist view of society, in which some rules and rights may be determined at the level of specific communities, whereas the political public sphere "sets apart an arena for the detection, identification, and interpretation of problems affecting society as a whole".[55] "Popular sovereignty" is not interpreted as a necessarily "single will" of "the people" but as an intersubjective communicative power, exercised, as also the Liberals argue, "by means of elections and voting and by specific legislative, executive, and judicial organs".[56] For Habermas the Liberal view offers too little guarantees for the legitimation of the law:

> "On the liberal view, democratic will-formation has the exclusive function of *legitimating* the exercise of political power. The outcomes of elections license the assumption of governmental power, though the government must justify the use of power to the public and parliament. On the republican view, democratic will-formation has the significantly stronger function of *constituting* society as a political community and keeping the memory of this founding act alive with each new election."[57]

According to Deliberative Politics "rights" cannot only be approached as tools for strategic action that could be used as in the model of the economic market. They are partly constituted through *communicative action* through a public political debate. Individual rights and collective decision-making are not opposites, as the Liberal–Republican discussion suggests. They are *interdependent*. According to Habermas, we have to combine private autonomy with public autonomy, private spheres guaranteed through individual rights co-exist with a public sphere that is organised through procedural rules:

> "Each form of autonomy, the individual liberties of the subject of private law and the public autonomy of the citizen, makes the other form possible. This reciprocal relation is expressed by the idea that legal persons can be autonomous only insofar as they can understand themselves, in the exercise of their civic rights, as authors of just those rights which they are supposed to obey as addressees."[58]

---

[54] *Ibid*, p 251.
[55] *Ibid*.
[56] *Ibid*, p 250, where Habermas refers to Art 20, s 2 of the Basic Law (Constitution) of the German Federal Republic.
[57] *Ibid*, p 249.
[58] *Ibid*, p 258.

The political public debate presupposes autonomous legal persons, but, on the other hand:

> "There is no law without the private autonomy of legal persons in general. Consequently, without basic rights that secure the private autonomy of citizens there is also no medium for legally institutionalizing the conditions under which these citizens, as citizens of a state, can make use of their public autonomy."[59]

However, not everything can be organised through law. Deliberative politics can only function properly within an open political culture. The law may provide the best possible conditions for the development of such a culture, but it cannot *create* this culture. Law has its limits.

It may not seem very appropriate to discuss these problems within a chapter on the structure of legal systems. However, it was my aim to show, first, to what extent the (perceived) structure of legal systems is dependent on underlying conceptions of law and democracy, and, secondly, that we need a theory that offers the best possible picture of legal practice. From this point of view it seems undesirable to limit the legal system to a pure set of "rights" or a set of "procedural rules" or even a set of "norms". Habermas' Deliberative Politics, and the communicational approach it includes, thus offers a richer theory (a) in that it accommodates both rights and procedures, primary rules and secondary rules, as mutually linked basic elements of legal systems and (b) in that it embeds law in its social and political context, which partly determines the very structure of law.

---

[59] *Ibid*, pp 260–61.

7

Methodology of Law ·

The specific nature of law does not only influence the scientific nature of legal doctrine when compared with other disciplines, it also influences the methodology of legal practice.

Generally speaking, we can state that each legal argument contains three components: deductive reasoning, inductive reasoning and value thinking.[1] With the *deductive* part of reasoning one reaches a legal solution by a logical deduction, starting from legal premises. With the *inductive* part of reasoning one starts from concrete facts and from desired results to reach general rules, a hierarchy of principles, etc. Finally, *value thinking* is also inevitable in legal reasoning. Even the choice of premises (in deductive reasoning) and the choice of the facts and values considered to be relevant (in inductive reasoning) are themselves value-laden.

The combination of these three aspects of legal reasoning is eg clear in the case of applying the legal concept "abuse of law" or "abuse of rights" to the following typical problem, which seems to have arisen in several countries in Europe.

A land-owner has erroneously built his house some decimetres over the boundary, on the land of his neighbour. According to most legal systems in continental Western Europe, the rights of the land-owner are very broad; they include the right to use, the right to build and to demolish. This implies, at least prima facie, the right to demolish the part of the building which the neighbour has erroneously erected on one's land. Most strikingly, this rather "absolute" power has been defined by Article 544 of the Code Napoléon (still as such valid in France and in Belgium):

> "Property is the right to use and to dispose of things in the most absolute way, as far as one does not use it in a way prohibited by the statutes or other regulations."[2]

Starting from such a clear premise a logical deduction seems to lead inevitably to the conclusion that the injured land-owner is himself entitled to demolish, or

---

[1] J Laakso, "Über die Dreidimensionalität des juristischen Denkens" in A Peczenik and J Uusitalo (eds), *Reasoning on Legal Reasoning* (Vammala, 1979), pp 75–85.

[2] "La propriété est le droit de jouir et disposer des choses de la manière la plus absolue, pourvu qu'on n'en fasse pas un usage prohibé par les lois ou par les règlements".

at least to force his neighbour to demolish, the illegaly constructed part of the building.

Nevertheless, in several countries, where such an injured land-owner has claimed the right to demolition, courts have decided otherwise. They have over-ruled the prima facie result of deductive reasoning by an inductive and value-laden argumentation.

It is in such cases that courts have elaborated the legal conception of "abuse of rights": something, which prima facie seems to be completely legal, is con-sidered by the judges to be unjust, taking into account the concrete elements of the case. If the building were to have been built fully on the neighbour's land no problem would have occurred and the claim of the injured land-owner would have been complied with. But in this concrete case the *bona fide* neighbour would be greatly harmed by a demolition, whereas the advantages for the injured landowner would be very limited. To all these judges it seemed much more reasonable to keep the building as it had been erected and to force the injured land-owner to accept a financial compensation.

Inductively starting from the concrete facts of the case, the judges have intro-duced the value of reasonable compensation of the injured right, taking into account the loss for the right-offender and the gain for the right-owner. In a second, "all things considered", argumentation, a new deductive reasoning is constructed, in which the statutory text no longer defines the rights of the owner, ie Article 544 of the *Code Napoléon* (that is now the main premise), but a newly introduced (moral) value. In the concrete case this value then overrules the literal application of the statutory text.

Besides those three basic components (deduction, induction, value thinking) legal reasoning also has some other characteristics.

Legal argumentation is *teleological*, goal-oriented. Law aims at a specific organisation of society. When creating, elaborating, implementing or adjudi-cating the law, a lawyer thinks from the perspective of this societal ordering, which governs his reasoning (or at least should govern it).

Legal thinking is *historically* oriented. When changing the law, even in revo-lutionary times, one essentially departs from the existing law, from basic rules and principles and from traditional concepts, conceptions and legal techniques. When looking for a solution to a legal problem, lawyers will always try to find precedents and use them as weighty reasons for their argumentation, even if such precedents are not legally binding at all.

Legal reasoning is *practical* and *concretising*. The elaboration of general rules and principles and of systems and theories is subordinated to the solving of concrete legal problems. The concrete, individualised case is at the core of legal reasoning. The specific, distinctive characteristics of a case are emphasised (especially, but not only, in English law to escape from binding precedents). Legal reasoning is thus opposed to any form of scientific reasoning, which for its part, abstracts from concrete, individual characteristics in order to find regular-ities, typologies, patterns, "laws".

Legal argumentation is of course *normative*. Lawyers do not try to give a causal explanation for a specific behaviour. They compare this behaviour with a normative model, which they find in the law. They analyse the legal rules from the perspective of the concrete characteristics of the case and deduce from it the behaviour one ought to follow. This model behaviour is then used for testing someone's concrete behaviour.

Legal thinking is *decision-making*. Even when, especially in case of judgment of evidence in court decisions, truth statements are made, making a decision seems to be as such more important than finding out the complete truth. Facts are proved, and thus are considered to have happened, or they are not. There is no room for probability. If necessary, legal fictions or other techniques (eg changing the burden of proof) are used to simplify reality and to consider a fact to have happened, even if perhaps it did not (eg the maxim *"pater est quem nuptiae demonstrant"*).

Legal thinking is *communicative*: it is based on, and implemented through, a constant communication between the different actors in the legal field: advocates, judges, legislators, administration, legal doctrine, etc.

Because of the complexity of legal thinking, legal methodology, inevitably, must be complex too. Theories on legal methodology tend to favour some aspects of legal reasoning, thereby neglecting other ones. Valentin Petev has rightly posited that legal methodology:

> "is neither of a purely logical nature, nor hermeneutical, nor topical; it offers a multitude of reflexions and actions aiming at an understanding and handling of the law that fits with its regulating function in a pluralist society in which identity and legitimation are constantly questioned. Such a methodology is open to diverging political and ethical positions in that society that influence the conception and practice of contemporary law."[3]

Currently, the mainstream approach is focusing on *argumentation*. It offers a methodology for sound legal *reasoning*, but it is generally not concerned with the question *what lawyers are looking for* and *how they can find it*. A strong relativism seems to reduce legal methodology to a theory of legal argumentation.[4] Eliminating false arguments or wrong deductions is very useful as such, but cannot offer a *positive*, full methodology for lawyers. This chapter cannot offer such a complete methodology either, but it will try to offer at least some building blocks for it.

---

[3] V Petev., "Quelle méthode? La méthodologie au seuil du XXIème siècle" (1990) *Revue de la recherche juridique. Droit prospectif* 757–67, at pp 759–60.

[4] A refreshing and well balanced approach, that escapes the extremes of strong relativism and false certainties, is to be found in K Greenawalt, *Law and Objectivity* (Oxford University Press, New York and Oxford, 1992), p 288.

7.2.1 Language as a Means of Communication

Language is basically a way to convey a person's thoughts to another person.[5] Linguistic utterances can only be studied in a meaningful way as a part of this communication process between the one who phrases the expression (the sender) and the one to whom the linguistic utterance is addressed (the receiver).[6]

Apart from this triangular relationship "sender–utterance–receiver" (see also above 1.2.2), there is also a "triangle of meaning" sign–denoted reality–meaning. The "sign" is the linguistic utterance. The "denoted reality" is the reality to which the sign refers. The "meaning" is (the result of) the link between both. This "triangle of meaning" refers to another dimension in the communication process: not to the relationship between communicating persons, but to the relationship between a linguistic utterance and reality.

This scheme is shown in Figure 7.1.

Actually, however, the meaning is not a relationship between a linguistic utterance and a reality. The meaning is a content which the *sender* has given to the linguistic utterance in order to give some message about reality. Conversely, the meaning may also be the result of the interpretation of the utterance by its *receiver*.

In the first case, we are confronted with an aimed meaning, a *sender-meaning*. When applied to statutes it is called "the will of the legislator". In the second case,

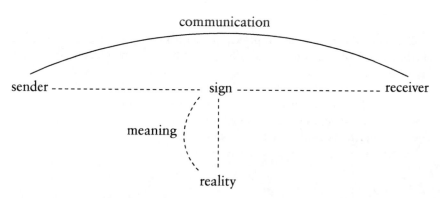

Figure 7.1: Triangle of meaning

[5] T Slama-Cazacu, *Langage et contexte* (Mouton, The Hague, 1961), pp 20–21
[6] CK Ogden and LA Richards, *The Meaning of Meaning* (Routledge & Kegan Paul, London, 1960) (1st edn, 1923), pp 205–6.

we have an interpreted meaning, a *receiver-meaning*, eg the meaning given to a statute by a judge when adjudicating on it in a concrete case. Within this receiver-meaning one may, moreover, distinguish between a "prima facie meaning" and a "methodologically determined meaning".

The *prima facie meaning* is the meaning spontaneously given to the linguistic utterance by the receiver, as a result of an unconscious interpretative reasoning. When a lawyer considers a legal text to be "clear and unequivocal", it just means that, on the basis of an unconscious interpretation, the text seems prima facie to be clear to its reader.

The *methodologically determined meaning* is the meaning given by the receiver to the linguistic utterance, on the basis of conscious interpretative research, by which the utterance is located in a larger context than the immediately perceptible, or at least immediately perceived, context. When eg interpreting a statute, this larger context encompasses, amongst others, a larger whole of legislation (systemic interpretation), legislative materials (*travaux préparatoires, Hansard*), the mischief of the statute (teleological interpretation) or historical developments (historical interpretation).

A lack of an elaborated theory on the concept of meaning and/or the implicit assumption of a highly questionable theory, constitutes a weak point in many theories on (the interpretation of) law. An example is Hans Kelsen, who saw the norm as the meaning of an act of will through which that norm is posited:

> "Someone who issues a command *intends* something. He expects the other person to *understand* this something. By his command he intends *that* the other person *is to* behave in a certain way. That is the *meaning* of his act of will."[7]

Hence, according to Kelsen, "it is more correct to say 'a norm *is* a meaning' than 'a norm *has* a meaning' ".[8] In such a view "meaning" is limited to the psychological sender-meaning, by this excluding any other type or conception of "meaning".[9]

The meaning given to some sign may be the result of a subjective, personal interpretation, but it is always based on a *meaning system* that is socially and culturally determined. Understanding (the sender-meaning of) signs requires a knowledge of the appropriate meaning system. In communication theory the knowledge of meaning systems and the ability to negotiate those systems within different cultural contexts is called "*cultural literacy*"[10]. Such meaning systems are the product of communication, through which the language, including a

---

[7] H Kelsen, *General Theory of Norms* (Clarendon Press, Oxford, 1991), p 32.

[8] *Ibid*, p 26.

[9] Another example can be found in Luhmann's writings, where "meaning" is cut loose from both sender and receiver and seems to live a life of its own. See for a criticism K-H Ladeur, "Perspectives on a Post-Modern Theory of Law", in G Teubner (ed), *Autopoietic Law: A New Approach to Law and Society* (Walter de Gruyter, Berlin and New York, 1988), pp 242–82, at pp 266–69, esp. n 5 at p 268.

[10] T Schirato and S Yell, *Communication and Culture* (SAGE Publications, London, 2000), pp xi and 1.

specific legal language, has been developed. At the same time, knowledge of the appropriate meaning system is a prerequisite for any adequate communication.

Just like law, language can only be correctly understood when seen as an interactively developing social construct. Language is learned and developed in social discourse. Language structures, grammar and vocabulary are constantly slightly adapted in the daily communicative practice of the language users. There is a constant tension between the language rules that have been socially determined in the past and their present use by an individual, a tension between social determinism and individual freedom. Even the most liberal use of language will have to stick to given rules and use words in a standard meaning if some communication is to be brought about. Language can only be conceived within a context of structured communication, be it for its coming into being, its being learned and used, or its development.[11]

7.2.2 Legislation as Communication

Language is by far the most important means for communication amongst people. Communication situations may present themselves in different forms: face-to-face or in public; oral or written; in power relations or on equal terms; in intimate relations or in impersonal relations, etc. Legislation is a specific form of communication, by which a legislator formulates norms, addressed towards a number of present and/or future (legal) persons, who are expected to respect and apply those norms. It is not only a transmission of information about the content of newly enacted rules, it is typically a *speech act*,[12] or a performative utterance, through which a legal change comes about. A newly published Act is not just informing about a change in the law, but also, by this very enactment, *creating* it. Therefore such utterances can neither be true nor false. They cannot give a correct or incorrect picture of an external reality, as the "reality" is made by the speech act itself. Seen from this point of view, they are by definition "true". Of course, legislation may be wrong in other ways: it may be invalid, it may be based on wrong information about the empirical reality the Act aims to regulate, it may be incoherent with other legislation, it may be badly drafted, it may be difficult to apply or to control offences, etc, but the enacted rules cannot be "false".

Legislation as a form of communication shows the following characteristics.

The enactment of a law is meant to be a *one-sided* communication process. The law-giver unilaterally imposes rules on the law-subjects, who, as such, may not react, no matter how. The opportunity to influence the content of legislation via the right to vote, could at the most be considered to be an indirect reaction.

---

[11] C Taylor, "Language and Society" in A Honneth and H Joas, *Communicative Action. Essays on Jürgen Habermas's The Theory of Communicative Action* (Polity Press, Cambridge, 1991), pp 23–35, at pp 23–29.

[12] On "speech acts" see JL Austin, *How to Do Things with Words* (Cambridge University Press, Cambridge, 1962); J Searle, *Speech Acts* (Cambridge University Press, NewYork, 1969).

The promulgation of legislation is part of a *power relation*, in which the legislator has the opportunity to impose his will on the law-subjects.

Communication via legislation aims at influencing the citizens' behaviour. This influence on behaviour takes place within the frame of a *normative* communication process. The citizens are forced to comply with the rules. In other power relations behaviour may be influenced without (pure) force, eg via psychological pressure (eg in love relations or with charismatic leadership). The relation towards legislation, however, is always one of pure force: the citizen may always ultimately be forced, directly or indirectly, with physical force, to comply with the rules of law.

These characteristics of legislation as a form of communication partly determine the way legislative texts should be worded and interpreted. The one-sided nature of the communication process thus requires a maximum of clarity in the formulation of legislative texts. In a standard conversation an equivocal utterance may be elucidated or corrected on the basis, eg, of a question asked by the conversation partner. As regards legislation such corrections can only be made indirectly (via court decisions or via politicians). In fact such feedback occurs very rarely and generally takes a lot of time.

If the legislator wants an optimum result from the communication process, ie a maximum of influence on behaviour, it is advisable for the legislator not to limit himself to the pure enactment of rules, but to add informative comment with justification, explanation and examples, placing the statute in a larger context, thus better informing and motivating the citizens to comply with the enacted rules.[13]

Finally, the normative character of the law requires that the interpretation of legislation is not limited to the prima facie receiver-meaning, eg arguing that the meaning of the statute is "clear" and thus would not need further interpretative research. When interpreting such a normative text one should at least try to find out the meaning that has been given to the legislative text by the legislator himself. Even if this sender-meaning may not always be decisive for the concrete decision in a specific case, one will at least need strong reasons for not (fully) following the sender-meaning of the statute.

7.3 METHODOLOGY OF LEGISLATION

7.3.1 Legislative Definitions

In all legislation one finds provisions by which words are defined. For example in article 8 of the Belgian Code on Civil Procedure, we find: "*Competence* is the

---

[13] Compare: "*Nous ne devons employer qu'une élocution facile, dont la précision et la clarté fassent tout le mérite . . . Le législateur travaille pour le peuple; il doit surtout parler au peuple: il a rempli sa tâche lorsqu'il en est entendu.*" (Cambacérès, rapport du Comité de législation, présenté devant la Convention française le 9 Août 1793, in Fenet, *Recueil complet des travaux préparatoires du code civil* (1827–1830), vol I, pp 2–3).

power of the judge to treat a demand brought before him". This definition shows how a word, with a broader or different sense in other contexts, gets a very specific meaning in (procedural) law.

Statutory definitions are thus linked to the relation between legal language and ordinary language. As one knows, legal language is a combination of ordinary language and technical language. "Pure" legal words, like "mortgage", "trust", "servitude" ("easement"), of course have to be defined in law. Sometimes this is done by an explicit definition (eg the definition of "property", quoted above 7.1). Sometimes the meaning of the concept just follows from the totality of the legislative provisions related to it, without there being some explicit and relatively short "definition" in the usual sense. As everybody is aware that the word *has* some specific legal meaning, its meaning will automatically be derived from the legal provisions in the relevant legal sources. There is no risk of confusion between legal language and (different meanings in) ordinary language.

This means that explicit definitions are especially needed when a word from ordinary language is used in law with a different meaning. Legislative definitions are *stipulatory definitions*, or performative utterances. They create some new meaning, in contrast with *lexical definitions*, that just describe the meaning as actually used in some language community. Dictionaries only contain lexical definitions, that *inform* about a standard meaning in such linguistic community. In legislation it only makes sense to formulate stipulatory definitions, as they are performative utterances that *create* a new, specific legal meaning, that differs from the standard meaning.

Often, both in the practice of legislative drafting and in judicial practice, words in legislation are indeed presumed to bear the meaning they have in ordinary language, unless they are explicitly defined in a different way.

This presumption is not, however, unproblematic. In every kind of language words partly derive their meaning from the context. Even if there is some standard meaning (the meaning given in dictionaries) language practice often refines the meaning of the word when used in some specific context, so as to (slightly) deviate from the standard meaning. This is also the case in law.

In fact, stipulatory definitions circumscribe the exact content and scope of a word. For example, in Belgian labour law "nightwork" is defined as "work done between 20.00 hrs and 6.00 hrs".[14] This brings certainty as to the scope of a vague concept, such as "night", which in daily language tends to be linked to "darkness", so that nights will be much longer in winter than in summer.

But a definition can also be worded in a different way, such as:

(a)   "It is question of X, when Y, Z", . . . take place." Example: "When two persons have debts against each other, a compensation takes place that extinguishes both debts, in the way and cases as explained hereafter." (Article 1289 *Burgerlijk Wetboek/Code civil*).

[14]   Art 35 *Arbeidswet/Loi sur le travail*.

(b) "X contains . . .". Example (Article 1 Belgian Cheque Act, 1 March 1961): "A cheque contains: (1) The denomination of cheque, . . . ; (2) The definite order to pay a determined amount; (3) The name of the one who has to pay; (4) The place where payment will be done; (5) The date and place where the cheque has been written out; (6) The signature of the person who writes out the cheque." By this, clearly a legal definition of "cheque" is given. This is confirmed by Article 2 of the same Act, in which it is stipulated that the document is not considered to be a "cheque" if one or more of these elements fail.

(c) "The conditions of application of concept X are . . .": the characteristics of a legal term indeed are nothing else but its *conditions of application and its legal consequences*.

However, it is seldom possible to enumerate all these conditions and consequences in one (even very long) sentence, under the form of a definition. This means that a definition of a legal term in legislation is often only a "working definition", which has to be completed by other elements to be found in the legislation. In Belgian law, for example, a settlement out of court (*"transaction"/"dading"*) is defined as "a contract by which the parties end a dispute or prevent a dispute from occurring" (Article 2044 *Burgerlijk Wetboek/Code civil*). In the Code it is, however, added that such a contract *should be put down on paper*. In a more complete, and thus more correct, definition this condition should be added.

On the other hand, the legal meaning of a term often follows from the conditions of application and the legal consequences as worded in the different stipulations in the Act or in different parts of the legislation. It is these legal rules that create the *legal meaning* of a term, not only, and even not in the first place, formal, explicit definitions. These rules are subject to interpretation, which may vary according to the context of adjudication of the law, just as with all legal rules.

All this means that a legal definition does not really fix the meaning of a term, it merely offers a starting point. If weighty reasons support another meaning, the interpreter may, without hesitation, deviate from the legislative definition. For example, this has been done by the Belgian Supreme Court (*Cour de Cassation/Hof van Cassatie*) as regards the definition of "cheque" quoted above. Somebody was prosecuted for having issued an uncovered cheque. He argued that the issued document was not a "cheque", as not all conditions enumerated in the definition of Article 1 of the Cheque Act were fulfilled. On his "cheque" no date was mentioned. The court considered that the penal judge was not bound by the definition in Article 1, even when applying the penal stipulations of the same Act. The court argued that:

"The penal judge is not strictly bound by the conditions of validity of a cheque listed in the Articles 1 and 2 of the Act of 1 March 1961. Notably, the omission of indicating the date and place of the issue of a cheque are not necessarily an obstacle for punishing the issue of an uncovered cheque, as this regulation has been established in view of protecting the citizen, facilitating exchanges and offering security to commerce. In order for a condamnation to be legally justified, it suffices therefore, that the issued document *has been considered to be a cheque in the common understanding.*"[15]

Taking into account the purpose of the law the meaning of "cheque" in ordinary language is, in this case, considered to prevail over the legislative definition.

7.3.2 The Formulation of Legal Norms in Legislation

Notwithstanding the normative character of the law, most legal rules in legislation appear to be worded in a descriptive way: "Education *is* free" (art 17 Belgian Constitution) instead of "education *should* be free"; "The spouses *draft* their marriage settlement as they like" (Article 1387 *Burgerlijk Wetboek/Code civil*) instead of "the spouses *may* contract a marriage settlement as they like".

At first sight, one might conclude that such provisions are descriptive instead of prescriptive. But this is obviously not the case. Until recently Article 8 of the Belgian Criminal Code stated: "Everyone condemned to the capital punishment will be decapitated". This utterance did not describe any concrete reality. Ever since the nineteenth century no single prisoner condemned to capital punishment has been decapitated.[16] Notwithstanding its apparent descriptive wording, this provision can only be read as a normative utterance, prescribing what *should* happen, not describing what is going to happen in reality. We thus have to conclude that in legislation normative provisions are hidden behind descriptive utterances. For a correct understanding of the meaning of statutory provisions this means that one should clearly distinguish between the text of an Act on the one hand, and the norm *behind* the text on the other.

7.4 INTERPRETATION OF STATUTES

Interpreting a statutory text is always a mixture of evaluative choices and relatively "objective", more or less methodologically underpinned, statements. When analysing the construction of statutes one has to distinguish between both aspects of legal reasoning, although in practical legal reasoning it is very hard to separate them.

This explains why the problems of statutory interpretation are often approached from the point of view of interpretation *arguments*[17] rather than

---

[15] Cass. 19 January 1976, *Pasicrisie* 1976, I, p 565.

[16] During and immediately after the World Wars they were shot. Outside wartime, capital punishment has always been converted into life imprisonment.

[17] Eg "the rational reconstruction of interpretational justification involves *presenting it as consisting in structured types of arguments which all belong within a coherent mode of justificatory reasoning*" and the emphasis on interpretive arguments throughout the book: DN MacCormick and RS Summers (eds), *Interpreting Statutes. A Comparative Study* (Dartmouth, Aldershot, 1991)

interpretation *methods*. However, precisely in order to make the distinction between evaluative and empirical elements it is necessary to distinguish between "objective", scientific *methods* on the one hand and "subjective" evaluative interpretive *choices* on the other. In most argumentation approaches we find a mixture of both. We can also word it in terms of "internal" and "external" perspectives. Argumentation analysis takes the internal point of view of how advocates try to convince courts of the soundness of their position or how judges try to convince the (losing) parties, higher courts and/or the public in general of the correctness of their decision. Here, it is rather the external position that is taken, starting from the question of what elements in statutory interpretation can be worded in terms of empirical "truth" and which ones inevitably necessitate some evaluative choice and cannot be approached in terms of "true" or "false" but only in terms of a "better" or a "worse" interpretation. It is obvious that argumentation theory will play a more limited role when it comes to prove the truth of an interpretative statement of the first kind, but will be of paramount importance when evaluative choices have to be justified. Argumentation theory will not be discussed as such in this book (albeit that its *importance* will be emphasised and briefly discussed in chapter 9).[18] When analysing the role of the judge and of legal doctrine it will only shortly be referred to, mainly to emphasise the importance of a *communicational approach* when studying legal argumentation, as opposed to a rhetoric approach, where an individual tries to convince a specific audience (a concept which includes Perelman's "universal audience" (*auditoire universel*)).[19]

In this part I will first give an overview of the methods which allow the interpreting judge to found his decision on generally acceptable, "objectively" sound reasons, when advancing some specific meaning of the statutory text under consideration. At the same time, this methodological framework draws the limits within which the courts enjoy discretion in interpreting statutes. In other words, the limits of methodology demarcate the widely different ways in which it is possible for the courts to construe the text of a statute on the basis of empirical

(quotation at p 19). This remark does not, of course, imply that I would disagree with these authors as to the importance of practical reasoning and argumentation in law (see eg their justification of the emphasis on argumentation at p 21), nor do I deny the problem of "how far such activities are or can be "value neutral" or value free" (p 22, where they add: "We shall not explore this intellectual minefield here."). Although these last two quotations are taken from comments on scholarly legal writing, they equally apply to judicial interpretation or legal interpretation in general.

[18] Actually, argumentation theory is an approach to law that encompasses literally all problems of legal theory, but looked at from the specific perspective of arguing and convincing, mainly within the frame of a judicial debate. Amongst the many interesting works on legal argumentation special attention may be paid to: R Alexy, *A Theory of Legal Argumentation. The Theory of Rational Discourse as Theory of Legal Justification* (trans R Adler and N MacCormick, Clarendon Press, Oxford, 1989), p 323; C Perelman and L Olbrechts-Tyteca, *The New Rhetoric: A Treatise on Argumentation* (trans J Wilkinson and P Weaver, University of Notre Dame Press, Notre Dame and London, 1969).

[19] Perelman and Olbrechts-Tyteca, above n 18, p 31, where this concept is defined as "a universality and unanimity imagined by the speaker, the agreement of an audience which should be universal".

facts and within the frame of generally accepted rules of linguistics and of logic and within the frame of the current paradigm of legal doctrine which governs the interpretive community of the legal system.

Secondly, I will try to give a more detailed overview of the interpretive choices the judge may, and often has to, make. This will be done by listing a number of interpretive opposites, within which the judge has to make a choice. This choice is sometimes made explicitly, sometimes only implicitly, and often even unconsciously.

7.4.1 Interpretation, Meaning and Context

When starting our analysis we have to take into account the fact that a statute does not have any scope in itself, but only derives its scope from the way in which its reader interprets it. Interpreting merely means "determining the meaning". As we have seen, meaning is the result of a link between a person, a sign and a reality. The concept of "meaning" itself, however, is not entirely unambiguous. For example, Ogden and Richards in their authoritative work *The Meaning of Meaning* offered 16 different definitions of the word "meaning".[20] A number of these definitions are totally impracticable as a concept which could be used for the purposes of interpreting statutes. Certain others enjoy a measure of practicability because they stress a particular aspect of the meaning of statutes. None of these definitions, however, are acceptable as being a correct and complete definition of what is to be considered as the "meaning" of a law.

As has already been argued above, a text must at all times be considered as a *communication* by the speaker or writer (the sender), directed at the listener or reader (the receiver): the triangle of meaning between sender, sign and receiver. The existence of this triangle of meaning is important in two respects.

First, a large number of communication interferences may occur, since the communication act, or sign, not only constitutes a translation of the sender's ideas, but has also to be translated by the receiver. Accordingly, the meaning attached to the communication by the sender and the way it is interpreted by the receiver do not necessarily coincide.

The existence of a possible and, to a certain extent, unavoidable discrepancy in meaning between sender and receiver moreover leads to the conclusion that a fundamental distinction must be made between the "*sender-meaning*" and the "*receiver-meaning*" of a statute. This distinction has its counterpart, in terms of interpreting the statute, in the so-called objective and subjective methods of interpretation.

Apart from this distinction between sender-meaning and receiver-meaning, we also introduced the concept of "*prima facie meaning*", ie the meaning given

---

[20] CK Ogden and IA Richards, *The Meaning of Meaning* (Routledge, London, 1960) (1st edition, 1923).

at first sight by the reader to the words, sentences or texts. Whenever there is mention of a clear law, this means nothing more than that it has a clear prima facie meaning attributed by the reader to this law; in other words, a meaning is attributed unconsciously. The fact that this prima facie meaning is clear, which automatically entails that there is a prima facie meaning for the receiver, by no means constitutes a guarantee that the sender-meaning and the receiver-meaning are the same. And it is precisely in order to ascertain whether both meanings actually coincide that the statute must in the first place be interpreted consciously and methodologically.

Following this analysis of the concept of meaning, we have to examine the elements which play a part in attributing a meaning to the statute. In attaching a particular meaning, a key role is played by the context. Such a context can be explicit or implicit, linguistic or non-linguistic, written or spoken, legal or non-legal. Linguistic science and communication science hold that the context exerts a fundamental influence on the meaning of words, sentences and texts.

Regarding the influence exerted by the context on the meaning of statutes, the following questions arise:

(1) To what extent can interpretations which take different contexts into account lead to one statute being interpreted in different ways?
(2) What options are open to the courts in involving several contexts in the interpretation of statutes?

In fact, the various traditional methods of interpretation of statutes come down to constantly locating the statute concerned in a different context; in each case, one particular context is deemed to be applicable, as the only, or at least most relevant context, in attributing a concrete meaning to a concrete statute.

(1) If a clear statute seemingly fails to be interpreted, this appears to entail that this statute has unconsciously been located in the context of the legal and social awareness and beliefs as experienced by the receiver, which make the seemingly appropriate meaning "clear". It is this unconscious process which prompts him or her to attribute a prima facie meaning which is qualified as being "clear". Here, there is no context that is consciously used; neither is there any "method" involved.
(2) The grammatical method is a method of interpretation by which a word is located in the context of the sentence, or by which a sentence is located in the context of the immediately preceding or following sentence(s). This method has also been called the linguistic[21] method.

---

[21] DN MacCormick and RS Summers (eds), *Interpreting Statutes. A Comparative Study* (Dartmouth, Aldershot, 1991), p. 26; J Wroblewski, *The Judicial Application of Law* (Kluwer Academic Publishers, Dordrecht, 1992), p 97. The relative terminological confusion appears from the following quotation: "The semiotic interpretation—in Germany usually called '*Wortlaut*', '*philologische*' or '*grammatische*' *Auslegung*—requires an investigation into the semantic content and the syntactic structure of a norm. Traditional German methodology identifies 'logical interpretation' as a canon separate from the semiotic. The function of logical interpretation is to ascertain

(3) The logical or systemic method places the interpreted statute in the context, either wholly or in part, of the existing set of statute law.

(4) In assessing the legislator's intention as it appears from the legislative materials, the statute concerned is located in the context of these documents.

(5) If an historical approach is adopted, the statute is placed in the context of developments in legislative history, or of the law in general, which took place either before or after the enactment of the statute.

(6) Finally, if the teleological or purposive method is employed, the law is interpreted by locating it in the context of the purpose or values underlying the statute, or a more general body of legislation, or the entire legal system.

It should be noted that most notably in methods 3 and 4 the statutory text is (exclusively) located in the context of other *texts*. This is partly also the case with method 5 (the genesis of the statute). Method 2 locates the text in the context of linguistic rules, more specifically rules of grammar, method 5 partly in reported historical events (and, thus, indirectly uses texts too), whilst method 6 refers to underlying aims and values or even current social changes.

Because of these different (kinds of) contexts it seems appropriate to distinguish the methods that are related to them, as, in fact, continental European legal practice has always done.[22]

7.4.2 The Plain Meaning Rule

According to an important, but slowly decreasing, part of legal doctrine and court practices[23] in Europe, the so-called "plain meaning rule" prohibits the courts from interpreting a clear statutory text. Such a rule, however, does not hold, either from a linguistic or from a theoretical point of view.

a norm's conceptual structures. Modern methodology treats this topic partly within the scope of semiotic and systematic interpretation, and partly within the scope of dogmatic argumentation" (R Alexy and R Dreier, "Statutory Interpretation in the Federal Republic of Germany" in MacCormick and Summers (eds), above, pp 82–83).

[22] On the first two methods there seems to be a consensus, save some variety in terminology, but not on the three other ones. In the Bielefelder project they are reduced to two methods ("teleological-evaluative" and "intentional" (MacCormick and Summers, above n 21, p 26), whereas Wroblewski reduces them to one single method, the "functional" one (J Wroblewski, *The Judicial Application of Law* (Kluwer Academic Publishers, Dordrecht, 1992), pp 103–7). It should be noted that MacCormick and Summers state that the categories adopted by the Bielefelder group are largely based on Wroblewki's analysis, whereas Wroblewki's book has been edited by MacCormick and Bankowski (who also participated in the Bielefelder project), who slightly adapted Wroblewki's terminology (eg "linguistic method", where in the Bielefelder book we can read, at p 26, that Wroblewki's own "preferred version of the terminology was 'semiotic' ").

[23] The European Court of Justice only occasionally referred to the "plain meaning" and only in the early years of its jurisdiction (eg: C1/54 *France v ECSC*, 21 December 1954 (ECJ) *Jurispr.* 1954–55, 1; C40/64 *Marcello Scarlatta v Commission Jurispr.* 1965, 215, esp. at 227). In most cases the court considered whether the "plain meaning" of the text was compatible with other elements, most prominently the purpose of the disposition (C6/60 *Humblet v Belgium*, 16 December 1960 (ECJ) *Jurispr.* 1960, 559, esp. at 575); the opinion of Advocate-General Darmon in C37/89 *Weiser v Caisse nationale des barreaux français*, 14 June 1990 (ECJ) *Jurispr.* 1990, 2395, esp. at pp 2409–15.

Criticism at linguistic level has already been gone into. Legal theoretical criticism can be summarised as follows:

The clear prima facie meaning attributed by the receiver to the law takes no account of the sender context and sender-meaning, and consequently basically ignores the legislature's intention. Naturally, this criticism is valid in practice only to the extent that the sender-meaning and receiver-meaning differ from each other. It is, however, precisely by interpreting in a methodological way the statute beforehand that this can be verified.

Secondly, it is not *because* the judge imparts a certain meaning to the statute which deviates from the meaning attributed to it by the legislator, that the former's approach to construction is wrong. It could well be, eg, that certain historical developments compel the courts to attribute a meaning to the statute which differs from that imparted by the draftsmen at the time when the statute was passed, so that it be applied appropriately to the concrete case in hand. Accordingly, it is not automatically wrong to apply the statute according to its receiver-meaning.

The plain meaning rule actually ignores the intention of the legislature of the time, there being no certainty that this has happened with a view to interpreting the law in such a way as to be more in line with present-day social requirements or ways of thinking. Since the meaning of a statute, which has been qualified as being clear, is merely a prima facie meaning, this entails automatically that any conscious location of the statute in any context, be it the sender or the receiver context, is absent.

It is an undeniable fact that, ultimately, the meaning of every word and every sentence in a statute is conditioned by the normative context, consisting of the legislature's intention on the one hand, and an appropriate social order on the other.

It is precisely for this reason that another rule, which is frequently found in doctrine and in case law, does not hold good, ie that the words contained in a statute must invariably be applied in accordance with their "normal" meaning.[24] In fact, the concept of "normal" significance covers a whole range of meanings which in many cases can be found to differ widely from each other. A distinction must be drawn not only between technical legal jargon and the everyday use of the language, but also between terminology in use at the time when the statute was passed, and present-day language. Finally, even the present-day use of the language reveals a number of possible differences in meaning resulting from everyday speech, which differ according to social or

---

[24] In Germany the emphasis on ordinary language seems to be based on the idea of the accessability of the law for the average citizen in areas such as criminal law or human rights. If, on the other hand, constitutional protection is better achieved on the basis of the meaning in technical legal language, the latter is preferred (see Alexy and Dreier, above n 21, pp 83–84) For the role of the "normal meaning" of words in judicial interpretation in other countries, see, in the same volume: p 220 (Italy), p 182 (France), pp 365–66 (United Kingdom), pp 273–274 (Poland), p 314 (Sweden), p 133 (Finland), pp 45–46 (Argentina), pp 412–13 (USA).

geographical circumstances. As transpired from the discussion on legislative definitions (above 7.3.1) the legal meaning of a word is determined by the sentence in which it appears, and the norm that follows from it, or from the combination with other statutory sentences. The "ordinary meaning" in which the interpreter reads the statutory text is nothing else but the prima facie-meaning, which can be used as long as there are no counter-indications. In case there are doubts about the technical or ordinary meaning of a word, the ordinary (or the technical) meaning may prevail on *non-linguistic grounds,* as, for example, the accessibility of the law for citizens in areas such as criminal law or human rights, which follows from the priority given to the individual's interests when conflicting with the interests of society or of the state in borderline cases.[25]

7.4.3 Methods of Interpretation

(a) The Grammatical Method

The context of the sentence or of the surrounding sentences is of course very limited for interpreting a word or a sentence in a statute. Grammatical analysis may at the most throw light on the syntactical structure and clarify the meaning at this syntactical level. As a real method, this approach is very seldom to be found in legal practice and is almost never elaborated in theory.[26] It should be distinguished from a literal interpretation of the wording of a text, which is not the result of any method, but only the application of the text in its prima facie meaning. With the grammatical method conclusions are drawn from a closer reading of the wording of the sentence and/or the neighbouring sentences.

(b) The Systemic Method

The systemic method entails the location of the interpreted word, sentence, text, in the larger context of the whole statute, of the whole legislation relating to some subject or problem, of a branch of the law or of the whole legal system. Within this broader context (para-)logical reasonings are used in order to reach a conclusion as regards the exact meaning of the interpreted text.

The legislative system, under which the courts apply principles of logic in order to attribute a particular meaning to a statute, however, is to a large extent a judge-constructed system.

This is not the case when a statutory text is compared to, and its interpretation determined by, another statute on a higher level in the hierarchy of legal sources (this is eg the case when a statute in a domestic legal system is interpreted in the light of an EU directive on the subject).

---

[25] This is explicitly the case in Germany (only) (see above n 24).
[26] An initial impetus has been given to it by Alf Ross, in his book *On Law and Justice* (Stevens, London, 1958).

In most cases, however, systemic interpretation aims at interpreting a statute within the context of other statutory texts on the same hierarchical level. Here, it is far from evident to what extent one statutory text could have more weight than, and influence in a more substantial way, another one, and why the opposite is not the case. This is especially so when the interpreter is confronted with an (important) time lag between the statutes under consideration. The hierarchy between these texts will be fixed by the judge. It will be his or her decision as to what extent eg the rule *"lex posterior derogat priori"* will be applied or not.

Another rule, used in the context of a systemic interpretation, is the rule under which exceptions are to be interpreted in a restrictive way. However, it is the court itself which determines in advance which law will be deemed to be the rule and which one will be qualified as an exception, and also which set of laws is to be considered as self-contained (eg property law, civil law, private law, or legislation as a whole?). It has, eg, been decided that civil (private) law is the "rule" and labour law the "exception", so that employer legislation should be interpreted in a restrictive way.[27]

Other (para-)logical reasonings used within the frame of systemic interpretation are: *a fortiori* reasoning, *a contrario* reasoning, reasoning *per analogiam* and the restriction of a statutory text the prima facie meaning of which is considered too broad.

All those "rules of logic" employed by courts when using the systemic method of construction are not coercive rules, but all contain important moments of choice, which means that, even if one locates the same statute in the same legislative context, it is still possible to arrive at mutually different and even contradictory meanings in relation to that very same statute. This can occur either by applying different rules of logic, or even by applying one rule of logic only, but which can be used in different ways in view of the available range of options.

If, eg, some situation is governed by a specific regulation and the judge is confronted with another situation to which the regulation as such does not apply, he may follow a reasoning *a contrario*: by limiting the scope of that regulation to those very specific cases, the legislator implicitly has excluded all other cases. But, if he applies a reasoning by analogy, he will reach exactly the opposite result.

When assessing the systemic approach to construction, one is led to the conclusion that this method does not constitute an adequate way of becoming acquainted with the sender-meaning of the statute, but is more of a means by which the interpreter seeks to realise a degree of internal coherence within the abstract set of legislative rules.

This is especially obvious with the interpretation *in pari materia*, used by the European Court of Justice to create coherence among comparable provisions of the three European Treaties through a construction by analogy,[28] or

---

[27] Vredegerecht (Justice of the Peace) Antwerp, 18 February 1959, *Tijdschrift van de Vrederechters/Journal des Juges de Paix*, 1960, p 98.

[28] See, eg, C21/88 ECSC *v Acciaierie e Ferriere Busseni*, 22 February 1990 (ECJ) *Jurispr.* 1990, 495, esp. at 523–24.

with comparative research of the law of EU Member States when the European Court of Justice interprets EU law.[29] Through such comparative research one tries to line up European law with a more or less common European legal culture.

A similar pursuit of coherence is to be found in the interpretation of domestic law in the light of EU law, which, according to the jurisprudence of the ECJ is a duty for national courts, at least as far as European directives are concerned.[30]. This implies both a coherent application of EU law in all countries of the European Union (internal coherence) and a re-interpretation of, even pre-existing, domestic law towards a more coherent European legal culture (external coherence with supranational law and with other national legal systems)

(c) The Use of Legislative Materials

By using legislative materials (*"travaux préparatoires"*, *"Hansard"*), ie the method by which statutes are located in the context of the legislative materials, one is especially concerned with discovering the legislature's intention.

Legislative materials are not always available to the public and can, in such cases, of course not be used by courts.[31]

Sometimes it is claimed that the text of the legislative materials can never outweigh the text of the statute, be it clear or unclear, because only the text of the statute has legislative force. What happens, however, is not a choice between these texts, but one text being used in order to interpret the other. In each case, the legislative materials merely constitute a context of interpretation, supplying information which is relevant to the meaning which is to be attributed to the law.

The legislative materials can be classified according to the nature of the information they have to offer. The first source of information is the evolution of the draft texts in the course of proceedings in Parliament, in other words, the genesis of the statute. The second is made up of the explanatory memorandum accompanying the various texts, as well as the criticism to which the text has been subjected inside and outside of proceedings in Parliament, the answers to parliamentary questions, etc.

---

[29] Although not often visible in the decisions of the ECJ, such comparative research plays a relatively important role: "The Court's abstention from references to comparative law in the grounds of its judgments should not obscure the fact that within the Court a considerable amount of time and energy is devoted to comparative law, although it is not specifically reflected in the judgments. The pleadings of the parties, particularly those of the Commission, often contain a discussion of the relevant problems from the point of view of comparative law and the Court frequently supplements this through its Research Department." (H Kutscher, *Methods of interpretation as seen by a judge at the Court of Justice*, Court of Justice of the European Communities, Luxemburg, 1976, I–28).

[30] C106/89 *Marleasing*, 13 November 1990 (ECJ) *Jurispr.* 1990, 4135 with the opinion of Advocate-General Walter van Gerven. An interesting article on the effects this duty may have on domestic law is W Dänzer-Vanotti, "Richtlinienkonforme Auslegung und Rechtsfortbildung", (1991) *Steuerliche Vierteljahresschrift* 1–15.

[31] This is, for instance, the case with a large part of the legislative materials of EU law, especially those related to the EC Treaties.

As an "objective" rule the condition could be formulated that these separate remarks and explanations are to be placed in the context of the complete legislative materials, more particularly in that of the genesis of the statute.

At first sight, this distinction is an important one, as any explicit intention by the draftsmen can only be found in the genesis of the law, whereas one can, at best, only derive an implicit statement of intention from isolated explanatory statements in the legislative materials.

This distinction is, however, rather a theoretical one. Legal practice reveals two facts: first, that as regards the genesis of the statute, the law-maker sometimes amends the statute without any conscious intention in relation to the meaning of the amended text, and second, regarding isolated remarks and explanatory memoranda, that some implicit statements of intention by the legislature, if placed in their proper context, can be put on the same footing as an explicitly-stated intention, since it reveals with near-perfect certainty the law-maker's intention.

An essential requirement which must be fulfilled with regard to the legislative materials as interpretation context, is that these documents must, where used in the construction process, always be employed in their entirety. By using them in a fragmented fashion, contradictory interpretations may occur in practice, according to the item in the legislative materials used as interpretation context.

The conclusion can accordingly be drawn that, on the one hand, the legislative materials constitute the most appropriate interpretation context in order to ascertain the sender-meaning of the statute, ie the legislature's intention. On the other hand, however, they still remain merely a part of the sender context, together with the legislative history and legal history in general, and furthermore merely serve to uncover the sender-meaning of the statute, ie the legislator's intention at the time when the law was passed, so that any important changing conditions or amendments in the law-maker's approach are left out of consideration.

(d) The Historic Method

When locating a statutory text in its historical context several kinds of "history" may be distinguished. I am using the term *legislative history* for the historical trend in successive statutes, whereas the evolution of successive draft laws which precede one particular statute is referred to as the *genesis of the statute*.

Moreover, the legislative historical context covers not only the developments in statute law which *precede* the statute that is being interpreted, but also developments which have *followed* the enactment of this statute in other, related fields and which can give rise to either a change in the legislature's approach, or some further vital information. This is what Pierre-André Côté calls "subsequent legislative history".[32]

---

[32] P-A Côté, *The Interpretation of Legislation in Canada*, 2nd edn (Les Editions Yvon Blais, Cowansville, 1991), pp 436–46.

In terms of the period preceding the passing of the statute, the legal history context refers to the antecedents of the interpreted rule (eg Roman law, early customary law, previous common law rules, etc), as well as the socio-legal and socio-economic developments immediately prior to the statute coming into being, and which have influenced the introduction of the text to be interpreted (eg developments in case law and in doctrine).

As far as the period following the enactment of the law is concerned, the legal history context covers material or social developments, which have occurred since the passing of the statute and relate to its context.

Here, we cannot analyse in detail these different possible historical constructions[33] and limit ourselves to the following conclusions that can be drawn from an analysis of the historical context:

(a) the historical context *before* the introduction of the law at times yields extremely relevant, but non-coercive, information regarding the sender-meaning of the statute;

(b) the historical context *after* the introduction of the statute points to the necessity in certain cases to use a purposive approach when interpreting the law, in order to be able to apply the law appropriately if circumstances change, if the legislator has adapted or changed his approach, as appears from related statutory texts, or if there are developments in society's way of thinking.

(e) The Teleological or Purposive Method

The teleological or purposive method takes the *objective of the statute* as interpretation context. In certain cases the interpretation of a statute in the light of the purpose of the statute, or that of the entire legal system, is a necessity, either for an adequate understanding of the statute itself, or in order to prevent absurd or unreasonable applications of the statute, often in the light of changed circumstances. It is interesting to note that, although (much) less visible in the case law of the national legal systems in Europe, purposive interpretation is by far the most used method by the European Court of Justice.[34]

Sometimes the necessity of a teleological construction is indirectly proven in a number of reactions shown by law-makers who, by means of an explanatory statute, sometimes react against such case law as has contravened the legislature's intention in interpreting the law in its prima facie meaning.

Conversely, this also appears from frequent instances where a law-maker has legalised judgments which had, by means of a teleological approach, set aside the prima facie meaning of the text.

---

[33] See for such an analysis: M Van Hoecke, *Norm, Kontext und Entscheidung* (Acco, Leuven, 1988), pp 165–93.

[34] See, eg C118/89 *Firma Otto Lingenfelser v Germany*, 25 June 1990 (ECJ) *Jurispr.* 1990, 2637, esp. cons. 13 and 14 at p 2657.

It is especially when applying the teleological method that the judge will play a more active role in the development of law. Here, a combined play between legislator and judge appears: on the basis of the aims set by the legislator the judge will "adapt" the conclusions that would normally follow from a literal application of the statutory text(s) to the case at hand, and "reformulate" the rule. This is more than a "combined play", it is an intensive cooperation between judges and legislators, based on an adequate communication between both, in which the reasons for legislating and the preconceived aims of the Act are made clear, or are at least to a large extent retrievable by the judge and in which the judge thinks along the lines set out by the legislator by "correcting" an inadequate wording of a statutory text or by implementing in a "new environment" the ideas put forward by the legislator. To this communication and cooperation between judge and legislator we will come back later (below 7.6). For this reason, however, the teleological interpretation method will be discussed somewhat more at length here.

(i) Interpretive Directives

In some legal systems there is even a rule which more or less imposes a duty upon the judge to use a purposive construction when determining the meaning which should be ascribed to the interpreted statute. As early as in Roman law one may find statements such as: "*Scire leges non hoc est verba earum tenere, sed vim ac potestatem*",[35] or "*Benignius leges interpretandae sunt, quo voluntas earum conservetur*".[36] The Italian and Austrian Civil Codes stipulate that one has to take into account the intention of the law-giver.[37] When interpreted in a narrow sense, the interpreter will focus on some psychological historical will of the law-giver; when interpreted in a broad sense, this rule can be seen as a support for teleological construction.[38] Occasionally it is explicitly stated that one should take into account the *aim* of the law.[39]

Well known is the "mischief rule" in England formulated by the Barons of Exchequer in Heydon's case in 1584:

"And it was resolved by them that for the sure and true interpretation of all statutes in general (be they penal or beneficial, restrictive or enlarging of the common law), four things are to be discerned and considered:

[35] *Digestae* 1.III.17.
[36] *Digestae* 1.III.18.
[37] Art 6 of the Austrian Civil Code; Art 12 of the Preliminary Provisions of the Italian Civil Code, which otherwise offers also two linguistic directives (the "proper meaning of the word" but also "according to the connection of that word").
[38] The whole variety of approaches between the most narrow and the broadest one seem to be found in Italian judicial practice (M La Torre, E Pattaro and M Taruffo, "Statutory Interpretation in Italy" in MacCormick and Summers, above n 21, pp 213–56, at pp 221–23).
[39] Art 31.1 Treaty of Vienna 1969; art 46 Bulgarian Act on Normative Acts; canon 17 Canon Law Code; Art 18 Louisiana Civil Code.

1st. What was the common law before the Act,

2nd. What was the mischief and defect for which the common law did not provide,

3rd. What remedy the Parliament had resolved and appointed to cure the disease of the Commonwealth, and

4th. *The true reason of the remedy,*

and then the office of all the judges is always to make such construction as shall suppress the mischief, and advance the remedy, and to suppress subtle inventions and evasions for continuance of the mischief, and pro privato commodo, and to add force and life to the cure and remedy, *according to the true intent of the makers of the Act*, pro bono publico."

In practice, however, this purposive construction is generally not used by English courts when the prima facie meaning of the statute seems to be "clear" and not absurd or unreasonable,[40] and when used it is limited by rather strict conditions.[41] Moreover, English courts will more easily broaden the scope of a statutory text through a purposive construction than limiting it.[42]

A similar rule is to be found in the New Zealand Acts Interpretation Act of 1924:

"Every Act and every provision or enactment thereof, shall be deemed remedial, whether its immediate purport is to direct the doing of anything it deems contrary to the public good, and shall accordingly receive such fair, large and liberal construction and interpretation as will best ensure the attainment of the object of the Act and of such provision or enactment according to its true intent, meaning and spirit."[43]

An almost identical wording is to be found in the Canadian Interpretation Act of 1985 (Article 12 and partly Article 10).[44] More than the English rule, this New Zealand and Canadian rule gives a clear priority to teleological construction, as opposed to other canons of interpretation.

---

[40] P Langan, *Maxwell on the Interpretation of Statutes* (Sweet & Maxwell, London, 1969), p 228.

[41] Lord Diplock in *Jones v Wrotham Park Estates Ltd* [1980 AC 74, [1979] 1 All ER 286. See also J Bell and G Engle, *Cross on Statutory Interpretation*, 2nd edn (Butterworths, London, 1987), pp 18–19 and 83–96.

[42] *R v Broadcasting Complaints Commission, ex p Owen* [1985] QB 1153 at 1174, per May LJ: "Whilst on modern principles of construction it is clearly legitimate to adopt a purposive approach and to hold that a statutory provision does apply to a given situation when it was clearly intended to do so, even though it may not also so apply on its strict literal interpretation, nevertheless I do not think that the converse is correct and that it is legitimate to adopt a purposive construction so as to preclude the application of a statute to a situation to which on its purely literal construction it would apply". Actually, this limits the purposive construction to an analogical interpretation and does not accept a teleological construction in its own right.

[43] See s 1(j).

[44] Art 12: "Every enactment is deemed remedial, and shall be given such fair, large and liberal construction and interpretation as best ensures the attainment of its objects".

Art 10: "The law shall be considered as always speaking, and where a matter or thing is expressed in the present tense, it shall be applied to the circumstances as they arise, so that effect may be given to the enactment according to its true spirit, intent and meaning".

Art 41 of the Québec Interpretation Act (1964) is even somewhat closer to the wording in the New Zealand Interpretation Act.

(ii) Reasons for Teleological Construction

Besides the ambiguity of the prima facie meaning of a statute, the clearly absurd or unjust result of applying the statute in its plain prima facie meaning is often a ground for looking at the aim of the statute.

The former Article 228 of the Belgian Civil Code stated that a woman had to wait at least 300 days after the end of her marriage before contracting a new marriage. The obvious aim of this rule was to avoid (legal) doubts about the fatherhood of children born during that period. One woman asked permission to marry earlier, arguing that it was medically proven that she was no longer able to become pregnant. Notwithstanding the clear prima facie meaning of the statute, the Court of Appeal of Ghent granted the permission.[45]

Another ground for looking at the aim of the statute concerns historical developments which have arisen since the enactment of the statute. Sometimes also here the immediate cause for a teleological construction is the absurd result of a literal interpretation.

The French Act of 1803 regulating the attribution of first names to newborn children remained valid in Belgium until 1987. This Act only allowed names "of famous persons in history" or of "saints, mentioned on calendars". On the basis of this statute a civil officer refused to accept the name "Dana". The court however, accepted this name, arguing that the aim of the legislator had been to avoid ridiculous or improper names. What is considered to be ridiculous or improper today is not necessarily the same as in the nineteenth century. Using names permitted by the 1803 Act is no longer a guarantee for realising that aim, nor should it be a limit, as name-giving practices have changed greatly since 1803.[46]

(iii) Types of Teleological Construction

(a) A statute is applied to a case, which does not fall under the prima facie meaning of the text, but completely fits with the aim of the legislator.

This kind of teleological interpretation is especially needed for applying a law to new techniques or new situations, which did not exist at the time of the enactment of the statute.

Articles 653 to 665 of the Belgian Civil Code regulate the rights and duties of neighbours (in towns) as regards the building of walls for separating their gardens. In case law the problem has arisen as to what extent concrete slabs may be considered to be a "wall", or equivalent to a wall built with stones. Concrete slabs were not known in 1804, so the only way to solve the problem is to look at

---

[45] Hof van Beroep Gent 2 April 1976, *Rechtskundig Weekblad* 1976–77, p 435.

[46] Rechtbank Brugge 7 January 1975, *Rechtskundig Weekblad* 1974–75, p 2144. It is interesting to note that the legislator, when changing this law by Art 1 of the Act of 15 May 1987, has now limited the rule to a prohibition of names which are "confusing" or which may "damage the child". It is left to civil servants and courts to decide in each concrete case what is acceptable or not.

the aim of the legislator. If this aim is guaranteeing that a wall, built by one neighbour, is strong enough to allow the other neighbour to build on it, then it is obvious that concrete slabs may not suffice. But in fact, the courts have stated that the aim was just to guarantee the privacy of the neighbours, when eg sitting in their garden. In this light, the courts considered concrete slabs to fall under the concept of "wall" and thus under the statute under consideration.[47]

(b) A statute is not applied to a case, although it clearly falls under the prima facie meaning of the statute, because it does not fit with the aim of the legislator.

Article 675 of the Belgian Civil Code states:

"One of the neighbours cannot, without the agreement of the other, install a window or an opening in a common wall, in any way whatsoever, even with a fixed window."[48]

Courts have been confronted with the question to what extent glass blocks should be considered to be a (fixed) window when applying this statute. The prima facie meaning of the text is very clear: it prohibits windows of all kinds, even fixed ones. Nevertheless courts have considered that glass blocks should not be considered as a window in the sense of Article 675. Also here the protection of the privacy of the neighbours had been the aim of the legislator. As far as one cannot really look through glass blocks, nor throw anything through them, this privacy is preserved, and glass blocks thus have to be considered, from this perspective, to be equivalent to stones rather than to a window.[49]

As already mentioned above, English courts are more reluctant to apply a purposive construction when it prevents a statutory text being applied to a case to which it should apply according to its literal wording.[50] In continental Europe no such distinction is made. In fact, from our analysis of "meaning" and "interpretation" it follows that such a distinction does not make sense. It can only be explained by some psychological block, based on the false assumption that the prima facie meaning of the literal wording of a statutory text has some coercive force on its own, independently from any purpose of the Act or any intent of the legislator or even any reasonable ordering of society.

---

[47] Rechtbank Kortrijk 5 March 1953, *Rechtskundig Weekblad* 1953–54, p 1817. For examples in English case law, see: J Bell, *Policy Arguments in Judicial Decisions* (Oxford University Press, Oxford, 1983), pp 88–90. For German law, see R Alexy and R Dreier, "Statutory Interpretation in the Federal Republic of Germany" in DN MacCormick and RS Summers (eds), *Interpreting Statutes. A Comparative Study* (Dartmouth, Aldershot, 1991), pp 73–121, at p 79.

[48] "L'un des voisins ne peut, sans le consentement de l'autre, pratiquer dans le mur mitoyen aucune fenêtre ou ouverture, en quelque manière que ce soit, même à verre dormant".

[49] Rechtbank Antwerp, 18 November 1969, *Rechtskundig Weekblad* 1969–70, p 1196. In Germany the Bundesgerichtshof has decided in the opposite way for the same interpretation problem (*Juristenzeitung* 1961, p 494 et seq) (see also Koch and Russman, (1982) *Juristische Begründungslehre* 128 et seq).

[50] See above n 6.

(iv) Types of "Aims"

In teleological construction, a distinction can be made between the narrower "subjective teleological method" and the broader "objective teleological method".

The *"subjective" teleological method* places the law against the background of the legislature's concrete intention in enacting the interpreted statute or the set of statutes of which the law concerned forms a part. Here, the accent in most cases lies on historical rather than on topical objectives.

The *"objective" teleological approach*, or systemic teleological method, for its part, locates the statute against the purpose underlying the entire legal system. This entails, amongst other things, that the court will base its interpretation on topical rather than on historical objectives.

As an example we may quote a case of Belgian social security law. A "househusband" claimed social security allowances on the basis of a statute which spoke only of "housewives".[51] The Antwerp labour court complied with his request, arguing that the legislator had recently enacted many statutory provisions in other branches of law aiming at equal treatment of men and women.[52]

It is not necessarily a conscious aim of a legislator which here governs the interpretation, but rather postulates such as the presumed rationality of the legislature, and the functional adjudication of the law. In the words of Karl Llewellyn: "It is a part of a Supreme Court's duty to keep Our Law Whole, and a working Whole".[53]

An example of such a broad teleological approach is the judicial decision in which the Brussels court had to interpret Article 76 of the Welfare Act of 10 March 1925, relating to children under the tutelage of the communal Public Welfare Service. The reasons given in the court's decision clearly show a much broader approach than just a systemic interpretation, by which only texts are compared, or just a legislative teleological approach, limited to the concrete aim of the interpreted statute. The starting point for the court's reasoning was the more general "interest of the child", the structure of family, and the organisation of tutelage by public bodies in our society. From the general spirit of the legislation relating to these domains, confronted with social reality (at least as perceived by the judges), some general legal principles are deduced, which then are used as the main context for the concrete statutory construction.[54]

By virtue of the difficulties experienced in ascertaining the exact purpose behind the statute, and certainly that of the legal system as a whole, and because of the somewhat distant nature of this "purpose", it would appear that the

[51] Art 165, § 1,1° en 2° Koninklijk Besluit (Royal Decree) 4 November 1963.
[52] Arbeidsrechtbank Antwerpen, 26 June 1979, *Rechtskundig Weekblad* 1979–80, 1058.
[53] K Llewellyn, *Jurisprudence: Realism in Theory and Practice* (University of Chicago Press, Chicago, 1962), p 229.
[54] Trib. Bruxelles 20 January 1956, *Journal des Tribunaux* 1956, p 673. This construction has been followed by other courts, eg Rechtbank Hasselt, 9 December 1960, *Rechtskundig Weekblad* 1960–61, p 1106.

courts also enjoy a great deal of liberty of interpretation when they employ the teleological method. Depending on the local, mostly national, legal culture judges will tend to use this liberty plainly or in a very cautious way, but overviews of case law in different legal systems also show that the personal view of the judges involved may play a determining role.[55] However, it should be clear that some of these views are simply wrong as they are based on erroneous assumptions of the (possible) "meaning(s)" of statutory texts. On the other hand, they are very revealing as regards the psychological needs of the judges concerned for "certainties", to such an extent that it blocks any critical reflection on the possible illusionary character of those apparent "certainties", such as the "obvious literal meaning" of a text.

7.4.4 Weighing and Using the Different Interpretation Methods

Every approach to construction, which uses but one method of interpretation, only takes account of a limited part of the global and relevant context. The meaning of a statute can be different, and even contradictory, according to the context in which the law has been located. Within the same part of a particular context, the law can be given a different meaning according to the method of interpretation adhered to.

Given this range of possibilities to choose from, the courts, in practice, can be said to enjoy a great deal of freedom of construction.

In general, it can be argued that the historical and teleological dimensions of the law strongly influence the scope of statutory interpretation.

The law indeed must of necessity have a purpose behind it.[56] Also every piece of legislation either complements or amends an existing law, or is the result of socio-historical developments, whereas, moreover, it is necessary to adapt legislation constantly to trends in society if the latter is to be regulated in an appropriate manner.

The historical and teleological dimensions of the law entail that the liberty of interpretation enjoyed by the reader of a statute from a linguistic point of view becomes even wider within a legal context.

It seems that only three formal requirements can be formulated, which can be expected of the courts in interpreting statutes:

---

[55] See, eg, for England J Bell and G Engle, *Cross on Statutory Intrerpreation*, 2nd edn (Butterworths, London, 1987), pp 68–111; for Canada: P-A Côté, *The Interpretation of Legislation in Canada*, 2nd edn (Les Editions Yvon Blais, Cowansville, 1991), pp 315–44; for some other countries, including the USA, France and Germany: DN MacCormick and RS Summers (eds), *Interpreting Statutes. A Comparative Study* (Dartmouth, Aldershot, 1991).

[56] It is revealing that sometimes it has been felt appropriate to remember this, most notably in the Québec Interpretation Act: "Every provision of a statute, whether such provision be mandatory, prohibitive or penal, shall be deemed to have for its object the remedying of some evil or the promotion of some good" (Art 41).

(1) The interpreter must locate the statute in as wide a context as possible; more particularly, he must take into account not only the sender context, but also the receiver context;

(2) when the receiver context appears to be relevant in any respect, the meaning of a statute must be defined in accordance with a dialectical interaction between the sender-meaning and the receiver-meaning;

(3) the interpreter must always take into account the social purpose behind the statute.

In order to restrict the conflicts and difficulties which may result from contradictions between the sender-meaning and the receiver-meaning of a statute, there should, moreover, be a close cooperation between the courts and the legislature.

The whole problem of the construction of statutes should be seen in the light of the role of courts in legal systems.

The judge is a policy-maker, a decision-maker within the legal system. As a judge, he must cooperate with the executive in realising the social order as envisaged by the law-maker. By the liberty of interpretation he enjoys vis-à-vis the statutes in his capacity as judge, he makes decisions on the actual scope of the more or less abstract legal system, which enables him, as well as the legislature and the executive, to pursue a policy, albeit on a different level.

Within the organisation of the legal system, the judge, in his relationship with the legislator, is to be considered as a *critical addressee of rules*. He is an *addressee of rules* in his capacity as receiver of statutes, even in cases where the rules contained in those statutes do not, as such, apply to himself. He is, moreover, a *critical* addressee of rules because, as an impartial outsider vis-à-vis the relationship between legislator and subject, and vis-à-vis the relationship between the subjects themselves, the statutes are to be assessed in the light of real situations, with a view to an optimal realisation of the legal order as conceived by the legislature. It should be pointed out in this regard that the courts, in performing this critical task, are continually in communication with the legislature and with other courts, and, in practice, also with legal doctrine as well as with the parties involved in the dispute and their lawyers.

It is precisely this intensive communication which must constitute a safeguard against arbitrary constructions and applications of statutes.

In order to promote this communication, it is, eg, advisable for the courts, and especially the Supreme Courts, not to confine their statement of reasons to a formal statement, but to endeavour, by using extensive arguments, to convince the parties involved in the case as well as other readers of the judgment that their judgment is the right one.

To this role of the judge and the communication between courts and other actors in the legal system we come back later (below 7.6).

7.4.5 Interpretive Choices, Interpretive Opposites

In scholarly writings on legal interpretation it is often emphasised that, statistic-ally speaking, judicial decisions mostly do not entail any problem of statutory interpretation.[57] In most cases the meaning of the statutory text is clear, not just in the trivial sense of a plain prima facie meaning for the judge, but in the broader sense that everybody involved (parties, their counsel, judges, doctrinal legal writ-ers, etc) *agrees* that this prima facie meaning is also the "final" or "true" mean-ing of the text. Just as a visit to a hospital does not give a correct picture of the health of the average citizen in the region, a scholarly discussion on hard cases is not representative of the adjudication of the law in daily court practice in the country. However, everything depends on the way the matter is presented. At first sight interpretation seems to be an exceptional activity in legal practice, whereas linguistically the potential divergences of meaning are unlimited. This paradox leads us to the hypothesis that the limited number of diverging inter-pretations is not in the first place due to indisputable empirical evidence of the "true meaning" of the statutory text, but rather to an *intersubjective consensus* on some reasonable or even "obvious" meaning in the light of a *common back-ground* (linguistically, culturally, historically, ideologically, etc).

A methodologically-founded interpretation seems, indeed, only to be able to lead to a rather negative result: a prima facie meaning may be invalidated as a result of methodological research, but such research may never "prove" the soundness of a proposed meaning of a statutory text.

Judges will inevitably always have to make interpretive choices, consciously or unconsciously, willingly or unwillingly.

Some of those choices are between opposite values or principles, some of which, in their turn, are basic choices which lie, explicitly or implicitly, at the basis of *each* statutory interpretation.

Hereafter I will list a number of such interpretive opposites. They may be dis-tinguished as "general interpretive opposites", offering choices which judges, to a certain extent, have to make each time they are interpreting a statute, and more "specific" interpretive opposites, which occur only occasionally, eg when some specific method of interpretation is used.

(a) General Interpretive Opposites

(i) Passive or Active Role for the Judge?

The paradigm[58] of legal doctrine and legal practice contains some theory about the division of labour between the judge and the legislator. Very roughly, at

---

[57] Eg E Bulygin, "Legal Dogmatics and the Systematization of Law" in T Eckhoff et al (eds), *Vernunft und Erfahrung im Rechtsdenken der Gegenwart/Reason and Experience in Contemporary Legal Thought*, Rechtstheorie Beiheft 10 (Duncker & Humblot, Berlin, 1986), pp 197–98.
[58] On the concept of paradigm see below 7.7.3.

least in European civil law systems, it means that the democratically elected legislator formulates the general rules, by which the judge, who is not to this extent "democratically legitimated", is bound. This judge is better placed to apply the general rules in particular cases and therefore enjoys some freedom of interpretation, but within rather narrow limits.

If this liberty of interpretation, or even liberty of policy-making is rather broadly interpreted by the judge, it may lead to a completely different construction of a statute in a particular case, when compared to the interpretation of another judge, who has a rather narrow view on his power as regards statutory interpretation.

Explicitly or implicitly the judge's own view on his role will thus influence, and partly determine, his construction of the statute under consideration.[59]

(ii) Will of the Legislator or Adequate Solution of the Case?

In line with the explicit or implicit theory of the state from which the judge is starting, and his conception of the role of the judge, he will often have to make a choice between following the will of the legislator, even if it leads to an inadequate (or even unreasonable or unjust) result in the particular case, on the one hand, or leaving (at least partly) aside the will of the legislator, in order to arrive at an adequate, equitable decision in the case he has to decide.

(iii) Legal Certainty or Equity?

The abovementioned interpretive opposite between the will of the legislator and an adequate solution is often also formulated in terms of a choice between "legal certainty" on the one hand, and "equity" on the other. Actually, the argument is mainly used to defend the application of the statute in its prima facie meaning, rather than the real will of the legislator. It is argued that the citizen decides to behave in one way or another on the basis of the content of the legislation as it appears from its text; when the judge does not apply this legislation in its "obvious" (prima facie) meaning, he shakes the citizen's trust in the legal system.

This argumentation, and, hence, the antithesis between "legal certainty" and "equity" is false. Very few citizens first read the law, or even consult a lawyer, before doing something. People mostly act in accordance with their (limited) knowledge of the valid law and in accordance with their moral beliefs, feelings of equity, reasonableness, and the like. They do not normally expect judges to apply the statutes in their literal sense, as they do not even know of these texts. What they, at least vaguely, expect is a reasonable, equitable judicial decision, if,

---

[59] This is already the case for the very large majority of judges who are reasoning within the limits of the current paradigm. This is still more the case for judges who do not accept this part of the current paradigm, as, eg has been the case in the last few decades of the twentieth century with the "*uso alternativo del diritto*" in Italy, the members of the "*Syndicat de la Magistrature*" in France or other "critical lawyers" in courts in other countries.

for any reason, they would have to conduct a trial before a court. "Equity" and "legal certainty" are thus, from this perspective, not opposites. They are rather different aspects of one and the same thing: a good, functioning legal system.

(iv) General Justice or Individual Justice?

The choice between "will of the legislator" and "adequate solving of a particular case" is also linked with a choice between two types of justice: general justice (*Normgerechtigkeit*) and individual justice (*Einzelfallgerechtigkeit*).

Treating equal cases alike, is a basic principle of justice. This equality principle, or non-discrimination principle, is written into most constitutions and in several international treaties on human rights. Departing from this equality principle, in order to decide otherwise in a particular case, seems to endanger the principle of justice, conceived as "general justice".

Equity, on the other hand, seems also to be an important value in law. More than justice, it aims at a reasonable solution in a particular case, without really taking into account other cases. This individual justice may thus sometimes conflict with general justice.

Here also, however, one may doubt whether there is a real antithesis between the two. If the judicial decision in the particular case is inequitable, unreasonable for one of the parties at the trial, this will also be the case in all other, similar cases. This means that courts are applying a theory of formal justice, not taking into account substantive justice. It, at least, is not obvious that this is the better approach.

If, on the other hand, the judicial decision appears to be unreasonable in a particular case, whereas it was not in other, similar cases, it simply means that the cases are not equal. They are probably similar, but some aspects are different. This means that the case appears to be very specific, and that the decision taken will not conflict with other, differing decisions in other, similar, but slightly different cases. Here, there is no problem of equality. Nevertheless, the decision may later be used as a precedent in genuinely comparable cases, so that, at least for the future, the problem of general justice may not be excluded.

But even if we have to relativise this opposition between general and individual justice, it plays an important role in everyday court practice. It, for example, also means that the judge should not overly take into account elements which may be important from a human point of view, but not from a legal point of view. If, eg, the judge allows a woman not to pay her debts, because her husband has left her, and her financial means have decreased considerably, the decision may seem equitable from the point of view of the woman. It will, however, conflict with the principle of equal treatment of debtors and, to a certain extent also, with individual justice to the creditor.

(b) Specific Interpretive Opposites

(i) Objective or Subjective Will of the Legislator?

The concrete aim of a statute is determined by the will of the legislator when enacting the law. This will of the "historical" legislator, however, becomes generally less relevant in court practices as the Act gets older. Especially where circumstances have changed, judges feel bound less by the obsolete will of the historical legislator. As a result of a historical and teleological interpretation some new "objective will" of the legislator is construed. Sometimes this is only a presumed will, based on a presumed rationality of the legislator, and not, eg, on the will of the current legislator, as expressed in recent statutes on related subjects.

No matter how this "objective will" of the legislator is found or construed, when following a historical and/or purposive method, the judge often will have to choose between both types of "will" of the legislator.

In favour of the historical will, it is often argued that the fact that the legislator did not change the law "proves" that the historical will remains valid, and that it is not the task of the judge to change the law. In practice however, it is obvious that no legislator is able constantly to adapt every legal regulation. Often legislative changes fail to occur, simply because in legal practice courts have interpreted the statute in accordance with some "objective will" of the legislator rather than on the basis of the obsolete "subjective will", so that there appears not to be any urgent need for a legislative change of the law.

(ii) Conservative or Progressive Interpretation?

Within the frame of a systemic interpretation, legislative texts are regularly interpreted by locating them in the context of statutory texts enacted at another moment in time. As long as a systemic interpretation is limited to one statute or one code enacted at one and the same time, one may reasonably presume a unity of purpose underlying all of these texts. This is less obvious, and even clearly not the case, when there is a more or less important time-lag between the different statutes. If there is an obvious or possible difference in the aims underlying the different statutes, the judge inevitably will have to choose between a "conservative" (static) or a "progressive" (dynamic) interpretation: are the more recent texts to be construed in the light of the older ones, or vice versa?

Above, I quoted a judicial decision in which labour law was considered to be "an exception" to the "common" civil law, and thus to be interpreted in a restrictive way. This is an obvious example of a "conservative" construction of statutes: the early nineteenth century civil law prevails over the twentieth century labour law.

On the other hand, Belgian courts have interpreted some, unchanged, articles of the 1804 Civil Code about family law in the light of a number of important recent legislative changes of large parts of this family law. Thus they interpreted, and to a certain extent "adapted", old statutes, according to the current will of the legislator, as it appeared from recent statutes in the same field of the law. From these new statutes a completely different view on the family, on the division of roles between men and women, on the extent of the "relevant" family (extended family versus parents plus children), can be deduced, compared to the one underlying the *Code Napoléon* of 1804.

(iii) Equity Rationality or Technical Rationality of Legislation?

A very common presumption used in case law in all countries, explicitly or implicitly, is some postulate of a "rational legislator". To a certain extent such a presumption of rationality is necessary in every kind of communication: if one were not able to presume that, eg, words are used in their ordinary meaning, unless the contrary appears in some way or another, communication in general would become very difficult. In interpreting the law, however, the presumed rationality of the legislator often tends to make the legal system more coherent than it actually is. The unity of the legal system being considered as an important value, judges sometimes try to achieve it as much as possible via statutory construction.

Two rather different concepts of rationality, however, may in practice lead to different, even opposite, interpretations of one and the same text.

First, there is a concept of "technical rationality". This appears in presumptions used, such as:

(a) "a word defined in one statute bears this meaning wherever it is used in any part of the legislation, unless another definition has been given in that statute", or

(b) "a word bears the meaning it has in common language, unless the legislator has defined it otherwise",[60] or

(c) "if the legislator uses two different words, even if they are more or less synonyms, they necessarily have different meanings", or

(d) "if the legislator abolishes a part of a statute, in which a word had been defined, this word ceases to bear the technical meaning previously defined, and should, from henceforth, been read in its ordinary meaning".[61]

The plain meaning rule also presupposes the presumption of a technical rational, even perfect, legislator, who always succeeds in perfectly formulating his will in clear statutory texts.

The postulate of a technical rational legislator also appears on the level of a presumed logical coherence of the legal system. It lies at the basis of most "log-

---

[60] This rule is commonly accepted and applied in Belgian case law.

[61] This rule has eg been used in the United Kingdom, in the case *Chapman v Kircke*, [1948] All ER, 556.

ical" reasonings, like "restrictive construction of exceptions", "*a contrario*", and "*a fortiori*".

It seems obvious that such a presumption of technical rationality may be used, but only if there are no doubts about its correctness in the case under consideration. Such doubts sometimes arise from the inequitable result of such a statutory construction. When the interpreter feels uncomfortable with the result of this interpretation, he may always reach the opposite result by using the presumption of equity rationality of the legislator.

The presumption of *equity rationality* of the legislator starts from the idea that the legislator is "just", "reasonable", "equitable", so that it is inconceivable that he would have wanted unjust, unreasonable solutions to legal problems. The conclusion that a statutory construction, based on a presumption of technical rationality of the legislator, leads to an inequitable, unreasonable result, from this perspective "proves" that the interpretation is not correct, because it cannot correspond with the true intent of the legislator.

(iv) Legal Pluralism or Unity of the Legal System?

Within a concept of the (perfect) coherence of legislation, the logical and axiological unity of the whole legal system seems to follow necessarily from the concept of a technical rational legislator. This, however, is not necessarily the case. Even when starting from this presumption of technical rationality, one might accept some pluralism within the legal system. It is, eg, obvious that in most legal systems in continental (Western) Europe, there is an important difference between the (liberal) ideology underlying civil law and the (socialist) ideology underlying labour law. In fact, there is often very little coherence between both parts of the law: neither on the axiological level (the underlying ideological fundamental principles), nor on the level of the terminology used. And it is very doubtful if such a coherence could ever be reached.

If we limit the presumption of technical rationality to parts of the legal system, it might have a more realistic basis, and we may avoid rather absurd conclusions like the abovementioned statement "that civil law is the rule, and labour law the exception".

(v) Technical Gaps or Evaluative Gaps?

"Real" gaps in the law very seldom arise. In a sense, a legal solution for a case may always be found.

As we have seen above, most legal systems are closed at a third level, the judge generally having full power to decide whenever a gap in the law may be found. But, of course, this solution already presupposes the existence of a "gap". It is a way of solving the gap problem, not of avoiding it.

A prima facie gap in the legislation, however, may often be "closed" by the judge, by using other legal sources, like the "general principles of law", or by interpreting the legislation, eg by analogy or by using a teleological approach, in such a way that the "gap" disappears. In this case, there is a (technical) gap in the statutes, but not in the law.

The gap may also be eliminated by using a rule which closes the legal system at a secondary level. Thus, if there appears to be a gap in penal law, eg, as regards computer criminality, it just means that the legislator has not yet regulated, in an appropriate way, the morally and socially improper use of modern techniques, and that it is highly advisable that he should do so as soon as possible. From the point of view of current valid positive law, however, there is no gap at all. Because of the rule *"nulla poena sine lege"* the judge will have to conclude that no crime has been committed and thus the accused has to be acquitted.

It is rather seldom that a technical gap in legislation may not be solved by using other sources or by interpretation. An example of a "pure" gap in the legislation would be one of a statute imposing on all citizens the duty to have upon them an identity card, the determination of the modalities of its issuing being left to the government, which up until now has failed to decide upon it.[62]

Just as gaps may "normatively" be closed by using general legal principles or some construction based on (general) aims of statutes or of (parts of) the legislation as a whole, in a similar way gaps may be "normatively" *created* by the interpreter. In legal practice, such "evaluative gaps" are more important than pure technical gaps.

As the example of "gaps" in penal law shows, the conclusion that "there is a gap" often means that the interpreter feels uncomfortable with a strict application of the legislation in its prima facie meaning. If someone, eg, were accused "of having breakfast each morning", nobody would think that there is a gap in the law because there is no penal regulation at all regarding "having breakfast". But if someone has, with the help of his personal computer and public telephone lines, broken into the computer of the Ministry of Defence and destroyed or changed vital military data, the lack of specific regulation will be felt to be a "gap", although strictly speaking there is none. In practice, moreover, attempts will often be made to "close" this, self-created, "gap" by interpretation by analogy, even if such a construction is prohibited in penal law.[63]

In general, each time the interpreter concludes, or just supposes, that the legislator did not have in mind the specific case under consideration when enacting the law, he may conclude that there is a "gap" in the law. The interpreter will argue that the text of the statute is formulated too narrowly, or too broadly, and that, if the legislator were to have been aware of the problem which has now arisen, he would have made a specific regulation, or exception, for such cases.

---

[62] Example suggested by Andrzej Grabowski.

[63] This transpires, eg, from the analysis of Belgian case law by Michel van de Kerchove in F Ost and M van de Kerchove, *Entre la lettre et l'esprit. Les directives d'interprétation en droit* (Bruylant, Brussels, 1989), pp 149–223.

Such a reasoning is very close to that which starts from the presumption of the equity rationality of the legislator.

If a judge only accepts pure, technical gaps as (real) "gaps", his interpretive choices will be much more limited than if he, explicitly or implicitly, consciously or unconsciously, considers it acceptable to "create" evaluative gaps in the law.

(vi) Restrictive Iinterpretation of Exceptions or *"Lex Specialis Derogat Generali"*?

When discussing the systemic method of interpretation the rule has been mentioned according to which "exceptions" should be interpreted in a restrictive way.

This "rule" entails several problems: What is the "rule" and what is to be considered to be an exception, or rather a new rule? What if there is an exception to an exception, thus requiring reapplication of the more general rule: is it, as an exception, to be construed in a restrictive way, or rather in a broad sense, as an application of a more general rule?

Moreover, it conflicts with another rule, used in the frame of systemic interpretation: *"lex specialis derogat generali"*, the more specific regulation takes priority over the more general one. The latter rule is based on the presumption that the more specific regulation is better adapted to the specific case under consideration than the more generally conceived rule.

The choice between both approaches, inevitably leading to opposite interpretive results, is to a certain extent comparable to the choice between "general justice" and "individual justice". Favouring the unity and the simplicity of the legal system has advantages in terms of reduction of the complexity of the system, by keeping, as much as possible, the scope of the main rules general. Favouring well-adapted regulations for each specific case has advantages from the point of view of optimum adequate ("reasonable", "equitable") solutions for individual cases.

(vii) Analogy or *a Contrario*?

Strictly speaking *a contrario* reasoning is only valid if the statutory text on which the reasoning is based explicitly excludes an analogous application to unforeseen cases. If a statute, for example, stipulates that *only* the owner of a good is entitled to do something, then one may conclude *a contrario* that the tenant is not allowed to do it.

Often, however, *a contrario* reasoning is applied when it is eg merely stated that "the owner is entitled to . . .", without excluding explicitly other persons. Sometimes it may reasonably be presumed that other persons or cases have been implicitly excluded, and in this case *a contrario* reasoning may prove correct, because the statute may, or even should, be read as if there were written *"only* (X is entitled to . . .)". In other cases, however, it is not at all obvious, or even rather doubtful, that the legislator really wanted to exclude all other persons or cases. In those cases *a contrario* reasoning has a very weak basis, and there may be as good, and even better, reasons for reasoning by analogy. One may argue that what the legislator had in mind was merely the most obvious category of people or cases to which the rule applied, and/or that he was not really aware of the category now under consideration (which undoubtedly is the case when the latter did not exist at the time of the enactment of the statute). Here, the interpreter is creating an evaluative gap, which, as a following step, may be eliminated by an analogous interpretation.

When reasoning by analogy it is always the interpreter's choice to conclude that the cases are equal from this peculiar, and for the application of the statute essential, point of view. If, eg, a statute stipulates "that all young men who are eighteen years old are eligible for military service" one might ask if this statute applies to young women or not. By reasoning *a contrario* obviously not. But, one could argue that equality between men and women is a fundamental principle in modern European legal systems, so that, according to this principle it would be appropriate to interpret the statute by analogy and thus to consider it equally applicable to men and women.

7.5 LEGAL PRINCIPLES AND INTERPRETATION

7.5.1 Legal Principles and Legal Rules

The distinction between legal principles and legal rules is at the core of many discussions in legal theory today. Attention has especially been paid to unwritten principles which underlie the written law. In his critique on legal positivism, especially on its weak, Hartian version, Ronald Dworkin argues that legal systems cannot be adequately understood if one limits oneself to the study of rules, as rules will sometimes be put aside by judges when they conflict with a general legal principle.[64]

In this part we will study the role of unwritten general principles in judicial decisions and their relationship with statutory interpretation. First, we will pay some attention to the distinction between "rules" and "principles".

The concept of principles has diverging meanings in legal practice and in legal writing.[65] In the context of our discussion a legal principle may be defined as a norm which is worded in general terms, has a broad scope and translates a value which is more or less basic to the legal system or parts of it. There are many legal rules, but the number of legal principles is rather limited. A principle will often be worded in vague terms, such as "good faith", "legal security", "fair trial", which in their turn refer to prevailing moral values and world views. In practice, there is

---

[64] R Dworkin, *Taking Rights Seriously* (Duckworth, London, 1978), p 22.
[65] See, eg M Atienza and J Ruiz Manero, *A Theory of Legal Sentences* (Kluwer Academic, Dordrecht, 1998), 3–4.

no clear cut distinction between what is concrete enough to be considered to be a "rule" and what is general enough to be a "principle". It is a matter of gradation.

Some principles are explicitly laid down in statutory law, especially in codes, which are meant to regulate broad domains of the law.

Some belong to a long doctrinal tradition and are worded as maxims, often in Latin. Their legal status is not always clear. Sometimes they are also to be found in statutory law, or at least backed by one or more statutory provisions, such as, eg, in most legal systems *"in dubio pro reo"* (the presumption of innocence of the accused); sometimes they are clearly rejected by a provision in a statute or a code and cannot be considered to be a valid principle in that legal system; lastly, some of them are rules of thumb, which are meant to guide the interpretation and application of the law, eg *"mater semper certa est"* or *"interpretatio cessat in claris"*, but, as both examples show, they are not necessarily true statements; they are often rather statements about (legal) science than about law, and, thus, not "legal principles" in the strict sense.

Since the second half of twentieth century, continental European courts have also applied "unwritten legal principles", which do not belong to one of the previous categories. They may find some limited support in statutory law, without the roots in legal tradition which maxims have, or they may have no such support at all and are directly referring to current non-legal values.

It is these implicit, "unwritten" legal principles, which courts have increasingly been accepting over the last decades, that we will discuss below.

7.5.2 Unwritten Legal Principles in Judicial Decisions

The use of unwritten general legal principles, which are accepted as a source of law by the courts, but which are not as such laid down in a statute or any formal source of law, is closely related to the interpretation of statutes.

My starting point is the evidence that in the course of the last few decades courts in several continental European countries have commenced to formulate and to apply "general principles of law" to fill gaps in the law[66] and even to "correct" statutory law.

In most legal systems there is some formal obligation for the judges to decide cases even if there is no legal rule available in the prevailing law.[67]

---

[66] In Belgium since the decision of the Supreme Court (Cour de Cassation/Hof van Cassatie) of 10 January 1950, in France since the *Aramu* decision of 26th October, 1945 of the Conseil d'Etat, in the Netherlands since the Act of 20 June 1963 conferring upon the Supreme Court (Hoge Raad) the power to apply not only the statutes but more generally "the law".

[67] Eg in France, Art 4 Code civil: "Le juge qui refusera de juger, sous prétexte du silence, de l'obscurité ou de l'insuffisance de la loi, pourra être poursuivi comme coupable de déni de justice". In Switzerland, art 1 Code civil: "La loi régit toutes les matières auxquelles se rapportent la lettre ou l'esprit de l'une de ses dispositions. A défaut d'une disposition légale applicable, le juge prononce selon le droit coutumier et, à défaut d'une coutume, selon les règles qu'il établirait s'il avait à faire acte de législateur. Il s'inspire des solutions consacrées par la doctrine et la jurisprudence."

Sometimes the legislator gives some guidelines or directives concerning the way the judge should decide when confronted with a gap in the legal system. On occasion, these rules refer implicitly or explicitly to the use of unwritten general principles of law.

Article 10, 3° of the Portuguese Civil Code, for example, formulates the directive for the judge to act as a legislator "according to the spirit of the legal system" (*espirito do sistema*). This implicitly refers to some general legal principles.

In Italy, Article 12 of the Provisions of the Law in General states still more explicitly:

> "In interpreting the statute no other meaning can be attributed to it than that made clear by the actual significance of the words, according to the connection between them, and by the intention of the legislature. If a controversy cannot be resolved by a precise provision, consideration is given to provisions that regulate similar cases or analogous matters; if the case remains in doubt, it is decided according to general principles of the legal order of the State".

An interesting variant is to be found in rules of international law, which do not confer upon the judge a universal power to formulate general principles and to apply them to a concrete case, but which refer to the common principles of national legal systems.

Article 215 of the EEC Treaty 1957, for example, refers explicitly to the "general principles common to the laws of the Member States" for determining the non-contractual liability of the Community in respect of its servants.

Article 38 of the Statute of the International Court of Justice refers more generally to "the general principles of law, recognised by the civilised countries" as one of the sources of international public law.

According to the written law, general principles of law seem, at first sight, to have a much more limited scope in European law than in public international law. In practice, however, it is the opposite which is the case. Because of the diversity of legal systems and legal principles in the world, one can hardly expect the International Court of Justice to reach a consensus on many common principles, certainly not when one is aware of the whole international political context and the limited role played by this court. On the other hand, general legal principles have become much more important in the decisions of the European Court of Justice than could be expected on the basis of the limited scope of Article 215 of the EEC Treaty. Just as in European national legal systems, the European Court formulates and applies general principles of law to fill gaps in EU law. Since these principles are partly deduced from those national legal systems, rather than from elements of the written EU law, the use of legal principles gains a comparative dimension.[68]

---

[68] H Kötz, "Allgemeine Rechtsgrundsätze als Ersatzrecht", (1970) *Rabels Zeitschrift für ausländisches und internationales Privatrecht* 671.

In most (national) legal systems, however, such as those of France, Germany, the Netherlands or Belgium, there are no statutory rules to indicate to the judge how to fill gaps in the law. It is especially in these legal systems that the growing use of unwritten legal principles by courts is most fascinating and revealing.

The judicial application of unwritten legal rules to fill gaps in the legal system has evolved in practice to the acceptance of a whole set of such unwritten legal principles, which are used not only to fill obvious gaps in the law, but also to limit and to reduce the scope of legal rules explicitly formulated in statutes. Two main problems arise from this judicial practice.

The first question is: where do judges find these legal principles, as they cannot as such be found in any formal source of law?

The second question is: how do these judges justify their practice when restricting the application of written law, being in conflict with rather vague general principles, which as such have never been formulated by the legislator? What is the relationship between traditional legal interpretation and the use of unwritten legal principles?

Another question which arises is how this extension of the use of unwritten legal principles by courts could be explained.

Lastly, it should be examined to what extent the judicial practice of applying unwritten legal principles could fit into a coherent theory of the adjudication of law by courts.

7.5.3 Types of Unwritten Legal Principles

Generally speaking, one can distinguish two types of unwritten legal principles as applied by courts. On the one hand, what could be called "implicit" or "structural" principles[69] are deduced, or at least claimed to be so derived, from the written law. On the other hand, what could be called "(purely) ideological principles" are not derived from the actual legal system. They refer to current dominant beliefs in society as to morals, politics or other non-legal ideologies.

(a) Structural Legal Principles

In a certain sense structural principles are hidden axioms of the logical structure of the legal system or of some branch of it. Their acceptance is necessary or at least desirable for the (optimum) coherence of this legal system. These principles are implicitly present in the legal system, even if the legislator may never have been clearly aware of them.

Some examples are the following:

---

[69] The term has been used by the European Court of Justice when referring to the general principles of EC law it was taking into account for filling a gap in European law (Court decision of 5 May 1981).

(a) The general principle of "good faith" has in several European countries been derived from one, or more, concrete rules, such as the obligation to execute a contract in accordance with good faith.[70]

(b) The binding force of contracts or international treaties can be deduced from the nature of these agreements. In civil law this binding force is a necessary consequence of the function of contracts in our society and more specifically in our economic system. In international law the principle *"pacta sunt servanda"* can be considered to be a logically necessary a priori which is inherent in the concept of "treaty". In a sense it is the *Grundnorm* of international law.

(c) The impartiality of the judge follows from the nature of the judicial function.

(d) The prohibition of taking the law into one's own hands can be deduced from the concept of the rule of law and the thereby implied monopoly for the authorities to enforce law.

(e) The prohibition of economic discrimination and the principle of economic liberty follow from the foundations of the EU legal order.

(b) (Purely) Ideological Legal Principles

Some of the abovementioned examples of structural principles have a clearly ideological nature (eg the principle of good faith). They are, however, structural because they find "institutional support"[71] in the codes or statutes. One can argue that the general principle has at least implicitly been accepted by the legislator, since he applied it in one or more concrete rules.

Purely ideological legal principles do not have that institutional support. They are the application of non-legal values or norms by the courts.

Examples for Belgian law are:

(a) The prohibition of abuse of rights.

(b) The reasonableness principle applied to the use of discretionary power by authorities.

(c) The legal security principle.

At the European level one can mention the equality principle in EU Law.[72]

---

[70] This has been the case in Italy, where the general principle of good faith has been derived from this rule as formulated in Art 1337 of the Civil Code and from Arts 128 and 1192 of the Civil Code (E Pattaro, "La completitud de los ordenamientos juridicos y los "principios generales del ordenamiento juridico del Estado", *Anuario de Filosofia Juridica y Social* (Buenos Aires), 1986, pp 204–305). In Belgium the same rule is laid down in Art 1134 of the Civil Code and has also been generalised by the courts. In Finnish law too, the general principle of good faith has been derived from the good faith principle in contract law (A Aarnio, "Taking Rules Seriously", in W Maihofer and G Sprenger (eds), *Law and the States in Modern Times* (Steiner, Stuttgart, 1990), p 183). The same has happened in Germany, where the principle is based on § 242 BGB.

[71] For the concept of "institutional support", see Aarnio, above n 70, with reference to Hannu Tolonen.

[72] For most European countries this principle is laid down in formal legal sources, particularly in Art 14 of the European Convention on Human Rights. Only within the EU legal system is it a purely ideological principle, as long as the EU has not formally adhered to that treaty.

In practice, ideological principles are generally applied only to restrict the application of some legal rules. They "correct" applications of rules, which in some specific circumstances are considered to be clearly unfair, unreasonable, unacceptable, when compared with some commonly accepted ideological point of view. Only when *clearly* conflicting with a *generally* accepted moral or political principle will the legal rule be disregarded and the non-legal principle be applied in the form of a, newly formulated, general legal principle.

Structural legal principles, on the other hand, often have broader scope. This makes them *guiding principles*, whereas ideological principles always function as *correcting principles*.

Before trying to explain the rise and the present role of the unwritten general principles as applied by courts, we need to compare this practice with the more traditional practice of interpretation of the law.

7.5.4 Legal Principles and the Interpretation of Statutes

(a) Interpretation by Analogy

One could argue that interpretation by analogy is nothing but a disguised application of unuttered general principles of law. When reasoning by analogy the interpreter applies a legal rule to a case which as such does not fall within the scope of that rule but which is on main points similar to the cases to which the rule is obviously applicable. To put it in another way: proceeding from a case to which the rule is clearly applicable one goes on to a more general legal principle, which by a further step is applied to the case which is not covered by the rule, but considered to be similar to the first case.[73]

In the twelfth century, for example, the glossators derived general legal principles (*regulae iuris*) from reasonings by analogy. Pattaro quotes an example from Bulgarus, one of the most prominent glossators of Bologna: the fish belongs to the fisher. When caught by a hunter, animals and birds living in freedom belong to the hunter. From these analogous cases the glossator derives the general principle which states that a *res nullius* becomes the property of the first one taking it.[74]

Generally speaking, it can be concluded that interpretation by analogy has traditionally been the most widely used technique to fill gaps in the law.[75]

---

[73] W van Gerven, *Beginselen van Belgisch Privaatrecht. Algemeen Deel* (Antwerp, 1969), p 58; P Foriers, "L'interprétation par analogie en droit belge", in *La pensée juridique de Paul Foriers* (Brussels, 1982), vol II, 817, 818; R Zippelius, *Einführung in die juristische Methodenlehre* (München, 1971), p 74; P Gérard, *Droit, égalité et idéologie. Contribution à l'étude critique des principes généraux du droit* (Brussels, 1981), p 184.

[74] E Pattaro, "Les principes généraux du droit entre raison et autorité", in P Vassart (ed), *Arguments d'autorité et arguments de raison* (Brussels, 1988), p 282. See also P Stein, *Regulae iuris: From Juristic Rules to Legal Maxims* (Edinburgh, 1966), pp 49–130.

[75] Foriers, above n 73, p 817. Compare also art 12 of the Italian Provisions on the Law in General, quoted above.

In German jurisprudence a distinction is made between "statutory analogy" (*"Gesetzesanalogie"*) and a more general "legal analogy" (*"Rechtsanalogie"*).

"Statutory analogy" denotes a reasoning by analogy, starting from a single statutory text, whereas "legal analogy" designates a reasoning by analogy, by which a more general principle is derived from several legal texts.[76] The last approach in particular is very similar to the "legal principles reasoning" (when using structural principles),[77] although (structural) principles too are sometimes derived from a single statutory rule. One could actually ask whether courts, at least where structural principles are concerned, could not have been able to reach the same results by using the more traditional interpretation by analogy, instead of introducing a new source of law. If the answer is yes, one has to ask what advantages can be found in this new approach, by comparison with the traditional methodology of interpretation. This question will be discussed below (in 7.5.8).

(b) Purposive Interpretation

Reasoning by analogy is very close to a teleological interpretation, in the sense that in both cases one is looking for a more general purpose of the rule. The analogy is found at this more abstract level of the (common) purpose.

Although the purpose of a rule and a general principle behind a rule are not the same, they are at the same meta-level above, or behind, the rule. In both cases this meta-level information is used to formulate a concrete rule.

As we have seen above, within the purposive interpretation method, one can distinguish between "subjective" or "statutory" teleology (*Gesetzesteleologie*) and a broader "objective" or "legal" teleology (*Rechtsteleologie*).[78]

By using a subjective teleological approach a statutory text is set against the concrete purpose of the legislator when enacting this text, against the purpose of the Act in general and/or the purpose relating to the article interpreted.

By using an objective teleological approach, the interpreter is not concentrating on the concrete intention of the legislator, which is a product of its time, but

---

[76] J Esser, *Vorverständnis und Methodenwahl in der Rechtsfindung* (Frankfurt, 1972), p 185.

[77] It is interesting to note that in the first draft s 1 of the Introductory Part (*Allgemeiner Teil*) of the German Civil Code (*BGB*) it was written that in cases for which the law contains no rules, those rules are to be applied analogically which apply to legally similar cases (*Gesetzesanalogie*), and that in default of such rules, the case should be decided according to principles embodied in the spirit of the legal system as a whole ("*Auf Verhältnisse, für welche das Gesetz keine Vorschrift enthält, finden die für rechtsähnliche Verhältnisse gegebenen Vorschriften entsprechende Anwendung. In Ermangelung solcher Vorschriften sind die aus dem Geiste der Rechtsordnung sich ergebenden Grundsätze massgebend.*") In the explanatory memorandum (*Motive zum Allgemeinen Theile*) it was added "*so ist die Entscheidung aus dem Geiste des gesammten, als ein Ganzes aufgefassten Rechtes abzuleiten (Rechtsanalogie)*". In the second draft the two general provisions on 'legal norms' were left out, as they were considered to be obvious, and, hence, superfluous. (Mugdan, B, *Die Gesamten Materialien* zum Bürgerlichen Gesetzbuch für das Deutsche Reich, vol 1, *Einführungsgesetz und Allgemeiner Teil*, Berlin: Decker's Verlag, 1899 (reprint Aalen: Scientia Verlag, 1979), pp LII, 365 and 568).

[78] M Van Hoecke, *Norm, Kontext und Entscheidung* (Acco, Leuven, 1988), p 204–11.

on more abstract purposes and principles which form the basis of the whole legal system or of some part of it. These purposes and principles are related by the interpreter to current ideologies which are dominant in society.

Whereas subjective teleological interpretation can be applied without any direct link to general principles of law, this is no longer the case with objective teleological interpretation.

The latter method can hardly be distinguished from the current formulation and use of general principles by the courts.

Using the distinction which Ronald Dworkin makes between "policy" and "principle",[79] we can conclude that subjective teleological interpretation places the legal text in the context of the "policy" or the concrete purpose of the legislator, whereas objective teleological interpretation tends to fall back on principles, taking less account of the concrete policies or purposes of the legislator at a certain time in history.

7.5.5 Legal Text, Rule, Principle and Political Theory

As we have emphasised above, a legal rule and a legal text are not one and the same. The text provides information about the rule, but is not itself the rule. This is precisely the reason why the interpretation of a statutory text may produce a result which may deviate from, or even be the opposite of, the prima facie meaning of this text.

It is, of course, desirable for a legal system to have a maximum degree of coherence between, on the one hand, the rules as intended by the legislator and, on the other hand, the prima facie meaning of the statutory texts as currently read by lawyers. Perfection, however, is never achievable, partly due to developments in society and the tremendous quantity of legislation.

Just as there needs to be good coherence between a legal text and a legal rule, the legal rules need to be coherent with the more basic legal principles, which are founding legal conceptions, branches of the law or the whole legal system.

Nor can legal principles be arbitrary. They also should be coherent, they should fit into a coherent ideology, in a non-contradictory political theory. Such a theory should contain not only a number of compatible principles but also some meta-principles indicating how to choose between two principles when they conflict in a concrete case.

An example is the balance between the principle of respecting national sovereignty and the principle of respecting human rights. These principles conflict,

---

[79] Dworkin defines a legal principle as "a standard that is to be observed, not because it will advance or secure an economic, political, or social situation deemed desirable, but because it is a requirement of justice or fairness or some other dimension of morality". He gives as an example the principle "No man may profit from his own wrong". A policy, on the other hand, is "that kind of standard that sets out a goal to be reached, generally an improvement in some economic, political, or social feature of the community". Example: diminishing the number of road accidents. R Dworkin, *Taking Rights Seriously* (Duckworth, London, 1978), p 22.

eg when applied to international intervention in national states because of the suppression of minorities. In national legal systems freedom of speech, for example, can sometimes conflict with the right to privacy.

The fact that these principles are largely accepted in a community does not suffice. In case of conflict one needs a new, meta-principle by which it can be decided which of two principles should have priority in the concrete case. But these are often hard cases for which it will be difficult to find a commonly accepted meta-principle. The problem cannot, however, be avoided. If there is no clear answer to the meta-principle question, one should at least depart from commonly accepted "procedural principles", which means, eg, using legal principles that are recognised as grounds for decision-making in practice, or giving some preference to the most coherent theory.[80]

7.5.6 General Principles as "*Ius Commune*"

The rise of general principles of law as a new source of law has sometimes been accounted for as being some kind of natural law revival. In the opinion of Paul Orianne, it has been seen as an alternative for the loss of natural law, but then *within* the systems of positive law[81]. Chaïm Perelman for his part, says it could be explained as an anti-positivist reaction of the courts after the Second World War.[82]

It is doubtful whether this should be considered to be the chief explanation for the rise of legal principles in judicial practice in many European countries. In my opinion, it is far more a way of accounting for the current importance of human rights in political and legal practice. Ever since the nineteenth century codifications, natural law never played any direct role in court decisions. General principles of law, on the other hand, do not nowadays fulfil a critical function as a touchstone for the morality of legal systems. At most, ideological legal principles are simply narrowing the (prima facie) scope of some legal rules. Structural legal principles cannot really conflict with the legal system, as they are derived from elements of this system. On the other hand, *human rights* are increasingly playing that critical role. They are really functioning as a natural law system, even if they have become part of the positive law, as is the case, eg, with the ECHR. Human rights are in fact considered to be inherent in each human being, to exist a priori, independently of the will or the benevolence of some legislator. They are the present natural law basis for criticising political or legal systems and political or legal practices. Compared with the positive legal status of general principles of law, the fact that human rights are laid down in international treaties has a much more symbolic and political value and a rather weak positive legal status.

Even so, there is a clear parallel between human rights and general principles of law. The fact that, during recent decades, these principles have increasingly

---

[80] Compare Aarnio, above n 70, p 13.

[81] P Orianne, *Introduction au système juridique* (Brussels, 1982), p 75.

[82] C Perelman, *Logique juridique. Nouvelle rhétorique* (Dalloz, Paris, 1976), p 137.

been formulated and applied by courts to complete, to sophisticate and to correct statutory law means that this practice fills certain needs. It is not very clear what precise elements have influenced this practice, but it certainly meets to some extent a revived need for an ethical framework for the law. Without any doubt, of course, this is the case with the increase in the importance of human rights, but it is clearly also the case with ideological legal principles and, to a certain extent, the ethically laden structural legal principles (such as the good faith principle).

The development of structural legal principles, however, cannot be explained by this ethical revival. A much more plausible hypothesis consists in considering the fragmentation of the law to be the main explanation of the rise in (structural) legal principles, for the growth of the number of rules inevitably increases the number of norm conflicts, and consequently, the demand for criteria to solve these norm conflicts. The formulation and use of general principles of law meets this need. Through these general principles a new *ius commune* is developing at the national level, reuniting a largely fragmentated law.

Before the nineteenth century codifications, it was Roman law which, in most European countries, played a unifying role with regard to the fragmented local customary law. Roman law contained the broad, unifying concepts and principles. To the extent that local customs derogated from them, they were interpreted in a restricted sense.[83]

Codifications, and particularly the French Code civil of 1804, were a synthesis of customary law, Roman law and new principles after bourgeois revolution. Thereafter the main legal principles were, for the first time in history, laid down in legislation and more precisely in the Civil Code.

The increase in legislation side by side with the codes, the secession of new branches of law, such as labour law, with a purpose of its own and a different underlying ideology, has made it increasingly difficult to use the Civil Code as a *ius commune*, coordinating the whole law.

Thus a new *ius commune* has been developed in the course of (the second half of) the twentieth century, in the shape of a—still growing and sophisticating—set of general principles of law. These legal principles are nowadays functioning as "closing rules", ie rules which guarantee the coherence and the completeness of the legal system. Huberlant thus writes:

"there is, thus, between the rules of one legal system not only a coherence that eliminates contradictions but also a harmony that follows from the general spirit which governs the system and manifests itself by the concordance of the chosen solutions . . . As a consequence, it is the harmony of a legal system that justifies the approach of the judge, who considers himself to be in a position to ascend from the concrete rules that constitute that legal system to its underlying principles, even if the latter are not expressed in any text; and it is for guaranteeing the preservation of the harmony of the

---

[83] WJ Zwalve, "Interpretatieproblemen vóór de codificatie", in *Liber Memorialis François Laurent* (Brussels, 1989), p 447–64.

legal system and for helping to elaborate it that the judge, in the absence of a text, invokes directly these general principles."[84]

7.5.7 Structuring Legal Principles

Structural legal principles and ideological legal principles each meet a different need and play a different role in legal practice.

Structural principles are mostly used *praeter legem*, ideological principles *contra legem*. Structural legal principles are mostly guiding principles, with broad scope, whereas ideological principles are only used as correcting principles.

Structural legal principles primarily meet the need for a new *"ius commune"*, in order to achieve coherence and completeness in the legal system, whereas ideological legal principles, just like the human rights, meet a revived demand for an ethical framework for the law.

The scope of structural legal principles is often limited to a branch of the law, eg administrative law, or procedural law, to mention the two branches with the widest applications of legal principles, whereas ideological principles are valid for the whole legal system.

A last distinction which can be made is the one between "aim principles" and "means principles". Means principles are means to implement a more general aim principle. The principle of the right to a second instance when a case has been decided by a court, for example, is a means to achieve the more general principle of the rights of the defence. The principle of the passivity of the judge is a means to achieve the principle of the neutrality of the judge. The principle *"patere legem quam ipse fecisti"* is a means to achieve the very broad equality principle. The prohibition of a retroactive enactment of the law is a means to achieve the principle of legal security. Van Orshoven even argues that all principles are implied by one general principle: the rule of law.[85]

It is noticeable that in some of these examples a more general, ideological aim principle is implemented in a specific branch of the law through a newly formulated means principle.

The distinctions between aim principle and means principle on the one hand, and between principles of a branch of the law and principles valid for the whole legal system on the other hand, will be useful in developing a hierarchical structure of legal principles.

---

[84] "il y a donc entre les règles d'un même système de droit non seulement une cohérence excluant la contradiction, mais aussi une harmonie qui découle de l'esprit général qui anime le système et se manifeste par la concordance des solutions choisies. . . . C'est donc l'harmonie d'un système juridique qui justifie la démarche du juge qui s'estime en mesure de remonter des règles particulières constituant ce système jusqu'aux principes généraux qui l'animent, même si ceux-ci ne sont exprimés par aucun texte; et c'est pour assurer le maintien et favoriser le développement de l'harmonie du système juridique que le juge, en l'absence de texte, invoque directement ces principes généraux" (C Huberlant, "Antinomies et recours aux principes généraux", in C Perelman (ed), *Les antinomies en droit* (Brussels, 1965), p 212).

[85] P Van Orshoven, "Non scripta, sed nata lex", in M Van Hoecke (ed), *Algemene Rechtsbeginselen* (Kluwer Rechtswetenschappen, Antwerp, 1991), p 75.

Personally, I think that such a theory should leave room for some ideological autonomy of the different branches of the law. If one accepts this, it means that complete coherence can only be attained at the level of branches of the law, not at the level of the whole legal system.

Lastly, we have to answer the question of the legitimation of the use of general principles.

7.5.8 Legitimation of the Judicial Use of Unwritten Legal Principles

Structural legal principles are derived from the legal system itself and thus have fairly strong institutional support. Even if the same result could almost always be achieved by using the more traditional interpretation by analogy and/or a teleological interpretation, the use of general principles of law has one great advantage: principles have a broad scope. Concrete interpretations only provide a decision in a concrete case, taking into account the very specific elements of the case. Interpretation is individualising judicial decision-making. The use of general legal principles, on the other hand, means generalising judicial decision-making. This generalisation offers a much better opportunity for structuring these principles in a coherent theory. Much better than individualised interpretations of very concrete statutes, principles can be widely discussed among lawyers and even among a broader public. They thus have much more chance of relying on a broad consensus, which consequently affords them another type of institutional support.

Ideological legal principles, for their part, are not derived from the legal system. They are non-legal, ideological principles, which are transformed by judges into legal ones. This practice could be legitimated, first by concluding that some adaptation and sophistication of the law by the judge is inevitable, and, from the point of view of the smooth functioning of the legal system, necessary; secondly, by accepting that the both following conditions should be fulfilled:

(a) ideological principles should only be used within the framework of a limited judicial review, for correcting (prima facie) statutory rules;
(b) they should rely on a broad consensus in society and/or (at least) among lawyers; this is the only way in which unwritten ideological principles can gain institutional support.

Both types of legal principles thus offer clearly a communicative advantage when compared to traditional interpretation. Both the wording of the principles and their implementation in concrete cases are widely discussed among judges and legal scholars and obtain by this a stronger basis and legitimation.

7.6 THE ROLE OF THE JUDGE

According to the traditional conception of the role of the judge, courts have to apply pre-existing rules, mostly statutory rules.[86] In this view, it is only exceptionally that they have some room for law creation, and this remains anyway within narrow limits. It is up to a democratically elected legislator to enact new general rules, it is said, whereas the task of the judge is confined to applying such rules to concrete cases. This relationship between courts and legislators has, at least over the last century, typically been seen in the context of their *democratic legitimation.* The legislator has been democratically elected, it is argued; judges have not. As a result, classical theory posits that it is up to legislators to determine the content of the law and not up to judges. The latter only should apply the democratically established rules, not change, let alone abolish, them.

However, this is a very formal approach to the conception of democracy. Today, most notably the protection of human rights may be conceived as an essential part of a more substantive conception of democracy. This entails a possible conflict between a *substantially* democratic judicial decision, protecting fundamental rights of a citizen, which, however, is not democratically legitimate from a *formal* point of view, on the one hand, and a statutory rule which is *formally* legitimate, but does not meet the *substantive* democratic standards as regards human rights, on the other.

In fact, constitutional courts have, in most countries, been introduced and installed in order to check legislation as regards its content, on the basis of fundamental rights of the citizen, as laid down in the constitution. This is just the next step forward towards a full implementation of the *rule of law.* If everybody and every institution are bound by at least some legal rules, some official body should be in charge of controlling whether or not they abide by those rules. If they do not, it should be possible to impose some kind of sanction in order to enforce the law. In the case of judicial review by a constitutional court this sanction consists of the annulment of the Act which is considered to be unconstitutional.

In the discussion about the democratic legitimation of such judicial review, several arguments can be put forward in favour of its being legitimate.

First, it could be argued that, if constitutional judges are not directly elected by the citizen, they are at least appointed by a directly elected body, such as, for example, Parliament itself.

Secondly, the power of judges, be it in a constitutional court or in other courts, is in any case much more limited than the power of legislators or governments. If *ordinary judges* "adapt" or "change" legislative rules, the scope of application of the newly worded rule *contra legem* is limited to the case beforehand. It does not become a *general rule* unless it is followed, on a free basis, in

---

[86] Even in the common law, judges are not presumed to create new law, but to apply "what has always been the law since times immemorial".

legal practice and/or by other courts, and as far as it is implicitly accepted by the legislator, by not reacting with a new and explicit statutory rule against "judicial usurpation".

If *constitutional judges* review unconstitutional legislation, they do not create any rule. They just, negatively, abolish a statute. By this, previous rules will come into life, so that indirectly judges seem to create "new" rules. But these old rules, generally speaking, will have been determined and enacted by a democratically elected Parliament, and never by the judges themselves. If this does not exclude the problem of formal democratic legitimation, it at least reduces its importance substantially, when compared to the question of the legislator's formal democratic legitimation.

Moreover, when weighing and balancing the positive and negative aspects of direct elections, it could be argued that a direct election offers fewer guarantees for the best judges being elected. Indeed, the qualities one needs for being a good judge are rather different from those one needs to become popular, and, hence, elected by the people. The way direct elections of judges work in practice in some countries, such as the USA, offer clear examples of this. If judges are almost never chosen by a system of direct elections, but instead appointed by government or Parliament, there must be good reasons for this. These reasons must be found in the weighing and balancing of the advantages and disadvantages of a system of election which offers a better formal democratic legitimation for judicial decisions, but fewer guarantees of their substantive quality, when compared to a system of appointment, which offers a weaker "demoratic pedigree", but more guarantees of the quality of the judges.

All this shows how the formal democratic legitimation is but one element in the discussion. It is not the only one, and even not the main one. It would be wrong to limit the problem of legitimation of judicial review of legislation to this formal element.

However, that is not the whole story. The problem of democratic legitimation cannot be limited to a weighing and balancing of formal and substantive legitimation either. It should be asked whether the problem, when worded like this, is not posited in an incomplete way. It departs from a linear, vertical approach, which proceeds like a Kelsenian deduction from some basic norm(s): if the "democratic pedigree" brings us back to a consensus by the citizen, then the judicial decision is considered to be formally democratically legitimate; if it brings us back to basic rights, previously enacted by a constitutional legislator, the judicial decision is considered to be democratically legitimate on the basis of its content.

In both cases some pre-existent "will" of "the people" or "will" of the "constitutional legislator" is presumed, which should legitimate today's judicial decision. However, I would like to argue that the legitimation of judicial decisions should be viewed in a *circular* rather than in a linear perspective. For this, one should accept that the general discussion about the legitimation of judicial decisions is different from a discussion about the acceptability of one single judgment. Limiting the analysis to such an atomistic approach almost inevitably leads to a linear approach in the Kelsenian sense. When viewing the problem from a systemic, global point of view, other functions and elements, which contribute to legitimate court decisions, come into the light. It is only within such a systemic approach that the circular perspective becomes visible.

The linear, *vertical approach* is based on the historical reaction against kings and judges, who were, from a democratic point of view, neither formally legitimate nor legitimate in terms of the content of their decisions. Even if only a very limited percentage of the population in nineteenth-century democracies were entitled to vote,[87] the legislation enacted by their Parliaments was clearly better legitimated than the legislation issued by the previous monarchs, at least from a formal point of view.

In the second half of the twentieth century one has become increasingly aware of the limits of such a purely formal approach to democracy. Such an approach, indeed, allows a "democratic" suppression, discrimination and even physical elimination of all kinds of minorities. As a result, fundamental rights have been taken more seriously, for instance, such as in Europe, by drafting and signing a treaty on human rights, which established an international court, the European Court of Human Rights. For the first time in history, it allowed an international court to condemn a state and its legislation on the basis of a violation of the human rights of its own citizens. Along the same lines of thought, at the domestic level, constitutional courts were established, with the power to annul parliamentary legislation when, according to the constitutional judges, it violates principles laid down in the constitution.

As a result, the vertical relationship between courts and legislators has evolved into a *circular relationship*. Instead of an absolute supremacy of (democratically elected) legislators over (not democratically elected) judges, we are now confronted with a circular relationship of predominance and inferiority between judges and legislators. The power of a constitutional court, for instance, is determined by the (constitutional) legislator. The legislator, in most cases, also appoints its judges. But the constitutional court itself has the final word as regards the interpretation of the constitution and the scope of the legislation submitted to the court's judgment.

As already mentioned above, this circular relationship is also to be found, within the European Union, between the Member States and the EU: none of them has a position of *sovereignty*: the Member States have given part of their legislative and judicial power to the EU, but only to a limited extent (which inevitably will remain the case, at least for a rather long period, because of the *subsidiarity principle*, introduced by the Maastricht Treaty).[88] The Member States remain "sovereign" in many areas, but they are subordinate to the

---

[87] Eg in Belgium it was around 1850 some 2 or 3%, whereas today it is over 70%.

[88] Art 3B EEC Treaty 1957, added by the Maastricht Treaty on European Union (7 February 1992), with effect as from 1 November 1993.

European level in an increasing number of other fields. Moreover, the key decisions at the European level are taken by ministers from the *national* governments.

At the European level, courts such as the European Court of Justice (within the European Union), or the European Court of Human Rights (within the ambit of the European Council and covering virtually the whole continent), have become strong constitutional courts. In the absence of any strong legislator at both European levels, courts have filled in the gap and established, through the interpretation of the respective European treaties, new general rules with a much broader scope, and sometimes a different content, compared to that which the parties to those treaties originally had in mind.

Because of the multi-level structure of the European Union (national and European) the circular relationship becomes even more complex when the *European judges* are controlling *national legislators*. The European judges, indeed, are demarcating the borderlines within which national legislators may operate.

Within the area of "constitutional" control of legislation, both at the national and at the European level, courts have sometimes explicitly obtained the power to formulate general rules, comparable to legislative powers. This, for instance, is the case when the court has the power to decide that a new interpretation of the constitution or of the treaty, which the court has posited in its decision, will be valid for the future only and could not be invoked for the period which was preceding the decision (unless a trial, in which a claim was based on it, had started before that date).[89] In such cases, it has been considered appropriate by the legislator to delegate some (more) limited legislative power to the constitutional court, notwithstanding its weak formal democratic legitimation.

A circular relationship may also be found at the level of the relationship between courts within the national court structure. In every legal system there is a hierarchical structure of the courts, in which the inferior courts are subordinate to the higher courts: in a strong way in systems with binding precedents, in a weak way in the other ones. Nevertheless, higher courts sometimes change their position on the basis of the fact that a previous decision was not accepted nor followed by the lower courts and/or massively rejected in legal doctrine.[90] Formal authority is sometimes overruled by arguments, indeed by substantive authority.

[89] Such decisions have been taken both by the European Court of Justice and by the European Court of Human Rights: 43/75 *Defrenne v Sabena*, 8 April 1976 (ECJ) *Jur.* 1976, (455) 481–82; *Marckx v Belgium* [1979] 11 EHHR 330 (ECHR). In Belgium, the Constitutional Court (*Arbitragehof/Cour d'arbitrage*) has the power to decide that some of the legal consequences of rules, which this court is annulling, will remain valid (Art 8 Bijzondere Wet Arbitragehof, 6 January 1989).

[90] This, eg is the case in Belgium, where it happens occasionally that the Supreme Court (*Hof van Cassatie/Cour de cassation*) reconsiders its jurisprudence, on the basis of a refusal of lower courts to follow an earlier decision of the Supreme Court. The *Hof van Cassatie*, then, will take over the interpretation, unanimously or largely adopted by the lower courts, in order to restore the "legal peace".

These circular relationships are not just a failure of the current legal system, a weakness, which would be the result of a degeneration of the legal systems from the point of view of (formal) democratic strength. They are one of the ways in which a new conception of democratic legitimation is currently developing.

The essential starting point here is that law is not something which is (completely) made at some point in time, and afterwards simply "applied" by officials, by citizens and by judges to concrete cases. *Law is constantly made, adapted and developed in legal practice*, and most prominently by judges. If a court adapts, and even changes, the content of a legislative rule, it is not, in so doing, usurping its role, but in most cases rather fully assuming its tasks and duties. Legislators cannot foresee everything, nor can they constantly adapt every statute to changed circumstances. It is precisely the task and the duty of the judges to fill in the gaps which every legislator must inevitably leave.

But the question then becomes: how can we legitimate such judicial decisions? There is no, or at least no strong, formal legitimation for such an active role of the courts. There is no strong substantive legitimation: fundamental rights are not necessarily involved. How then could we legitimate these judicial decisions? The answer is: through *deliberative communication*.

Just as *law* is constantly made in and through legal practice, *legitimation* too is constantly achieved through deliberative communication. In a trial, parties are exchanging arguments and evidence. They probably do not try to convince each other, but they certainly try to convince the judges. In some cases judges will ask questions and require more information from one or more parties. Through this process of communication between parties and judge(s), some "judicial truth" arises. If the court offers convincing reasons for its decision, it may well be that both parties accept the judgment. This is a *first "communicative sphere"*.

If the court decision fails to convince both parties, and if one of them takes the case to a higher court, the communication process is broadened: the higher court will not only take into account the arguments and evidence offered by the parties, but the earlier decision by the lower court as well. This is a *second "communicative sphere"*.

Even outside the context of an appeal, judicial decisions have to locate themselves in a larger structure of previous decisions in similar cases. As a rule, they will follow such precedents. If they do not, they will have to give reasons for it. These reasons in their turn will probably be discussed in legal doctrine and/or followed or overruled by future judicial decisions.

Sometimes, the case is considered to be interesting enough to be published. As a result, legal scholars will give their comments, criticising and/or supporting the decision, putting it in a broader context from which its value or its weakness appears, etc. Those comments may, in their turn, influence future decisions of the same court and/or of other courts. This is a *third "communicative sphere"*.

On rare occasions, a case may attract the interest of the media and be discussed within a non-legal audience as well. This is the *fourth "communicative sphere"*.

Finally, albeit very rarely, a case may be discussed in society at large, because it involves current fundamental ethical or political issues (eg abortion, euthanasia, immigration, racism, etc). In such cases there is a very large involvement of the citizen in determining (the content of) the law. This is the *fifth* and largest *communicative sphere*.

These different types of cases and of communication processes create different, and always wider, spheres of deliberative politics. They offer various forms and degrees of a *"public forum"*. The more technical and individual the matter is, the more limited the deliberative sphere will be, as there is only a weak interest for the community at large. The more ethical and political the matter is, the more it will be of greater general interest, so that it is desirable to discuss it amongst a larger audience. The same goes for rather technical matters which are of a general importance, because the decision may, as a precedent, affect many others. Here too, a broader debate is desirable.

Democratic legitimation of judicial review, and of judicial activism in general, is offered by these deliberative processes. It is the *public forum* function, through which public control, criticism and debate become possible. This *public forum* function is also to be found in Parliaments.[91] It is at least as important as the rule-making function on the basis of democratic representation. One could ask what would be the worse situation: (1) an open society with full access to any kind of information and a wide range of opportunities for political discussion, also as regards Parliament, although this Parliament would not have been democratically elected, but, eg, constituted on a hereditary basis, or (2) a democratically elected Parliament, which would be working in secret, with no information to the public (except the result of the parliamentary work, notably legislation as such) and no public debate whatsoever?

If we would have to choose amongst these two alternatives, it is obvious that we would be better off with the first one. The reason is that such a public debate *outside* Parliament is a necessary condition for making democratic elections possible. In the absence of open information and debate, elections cannot be meaningful. On the other hand, it is very probable that the public debate in the society with a Parliament, which is not democratically elected, will eventually lead to democratic elections. This example shows how public debate is a necessary condition for democracy and, hence, for democratic legitimation.

In ideal circumstances, the various deliberative spheres guarantee the best audience, or community, for this communication and legitimation process: technical matters within a community of professionals, highly ethical and/or political matters within society at large. It clearly offers the advantage of limiting, where necessary, both the number and the plurality of participants in

---

[91] "In particular, when policy requires legislation, parliamentary approval is needed. National parliaments, apart from exercising these "power functions", also fulfil a "public forum" function described variously as information, communication, legitimation etc." (JHH Weiler, U Haltern and F Mayer, *European Democracy and its Critique. Five Uneasy Pieces*, EUI Working Paper RSC No. 95/11 (European University Institute, Florence, 1995), p 5).

deliberation. Such a plurality of deliberative spheres also solves the problem of the cognitive capacities of citizens presupposed by the conception of deliberation. Finally, it refines the position according to which judicial debates must become open to the general public and not remain restricted to the immediate parties, so as to broaden democratic legitimation. Such a large openness is only desirable in cases belonging to the third, fourth or fifth "communicative shpere", not in the majority of cases.

The assumption that court decisions would be "undemocratic" because "legal debates are not open to all citizens" thus seems to be incorrect, as it erroneously narrows the concept of "democratic legitimation" to one single atomistic and populist approach. It considers legitimation within the narrow context of the concrete case only. Moreover, it requires a direct or indirect involvement of *all* citizens in the judicial debate. It is obvious that democracy does not mean that everybody has to decide about everything. Delegation and adequate division of labour are unavoidable if one wants to limit the impact of manipulation on apparently "collective" decisions.

All this is not just a matter of trying, defensively, to legitimate to some extent a judicial power, which otherwise would suffer from some "democratic deficit". The way legal practice works, as a permanent deliberative community, through which new legal concepts, new rules, new principles, new interpretations, new theories are proposed, discussed, elaborated and finally accepted, shows that it also, qualitatively, offers an *added value*, compared to law making through delegation, which is (only) formally legitimated. It confirms that, as Michael Sandel wrote, "when politics goes well, we can know a good in common that we cannot know alone".[92] It is true that in the short term some "wrong" decisions, some "accidents" may occur, but in the long run such deliberative law-making has proven to create better law.

7.7 THE ROLE OF LEGAL DOCTRINE

7.7.1 The Importance of Legal Doctrine

The importance of legal doctrine for the development and legitimation of legal systems has until now been highly underestimated.[93] In civil law systems this fact inevitably follows from the theory behind the codifications and the preponderant role it implies for statutory law. If there is almost no room offered for law creation by the courts, then certainly nothing is left for a legal doctrine, which lacks any official status or formal legitimation. In the common law, on the other

---

[92] M Sandel, *Liberalism and the Limits of Justice*, 2nd edn (Cambridge University Press, Cambridge, 1998), p 183.

[93] A notable exception is Max Weber (see his "Rechtssoziologie" in *Wirtschaft und Gesellschaft. Grundriss der verstehenden Soziologie*, 5th edn (JCB Mohr, Tübingen, 1972), pp 387–513, esp. at pp 504 and 509–11.

hand, academic legal doctrine started to develop only recently, so that, in the past, it could not play any significant role in the development of the law or its legitimation.

However, as follows from the previous discussion, legal doctrine is of paramount importance, both for the development and for the legitimation of legal systems.

Professional institutionalisation is not a condition for the existence of a legal system, but it is an important criterion for determining its *level of development*. Fully developed legal systems, it has been argued, embody three categories of legal professions: professional law-makers, professionals of the administration of justice and professionals of legal doctrine.[94] When comparing, from this point of view, international law with, for instance, the law of highly professionalised sports organisations, it transpires how important a professionalised legal doctrine is in order to be recognised as a legal system. Of course, both types of legal system lack the degree of development advanced state legal systems have, and, because of that reason, they are generally considered to be only "incomplete" legal systems. But, incomplete in what sense? International law has a highly developed legal doctrine, a well developed institutionalisation of law-making (albeit rather contractual through treaties than statutory through international public organisations), a limited number of international courts, and overall a weaker efficacy when compared to many other types of legal system, including state law and sports law. Sports organisations often have a well developed institutionalisation of law-making and of its adjudication, but they lack an own legal doctrine. All lawyers, and probably all other people too, will consider international law to be closer to a "real" or "full" legal system than the law of a sports organisation, however institutionalised the latter may be. Part of the reason for that perception is the presence of a highly professionalised legal doctrine in the one case and its (complete) absence in the other. If legal doctrine were not relevant for the identity of a legal system, some sports organisations would obviously have a stronger position from our perspective than the rather weakly institutionalised and professionalised international law.

For the *development* of law, legal doctrine is indeniably of paramount importance. (Lasting) codifications have only been made possible thanks to the work of legal scholars during many decades or even centuries. During the whole of history legal systems with a highly developed legal science have influenced and even partly replaced less developed legal systems. Even a rediscovered Roman law in eleventh-century Italy succeeded in dominating most of the private law in Europe during the following centuries, because of its doctrinal superiority. Over the last centuries the cross-fertilisation of European common law and continental law has been almost exclusively a one way influence from a doctrinally more sophisticated continental law on a scholarly less developed common law.

---

[94] See above, 3.3.3 on professional institutionalisation.

It is mainly in legal doctrine that technical *legal language* and *legal methodology* are developed. Of course, some doctrinal work is done by legal practitioners when drafting an Act or a court decision, but such a work, however remarkable it may be, inevitably remains at a weakly developed level if it is not backed by a professionalised legal doctrine. Again, this transpires from a comparison of the English common law with its continental counterparts.

Both for the development of law and for its *communicative legitimation*, legal doctrine interacts with the legislature and the judiciary. This interaction is a necessary condition for the relevance of any doctrinal work on law. It is not merely a division of labour, in which each of the legal professions has its own task. The development of law is only possible if they use each other's work as building blocks for their own sphere. Legitimation of judicial decisions will to an important extent be determined by their, implicit or explicit, acceptance in legal doctrine and their implicit acceptance by the legislator.

7.7.2 The Task of Legal Doctrine

Legal doctrine basically performs two tasks, ie the description and the systematisation of the law.

(a) Describing the law

As already mentioned above (in 5.4.1), legal doctrine can be seen as an *empirical science*, that is concerned with questions of truth as to the existence of norms and of their exact meaning. As in each scientific discipline, the first stage of scientific research in law consists of describing the research material. However, such a description is never completely neutral and "objective", as we noticed above when discussing the definition of law (above chapter 2). Every knowledge of reality is an interpreted knowledge, coloured and structured by a theory. Such knowledge, thus, is never absolute. It is nothing more than a hypothesis that will be considered proven, but only for the time being, as long as it has not been falsified, or as long as the theory on which it is based has not been falsified. The same is true for legal science. Statements about the law are nothing else but hypotheses about the *existence, validity* and *content* of legal norms.

Hypotheses about the existence and validity of legal norms refer to a *theory of legal sources*. Which institutions have the power to enact rules and how, is the question which is at the core of such a theory. It would be mistaken to think that the power to enact valid legal rules is completely determined by the legal system itself. At least the acceptance of the founding constitution and of its interpretation by the legislator is an *external* statement, which cannot be determined by the legal system itself. But the same goes for when judges and/or legal scholars accept *new* legal sources, that were not part of the legal system before, or a different hierarchy amongst them, such as the validity of *unwritten principles of law* or the *precedence of international law over domestic law*.

Hypotheses about the content of the law refer to a *theory of interpretation*. The most elaborated legal methodology, in all legal cultures, is precisely the methodology of interpretation. That is why it can be argued, as Aulis Aarnio did, that legal doctrine is a "science of meanings".[95] Describing legal norms, thus, inevitably means interpreting them, whether consciously or unconsciously, intuitively or methodologically. It is that theory of interpretation that will determine the possible meanings of a legal text, rather than the text as such.

(b) Systematising the Law

Legal scholars are faced with a variety of data that have to be systematised into a more or less coherent whole:

(a) normative legal texts, such as legislation, treaties, general principles accepted or enacted in such texts, contracts, wills, binding precedents, and so on;
(b) legal language, with a typical standard meaning of legal concepts;
(c) the adjudication of law, most notably through judicial decisions;
(d) to a lesser extent, foreign or previous legal systems, through comparative law and legal history.

These data have to be systematised for different reasons.

A first one is the rationalisation and simplification of the legal system, which is increasingly needed the more the legal system becomes complex. Such a reduction of law's complexity is realised through the construction of more general rules and concepts extracted from a larger number of more concrete rules and concepts. With the help of such rules and concepts with a wider scope it is possible to order the legal material better and more logically.

A second reason is the need for the integration of case law into statutory law, or, in the common law, to some extent the other way around (integrating new statutes into the system of the common law). This means an interpretation of judicial decisions so as to make them fit with the logic of the whole of the legal system, or a critique which involves a rejection of the legal construction used by the court, or by another scholar, or even by the legislator, because it is considered to be incompatible with the law's systematicity.

A third reason is that such systematisation as described above allows the lawyer to find solutions for legal problems that are not explicitly to be found in the existing legal rules, or, to put it differently, to fill (apparent) gaps in the law.

Fourthly, systematisation is often needed for making competing legal systems compatible, or even for integrating them into one whole, such as converging local customary law with Roman law and Canon law in medieval Europe, or, nowadays, domestic legal systems with European law or, at world level, national commercial law with international trade law.

---

[95] A Aarnio, *Denkweisen der Rechtswissenschaft* (Springer, Vienna and New York, 1979), p 49.

A fifth reason is the need for "external" systematisation: the law has to fit with its societal environment. Through interpretation and (re)systematisation lawyers are able to adapt the existing legal rules to changed circumstances and changed world views.

Just as hypotheses about the existence, validity and content of legal norms are formulated at the level of the description of the law, *theory building* is carried out at the level of the systematisation of the law.[96] At a first level, internal doctrinal theories are worked out, about, for instance, the scope of "property" and its possible use in adjacent areas. At a second meta-level, theories of legal sources and of legal interpretation are worked out, that offer the framework within which the other theories can be constructed. The latter are, in their turn, the framework for concrete hypotheses on the exact meaning of a specific rule.

7.7.3 The Paradigm of Legal Doctrine

All this means that legal doctrine is not just dependent on legislation and court decision for the "relevance", "correctness" or "legitimation" of its work. This is also true the other way around. It is the consensus among lawyers that largely determines the framework within which legislators can make rules and determine their possible scope, in other words their "relevance", "correctness" or "legitimation". An example: during the Second World War (part of) the Belgian government, residing in London, enacted statutes that during normal times, without any doubt, would have been considered to be clearly unconstitutional, as statutes can only be enacted by Parliament and need, moreover, Royal Assent. Nevertheless this governmental "usurpation" of the legislative power has been accepted and validated by the Supreme Court[97] and was never criticised in legal doctrine. If that should have been the case on a large scale, the government certainly would have felt compelled to "legalise" the criticised Acts by asking for a formal decision from Parliament, that would fulfil all constitutional requirements. Because of the silent agreement of legal doctrine after the acceptance by the judiciary, there was no need to do so.

The legislature and the judiciary anticipate possible generalised doctrinal criticism and will try to offer a result that will be acceptable for at least an important part of legal doctrine.

It should be repeated that all this is not done in isolation from each other, but through constant interaction and communication between legislature, judiciary and legal doctrine. They all act (partly) within the framework determined by the two other actors in the elaboration of the law, but this framework is constantly

---

[96] See on this Aarnio, above n 95, pp 66–67. See also A Aarnio, *Philosophical Perspectives in Jurisprudence*, Acta Philosophica Fennica no 36 (Helsinki, 1983), p 216, where he defines a theory in legal doctrine as "a set of concepts and propositions which systematize legal norms in a certain way".

[97] Cass. 11 February 1919, *Pasicrisie* 1919, I; Cass. 11 December 1944, *Pasicrisie*, 1945, I, 65.

adapted and refined on the basis of new legislation, or new court decisions, or new doctrinal theories or positions.

Legislators and courts play a preponderant role in determining the existence and scope of legal rules. Courts will be of crucial importance for the acceptance or rejection of doctrinal theories and interpretations, and, hence, for making them parts of the law or not. Legal doctrine, for its part, plays a decisive role at the level of the meta-theories: theory of legal sources, theory of interpretation, theory of argumentation, and legal methodology in general. It is in scholarly legal writing that the external borders of the legal system, and of its working, are drawn, that the hard core theory of the legal system is elaborated within which more concrete theories about positive law may be worked out. In other words, it is in legal doctrine that the *paradigm of the legal system*, or, perhaps more broadly, the paradigm of the legal culture concerned is determined, accepted and, from time to time, slightly changed (or more radically in revolutionary times).

It is Thomas Kuhn who, in the philosophy of science, developed the concept of "*paradigm*", which refers, amongst others, to the hard core of scientific theories.[98] It is the common framework within which theories are developed and scientific discussions are pursued. It implies a common scientific language, a common set of concepts, and a common basic world view. If one does not accept the commonly used concepts and/or the commonly accepted ideology, it is no longer possible to develop theories *within* that science as it has traditionally been conceived. Sometimes this deviant scientific behaviour attains a notable measure of success. This can be perceived as being the start of a "scientific revolution", such as, eg, the Copernican revolution, when it was accepted that the sun, and not the earth, is the centre of our solar system.[99]

Lawyers also have their "paradigm",[100] their hard core of shared understandings, of basic theories and concepts, a common language, and a common methodology. Or, to put it differently: they share *a common legal culture* within

---

[98] TS Kuhn, *The Structure of Scientific Revolutions*, 2nd edn (University of Chicago Press, Chicago, 1970).

[99] Note that the Copernican theory has been incorporated in our language, as we talk of a "solar" system rather than of a "planetary" system, and we do not use at all the word "earth system".

[100] Within legal theory, some attention has been paid to the concept of "paradigm", be it roughly limited to the question of the historical development of legal science and the question to what extent legal science has been faced with scientific revolutions. It is interesting to note that this topic was very fashionable during the 1980s, but does not seem to have attracted much attention after that. See, eg A Aarnio et al, *Paradigms, Change and Progress in Legal Dogmatics* (Gummerus, Jyväskylä, 1983); A Aarnio, "On the Paradigm Articulation in Legal Research", in I Tammelo and A Aarnio, *Zum Fortschritt von Theorie und Technik in Recht und Ethik*, Rechtstheorie Beiheft 3 (Duncker & Humblot, Berlin, 1981), pp 45–56; J Wroblewski, "Paradigm of Legal Dogmatics and the Legal Sciences", in Z Ziembinski (ed), *Polish Contributions to the Theory and Philosophy of Law* (Rodopi, Amsterdam, 1987), pp 75–88; A Peczenik, *The Basis of Legal Justification* (Lund, 1983), pp 129–34; E Zuleta Puceiro, *Paradigma dogmatico y ciencia del derecho* (Madrid, 1981); M Flodin, "The Possibility of Revolution in Legal Science", in Z Bankowslki (ed), *Revolutions in Law and Legal Thought* (Aberdeen University Press, Aberdeen, 1991), pp 175–82; J Uusitalo, "Legal

some legal community. Such a common legal culture includes shared under-standings on, at least, the following points.

(a) A concept of law: What is law? How is it related to other social norms?

(b) A theory of valid legal sources: Who has the power to create law, and under what conditions? What is the hierarchy of the legal sources? How, and by whom, are problems of conflict between legal sources solved? What is the respective role of the various legal professions? Are non-legal texts or deci-sions, such as religious ones, direct sources of law?

(c) A methodology of law, both for the making (at least if there is any deliber-ate law-making in the legal orders concerned) and for the adjudication of the law. This consists in the first place of a theory of interpretation of the law. To what extent do the adjudicators of the law have the freedom and/or the duty to interpret the law? Which methods of interpretation may be used? Do they have any hierarchical relationship? What is the standard style of writing, eg, for statutes or for judicial decisions?

(d) A theory of argumentation: Which kind of arguments and of argumentation strategies are acceptable? Are these strictly legal elements, or social, eco-nomic, political, ideological, religious ones as well?

(e) A theory of legitimation of the law: Why is law binding? What if it conflicts with some other, non-legal, social norms, such as religious norms? What kind of legitimation may give binding force to the legal rules: a purely for-mal legitimation or (also) an ideological legitimation (eg moral or religious values)? What kind of legitimation gives the whole legal system its binding force? Is it sociological, historical, or axiological legitimation? And, in case of more than one kind of legitimation, in which combination, and under what conditions?

(f) A common basic ideology: common basic values and a common basic world view. A common view on the role of law in society and on the, active or pas-sive, role of lawyers. A view on which problems are considered to be *legal* problems, to be solved properly by the legal system, and not just, eg, moral or economic problems, which remain outside the realm of the law. For west-ern legal orders this includes, amongst others: a rationalist and individual-ist view on man and society;[101] a positivist view on law: law is generally considered to be valid, independently of its moral content (except in very

Dogmatics and the Concept of a Scientific Revolution", in Bankowski, above, pp 113–21; M Jori, "Paradigms of Legal Science", (1990) *Rivista Internazionale di Filosofia del Diritto*. 230–54.

Specifically on the historical development of science, from the point of view of pradigm, see W Krawietz, "Zum Paradigmenwechsel im juristischen Methodenstreit", in W Krawietz et al, *Argumentation und Hermeneutik in der Jurisprudenz*, Rechtstheorie Beiheft 1 (Duncker & Humblot, Berlin, 1979), pp 113–52; NE Simmonds, "Law as a Rational Science", (1980) *Archiv für Rechts- und Sozialphilosophie* 535–55. See also HH Jakobs, *Wissenschaft und Gesetzgebung im bürgerlichen Recht* (Ferdinand Schöningh, Paderborn, 1983), p 164.

[101] M Van Hoecke and M Warrington, "Legal Cultures, Legal Paradigms and Legal Doctrine: Towards a New Model for Comparative Law", (1998) 47 *The International and Comparative Law Quarterly* 495–536, at pp 498–513.

exceptional cases, such as nazi law, or abuse of rights); an instrumentalist view on law: law is not a spontaneously emerged social ordering, but a technique used by the ruling power to steer the society.

Part of these theories are worked out and discussed openly, such as the theories on legal sources or on legal methodology. Another part of them, such as the conception of the law or the common ideology, remain largely hidden and tend to belong to the unconscious assumptions of the (average) lawyer. Finally, some other theories, like the theories of argumentation and of legitimation, take an intermediate position and are occasionally discussed within legal doctrine, but not in a systematic way.

Such theories, especially the more hidden ones, are deeply rooted in a legal culture, and often in a long tradition too. They are the work of a long-lasting communication among lawyers, between generations on the one hand, and between lawyers and the external world on the other. Indeed, they partly take over elements of the general culture within their society, but only partly: lawyers tend to develop their own, undeniably more conservative, common ideology (which, of course, still allows many divergences on points that are not part of that common basic ideology).

One should not underestimate the importance of such shared understandings. It is mainly these paradigmatic theories that strongly limit the number of interpretation problems, interpretation discussions and possible alternatives for the meaning and the scope of the law. Explicitly or implicitly, it is to an important extent legal doctrine that co-determines, refines and structures these theories and their mutual coherence.

8

Legitimation of Law

Legitimation of law has already been discussed occasionally in earlier chapters (especially above 6.3 and 7.6). Here, I will partly summarise my conclusions and integrate them into a more structured analsis of this topic.

8.1 THE IMPORTANCE OF LEGITIMATION FOR LAW

The strong links of law with the society it organises and, hence, its lack of substantive autonomy vis-à-vis that society raise, by definition, questions of legitimacy (above 3.6): why can people be forced to act according to legal rules, if they do not want to? How can it be legitimated that they are sanctioned when they do not abide by the rules? How can it be justified that certain persons or bodies are allowed to enact such rules or to determine their content and scope whilst applying them to a concrete case, with positive or negative consequences for others?

The legitimation of law is most important for legal systems that structure a political community, such as, most notably, state legal systems. At the opposite of the other legal systems, here there is no freedom to enter or to leave the "organisation". Such legal systems are applicable to everybody within a determined territory.[1] The only way to escape a state legal system is to leave its territory.[2] With other legal systems, such as a church or a sports organisation, it always is possible to leave the organisation, so as to escape from the applicability of its rules, with much less impact on one's life, even if, in some cases, it still may have important psychological and/or financial consequences. This stronger impact of state legal systems and their monopolistic position creates a stronger need for legitimation than is the case with non-state legal systems. As argued above (in 3.4) political communities, and hence state legal systems, determine the debates about the basic organisation of society within their territory. They determine a common world view with its hierarchy of values. They have the monopoly of military force that is considered to be "legitimate", at least to the extent that the legal, or rather political, system is considered to be "legitimate".

---

[1] For our reasoning we can leave aside marginal exceptions such as diplomatic immunity, which anyway never means a *complete* escape from the domestic law.

[2] In some cases even this will not suffice, eg after having committed a crime that is also internationally considered to be a criminal act.

In this chapter we will concentrate on the legitimation of *state* legal systems, as discussion on the matter in fact does.

In this book it has been repeatedly argued that legitimation is not, or at least not any longer, a matter of linear hierarchical "pedigree" but rather a circular, inter-dependent, reciprocal legitimation of all main actors in the legal system. By this, legitimation gets a pluralist dimension. Instead of concentrating on some ultim-ate legitimating ground, such as a God, a natural law system, a basic norm or any kind of official ideology, we have to face a network of mutually legitimat-ing actors, most notably legislators, courts and legal doctrine. *How* this legit-imation functions will be discussed below (in 8.3). Here, I want to point to the *plurality* of elements that may contribute to the legitimation, but have in their turn to be legitimated.

As we have seen (above 6.1), "legitimation" of a legal system as a whole can only be a kind of *weak legitimation*, an actual acceptance of the legal system as a fact, an identification of its being a "legal system". In this sense legal systems are recognised by others, without necessarily being legitimated in a strong sense, as a morally good system.

Legitimation in its full sense can only apply to *parts* of the legal system. Moreover, different types of (sets of) rules and principles will require divergent types of legitimation: moral, political, economic, etc. Some will require sub-stantive legitimation, for others a formal one may suffice.

The first, and main level on which law has to be considered as to its legitima-tion is the set of its underlying values and world view. The main touchstone for this will be the prevailing culture in the society to which the law applies.

A second level is the political one. When talking about the (moral) legitima-tion of legal systems as a whole, it is very often this *political* system which is meant, in other words, those parts of the legal system which are directly linked to political decision-making. A divorce pronounced by a court in a fascist coun-try may very well be accepted as "legitimate" even if the government and its pol-icy are vigorously attacked on moral grounds.

Here, it is interesting to note how politics and law legitimate each other: law relies on a legitimate political power for its own legitimation, but political power in its turn is legitimated on the basis of the *legal* procedures through which it is organised (above 4.1.1). It is through this political legitimation that *legislation* is *formally* legitimated and, in pluralist societies, to a large extent also legitimated as to its content.

To the extent that they produce law, courts need their own legitimation as well. In any conception of the judge's role, courts produce law at least in the sense of concretising a general rule and applying it to concrete facts. In most the-ories it is also admitted that courts create new law, at least occasionally and to some extent. The more one accepts a creative role for the judge in the production of law, the more court decisions need legitimation.

Legal doctrine does not need legitimation as such, as it has no power to produce law or any compulsory effect whatsoever. However, it functions as an important legitimating forum for judicial decisions (above 7.7.3).

As transpires both from what has been written above (especially chapter 7) and from scholarly publications, besides the debate on political legitimation, it is mainly the court's decisions on which discussions about legitimation concentrate. Here again, there is a multitude of elements in judicial decisions around which questions of justification may arise: the use of some interpretation method rather than another one, discarding the subjective will of the legislator in favour of some construed "objective" purpose of the law, the use of unwritten principles of law, and so on. Within each of those approaches more specific legitimation questions can be asked, such as the reasons for preferring a specific value or principle above other ones. It appeared from our analysis above (in 3.7) that legal systems are open systems, not just in exceptional cases but in a systematic way and at many levels and many points. For this reason external justification is not only needed at the end of the chain or hierarchy with some closing set of values or some basic norm. A legitimation is required at every point where there is a use or influence of external data that co-determine the result of the judge's reasoning. This places the whole discussion on legitimation in another perspective. Traditionally legitimation was considered to be largely a problem of an internal and formal legitimation *within* the legal system, with only at the end a consideration of the entire legal system against a set of (moral) values. That the situation is far more complex appears also with the impact of human rights in legal systems, most notably in the European ones, governed by the European Convention on Human Rights. In 1950 this Treaty was created with the view of preventing new fascist regimes coming into being in Europe. The Convention was conceived as a kind of positivated natural law system that could be used as a touchstone for undemocratic political regimes. The number of cases brought before the European Court of Human Rights has increased dramatically since 1950, not because of the deterioration of the moral quality of the legal systems concerned, but because human rights have affected the farthest corners of the domestic legal systems.[3] In all those cases the European Convention is not used for accepting or rejecting legal systems as a whole in view of their (non) conformity with the set of human rights it incorporates. Specific human rights, such as, eg, the right to be judged by an impartial court, are used to criticise and to correct a very specific practice, a "detail" in the whole legal system. An example is the (possible) lack of impartiality of a judge, who

---

[3] There have, of course, been other elements that partially explain the rise in the number of cases, such as the increased number of states that have become members of the Council of Europe, a simplified procedure which offers direct access to the court for the citizen, and an increased wealth and procedural assertiveness of the average European citizen. However, even taken together they cannot sufficiently explain the exponential growth of cases.

was already involved in the case in first instance and was afterwards a member of the court who dealt with it at appeal, as in the course of the trial he had been appointed to that higher court. Even if, by and large, the domestic legal system is respecting the basic values incorporated in the European Convention on Human Rights, it is examined at all levels as to its conformity with the Convention *in every respect*. From time to time, the national legal system will thus be forced to adapt its regulation and practices in order to reach that total conformity, in other words its full substantive legitimation.

8.3 TYPES OF LEGITIMATION

By "legitimation" we understand the *normative* validity of the law, its being accepted as rightly *binding*. This is stronger than a *sociological validity*, the fact that the law is generally followed, that it is by and large accepted by those to whom it applies, at least in the weak sense of a forced acceptance (see above 3.5 and 5.3). Here, we are concerned with legitimation in the sense of strong accept- ance ("complete" or "conditional"), not only by those to whom the law applies, but also to some extent by the "external world". This problem of "legitimation for outsiders" arises when a legal system is considered to have transgressed the borders of a minimum morality (eg fascist systems) or to be in conflict with the "international public order" (eg the validity of transfer rules in sports organisa- tions, when against (domestic, European, international) basic rights). By far the main discussion on "legitimation", however, is about a *strong* acceptance *by those to whom the law applies*. We will limit ourselves to this type of legitima- tion problem.

The acceptance of a legal system or parts of it (rules, court decisions) by its legal subjects is broader than a pure moral acceptability. We should approach it from the somewhat broader perspective of its *societal acceptability*. To be widely accepted in society, the content of the law or of the judicial decision must meet certain minimum moral standards that are prevalent in that society. However, this acceptability is not just a moral matter. It is a mixture of morals, sociology and pragmatic reasoning. Morally neutral forms and procedures may be decisive for such acceptability. One can, of course, accept that following cer- tain kinds of procedures and other formal rules, may have some moral value in its own right, as it makes it more probable that the *content* of the rules which will be the outcome of such procedures will also be *morally* acceptable.[4] Nevertheless, the *moral* value of procedural rules is limited. Moreover, posi- tivist legitimation tries to avoid morality as a decisive touchstone for the valid- ity of law and offers amoral legitimation theories. Therefore, it seems appropriate to look at the problem from a broader perspective.

[4] This aspect of legal processes has especially been emphasised by Lon Fuller (see RS Summers, *Lon L. Fuller*, Series "Jurists: Profiles in Legal Theory" (Edward Arnold, London, 1984), esp. at pp 28–31, 76 and 102–3).

We discussed at some length the opposition between formal and substantive legitimation in the discussion on "conceptions of democracy" (above 6.3). One of the conclusions was the actual intertwinement of form and substance: in current democratic legal systems the structure of these systems is largely determined by *substantive* procedural principles. Here, I will shortly discuss the formal approach and the substantive approach to legitimation, including their weak points, and for which *communicative legitimation*, as a third type of legitimation that will be discussed, may offer a better alternative.

8.3.1 Formal Legitimation

Substantive legitimation of legal systems is a relatively rare phenomenon in history. Most kinds of legitimation have been, and are nowadays, of a formal nature. In societies deeply rooted in tradition reference to historical roots of the law, which had been valid "since times immemorial" may formally legitimate (some of) the primary rules and/or the secondary rules of the legal system. In societies in which there is a strong link between law, morals and religion reference to the, direct or indirect, divine origin of the law will offer a formal legitimation.

In Modern Times *rational* types of formal legitimation have been worked out that could replace, in Europe, the lost belief in a divine origin of the law.

In a first period (sixteenth and seventeenth centuries) attempts were made to prove the need for a strong political authority, with the power to enact legal rules. The *content* of those rules was considered formally legitimated because of the presumption that they served the *general interest*. Even an unjust decision or rule was considered to be better than anarchy (Hobbes) or a weak political power (Machiavelli). Individual interests could be sacrificed for the common interest of the community or state. The rules enacted by a king who served that (presumed) common interest were, for that reason, sufficiently legitimated. This kind of legitimation is typically formal, as the *source* of the rule or decision counts, and not its content. However, there is some reference to a substantive legitimation in that the king will be legitimated only if, by and large, his policy indeed serves the common interest (however this has to be defined). This substantive legitimation is not a moral but a sociological one. A good king is a strong, efficient king who can avoid anarchy and keep out foreign armies, even if his rules or decisions are morally difficult to accept. On the other hand, a weak king, on this approach, is a bad one even if he is acclaimed for the high moral value of his rules and decisions.

In a second period this sheer necessity of having some strong political authority no longer sufficed. There was a need for a legitimation of this political power, and of the legal rules it produced, that was based on some, at least presumed, *consent of the citizens*. It was Jean-Jacques Rousseau who introduced the concept of the "social contract", by which the citizens were presumed to have agreed to delegate their "sovereign power" to some representatives, eg a Parliament, representing henceforth the "collective will" of "the" people. In this model the presumed consent is clearly a fiction, as it also is in more refined theories modelled on the concept of "social contract", such as John Rawls' theory of justice. The important shift was that the initial "sovereign power" moved from the monarch to the individual citizen. Henceforth, legitimation of political and legal systems had to be linked, in one way or another, to the *consent* of the *individual*, which, at the same time, made legitimation a *permanent problem* for the law, as there never is actual consensus of everybody on everything.

Since Rousseau, all legitimation theories have to solve this problem of the justification of enforcement of the law against the will of an individual or a minority group.[5] They all have in common a presumption of *rationality* on behalf of the citizens and the acceptance of a principle of *equality*. In that sense these theories are never purely formal, they are built on a minimum of *substantive* assumptions.

Rousseau's theory was defective because it took over Bodin's conception of "sovereignty" when applying it to the "sovereign people". According to Jean Bodin, "sovereignty" means "the absolute and eternal power of a republic".[6] This definition has, rather uncritically, been used ever since and created a lot of confusion and artificial problems, including the discussion on the relationship between the European Union and its Member States in the course of the last few decades. The conception laid down in this definition has two consequences. First, "sovereign power" is located at the level of the state. This has reinforced considerably monist approaches to state and law (see above 3.4). Secondly, and most importantly, the power to create law is conceived as an absolute and indivisible power, which can be attributed to one single person or body only.[7] In the case of an absolute monarch this seems obvious, but once this type of "sovereignty" is transferred to "the people" it almost necessarily implies an unlimited dictatorship of a majority (and in practice even sometimes, if not mostly, a minority) over the rest of the population. It leads, as with Rousseau, to a concept of "general will" with a binding force for everybody who has agreed with the "social contract". For Rousseau such an agreement is given implicitly by simply staying in the territory of the State.[8] Hence, by simply living in a state one

---

[5] Some theories have even tried to legitimate the enforcement of rules against a *majority* of the population, eg by defining the political party as the "vanguard of the proletariat" (marxism) or any other group as the "enlightened" leaders of the people, who know better what is good for them than the people themselves. We will not discuss this kind of legitimation theory here, as it is not part of the *scholarly* debate.

[6] J Bodin, *De la République* (Paris, 1583), book 1, ch VIII, p 122.

[7] The same approach to the concept of "sovereignty" is to be found with Hobbes. See, for a critical comment E Lagerspetz, *The Opposite Mirrors. An Essay on the Conventionalist Theory of Institutions*, Law and Philosophy Library vol 22 (Kluwer Academic Publishers, Dordrecht, 1995), p 113 et seq.

[8] JJ Rousseau, *Du contrat social* (Geneva, 1762), book IV, ch 2, [6]. For an English edition, see, eg JJ Rousseau, *Of the Social Contract or Principles of Political Right* (ed. V Gourevitch, Cambridge University Press, Cambridge, 1997), at p 124.

is presumed to accept a priori any rule and any decision taken by official bodies, however unpleasant and unacceptable they may appear. The sheer majority based on democratic elections thus formally legitimates any content of the law.

In the elaboration of the modern states this positivistic conception of law has been partly balanced by the natural law idea of *human rights*. This opposition between two rather incompatible approaches has been at the core of most debates on the conception of the state, on its legitimate power to govern the private lives of the citizens and the (im)possibilities for the individual to oppose legal regulation and decisions. It is the opposition between a formal and a substantive approach to the legitimation of law.

In the modern formal approach to legitimation, emphasis is increasingly laid on the *procedures* that are used for determining "the collective will of the people", for judging the validity of legal rules and judicial decisions.

It is most prominently Niklas Luhmann who worked out a fully positivistic formal legitimation theory, in fact much more than Kelsen, who still left room for non-legal (moral, political) discussions on the legitimation of law, even if they were considered irrelevant for a lawyer *as a lawyer*. Luhmann defines "legitimacy" as "a generalised willingness to accept yet substantively undetermined decisions within some limits of tolerance".[9] His starting point is the complexity and plurality of current societies, which make it impossible to find a common moral basis for the legitimation of legal and political systems. Hence, according to Luhmann, it is *within* that legal or political system that such legitimation has to be found, more precisely in the *procedures* through which law is produced.[10] If a legal system succeeds in organising its procedures for the creation and application of the law in such a way that all those concerned are convinced that they have equal chances to see their legal point of view accepted, or at least that the result, even if negative, will be acceptable for them, then such a generalised willingness will exist. Legitimation is linked to the recognition of the binding force of legal *decisions,* not of the principles underlying them—in other words, the acceptance of the *secondary rules* of the legal system, rather than its primary rules. The recognition of the binding force of legal rules and decisions implies that those who are concerned are willing to use these rules and decisions as starting points for their future behaviour and expectations.[11] This recognition is not a matter of individual acceptance, but of a *social and psychological climate* by which such recognition is institutionalised to such an extent that it is considered as self-evident.[12]

It should be obvious that with Luhmann "legitimation" is to a large extent reduced to a climate of *legal certainty*. This type of legitimation is only a weak one, which can be effectuated at the level of forced acceptance. Prisoners in a

---

[9] N Luhmann, *Legitimation durch Verfahren* (Luchterhand, Berlin, 1969), p 28.
[10] *Ibid*, pp 30 and 251–52.
[11] *Ibid*, p 33.
[12] *Ibid*, p 34.

concentration camp will "accept" the rules and decisions of their tyrants, just to survive. They, indeed, will use them "as starting points for their future behaviour" and build their expectations on it. But this does not mean that they accept those rules and decisions in a strong sense, in other words that they consider them as "legitimate". However, Luhmann is right that a legal system may itself largely create its own social acceptance by making appropriate, reasonable, fair rules and procedures. Such fair (formal) procedures that offer equal chances to everybody are, indeed, likely to create better (substantive) law, but they are not a sufficient guarantee for it. It also seems true that in our current societies it is easier to reach a consensus on the most appropriate procedures for making and applying the law than on the most appropriate substantive law. This can facilitate and limit the discussion on substantive legitimation, but it cannot exclude it.

Lon Fuller has listed eight procedural principles that should help to produce better law and to limit arbitrariness in legal decision-making: the rules should be (1) general, (2) publicly enacted, (3) not retroactive, (4) clear and understandable, (5) not contradictory, (6) workable, (7) stable, and (8) in accordance with the actual policy of the authorities.[13] However, more than being a guarantee for the "morality" of law, these principles assure the *efficacy* of law. As Wolfgang Friedmann has rightly noticed, the legal system of nazi Germany fulfilled each of these criteria, except to some extent the second one.[14]

Nevertheless, these approaches try to some extent, intentionally or not, to build a bridge between a formal and a substantive legitimation (a) by giving *formal* conditions for facilitating *substantive* legitimation, and (b) by accepting *substantive* principles and values (equality, legal certainty, fairness, reasonableness) that should govern the *formal* procedures for the production and application of law.

Republicanism, as we have seen (above 6.3), goes one step further. This approach does not limit itself to advocating free *access* to procedures and *formal requirements* for these procedures. They are seen as a *means* for reaching an important democratic good, the creation of a *public sphere* "within which persons can achieve freedom in the sense of self-government by the exercise of reason in public dialogue".[15] By this, Republicanism comes close to a communicative approach. However, both Republicanism and Liberalism word their positions too much in terms of (mutually exclusive) opposites: individual rights versus collective decision-making, private sphere versus public sphere. They do not succeed in transcending the old oppositions between positivism and natural law theories, between formalism and substantivism, individualism and communitarianism.

---

[13] L Fuller, *The Morality of Law* (Yale University Press, New Haven, 1969), p 138.

[14] W Friedmann., *Legal Theory*, 5th edn (Stevens, London, 1967), p 18.

[15] F Michelman, "Political Truth and the Rule of Law" (1988) 8 *Tel Aviv University Studies in Law* 284.

8.3.2 Substantive Legitimation

Substantive legitimation is mainly required for concrete rules and decisions, whereas legal *systems* are to a large extent formally legitimated. However, as we have seen, a purely formal legitimation of law is not possible, as in one way or another even such a formal legitimation is inevitably based on substantive values and principles.

All kinds of theories that have advocated the necessity of a substantive legitimation of law have tried to offer some minimum criteria for the moral acceptability of law, not some morality of excellence or aspiration that could guide legal systems as a regulative ideal for the best possible law.

In the past, such theories have been presented mostly in the shape of "natural law theories" of different kinds (divine, rational, empirical). Today they are generally presented as *human rights* theories, which are to a large extent laid down in positive law (constitutions and international treaties). These human rights catalogues have seen a development too. They started as a set of *individual rights* guaranteeing individual freedom (free speech, free press, free associations, freedom of religion, etc) and political participation through elections (actively through the right to vote, passively through the right to be a candidate for a political mandate). Such formal rights of freedom and equality, however, cannot be sufficient conditions for bringing about *actual* freedom and equality. Therefore, they have been supplemented by sets of "socio-economic" human rights (right to health, to housing, to work, etc). Such socio-economic rights, however, are difficult to introduce into a legal system as claimable rights, as they presuppose appropriate economic conditions that cannot be guaranteed by any legal or political system as they largely escape their control. Therefore, such rights are rather seen as a "morality of aspiration" that should guide governments, without really offering any guarantee to the citizens. They contain at the most some minimum conditional claims, such as the right to be placed on a waiting list for obtaining suitable housing (as far as is available) rather than an enforceable claim to receive (immediately) suitable housing whenever needed (which would include a duty for the authorities to build and to maintain appropriate flats and houses). When judging the "legitimation" or "moral quality" of legal systems in the light of such socio-economic rights, it is obvious that the conclusion will not be a binary one (legitimate or not) but a matter of degree, as some legal systems will come closer to the ideal than other ones, without any legal system fulfilling the ideal for 100 per cent and none for 0 per cent.

The human rights of the first generation, on the other hand, offer minimum conditions, which should, according to these normative standards, be fulfilled by any legal system. Presently there seems to be a worldwide consensus on such a minimum, even if the concrete interpretation of specific human rights may diverge, especially when it comes to balancing individual interests with collective or state interests.

This balancing of individual interests with collective ones points to the weak element in the liberal rights theory, ie its atomistic conception of the individual, cut loose from the community in which the individual lives, and which that individual needs in order to use his or her freedoms in a meaningful way. Environmental problems in particular, have made us aware of the impossibility of avoiding locating individual freedoms and their limits in a context of *collective* interests. On the other hand, one should avoid turning the individual into a slave of the collectivity, thus potentially eliminating any individual freedom. Therefore it seems appropriate to distinguish, as Habermas argues, between a *private sphere* of (a large) individual freedom and a *public sphere*, where these individual interests are subordinated to the common collective, but to a large extent also individual, interest.[16] This public sphere has to be conceived as a plurality of many "public spheres": local politics, regional politics, national politics, international politics, economics, labour, leisure, etc. These spheres are neither "given" nor static, they are constantly made, maintained and adapted through communication among those who belong to that sphere, directly in smaller communities, often indirectly (eg through mass media) in larger ones. We will come back to this below.

It is interesting to note the development of another kind of human rights, apart from classical freedom rights and socio-economic rights, ie *procedural rights*. This shows a coming together of formal and substantive legitimation, even if these procedural rights are not linked to political decision-making, to the production of law, but to its adjudication, and mainly as to criminal law. Trials that do not fulfil minimum *formal* requirements as to procedure are, for this reason alone, not legitimate from a *substantive* point of view. Again, this shows the intertwinement of form and substance.

In the area of the *adjudication of the law,* I want to point to another discussion related to the substantive legitimation of law.

Ronald Dworkin has developed his *"right answer thesis"*. Opposing, as a Liberal, the Republican relativism of rights and their interpretation, he argues that we should distinguish between the "right answer" to a legal question and the actual possibility for the judge to find it. If only a superjudge, Hercules, is able to find the one right answer and "normal" judges are not, it does not mean that the right answer would not exist, but only that we are never sure whether we have found it or not. Again it is interesting to see how Dworkin conceives this search for the one right answer as a collective endeavour, not as purely individual brainwork: a chain-novel rather than isolated individual writing. Of course, the obvious criticism is that (a) it is impossible to prove that there would be only *one* right answer, and (b) that, even if this would be the case, it becomes irelevant if in practice it is impossible to find it anyway, or at least to be sure that it has been found. I think that such criticism misses the point of a "perfectionist" approach like Dworkin's. The main quality of this kind of theory is that it

---

[16] See above 6.3.

points to the necessity to *believe* that there *is* one right answer, that there is some "objective truth", which is *equally* valid for everybody. This belief is important to strengthen the feeling and conviction that legitimation is not an isolated individual(istic) matter, but that we have it in common, be it as an objective truth or as a social construct. However, the way for "finding" the (presumably) one right answer cannot be the superjudge, the Hercules, but only communicative argumentation, in which we *together* try to find the currently best possible answer.

This implies some, probably inevitable and even necessary, tension between "absolute truth" and time- and place-bound "relative truth", between a regulative ideal and social contingency.

8.3.3 Communicative Legitimation

Social models of legitimation, which are based on some sociological necessity or desirability as regards law, generally point to two important aspects of legitimation:

(a) the acceptance of the basic principle of *equality* of all people for participating in the legitimation process, and
(b) the assumption that legitimation is largely a *social construct*.

However, such theories that are based on claimed sociological facts are often just theoretical a prioris or constructs (eg Hobbes' *homo homini lupus*, Rousseau's social contract, Rawls' veil of ignorance) and not linked to any actual acceptance or other kind of sociological legitimation.

The main advantage of a theory such as Luhmann's is that it is based on neutral, fair procedures as a means for creating a social psychological climate of *actual* acceptance of the law. Its disadvantage, however, is that it is limited to *formal* elements and unable to cope with hard cases, such as the protection of minorities or the (lack of) legitimation of other "socially accepted" discriminations.

Fuller has tried to overcome such a purely formal approach by linking form with substance, albeit in a limited way: good procedures follow from substantive values (eg equality) and tend to create intrinsically better law.

Modern, rationalist, natural law theories and the classical human rights theories (of the first generation) that rely heavily on them, tend to approach legitimation from a strong individualistic perspective.[17] However, just as with rights,[18] it is impossible to conceive legitimation otherwise than socially. When, for instance, I consider a rule or decision to be highly unjust, but nobody else

---

[17] This individualistic approach has imbued most of Western legal thinking. See eg Joseph Raz in his *The Authority of Law*, where legitimation is analysed as "the obligation to obey the law" seen from the point of view of the individual, cut loose from any community (Clarendon Press, Oxford, 1979), pp 233–89.
[18] See above 3.1.

agrees with me, I will, as a reasonable man, start to doubt whether my position is correct. Even if I still think that I am right and all the others wrong, I will probably "accept" the law in the weak sense of "forced acceptance" just to avoid social isolation. If I still think that I should oppose the law, it is very likely that I will end up in jail, or, much worse, in psychiatric care. In both cases the quality of my life, being both physically and socially isolated, will be much worse than in the case of any form of acceptance of a law that I consider unjust, but all others do not.

(a) A Framework for Communicative Legitimation

On the basis of what we have discussed up to this point, we may conclude:

(a) that legitimation is a social construct, in which
(b) all human beings (should) participate on an equal footing, and
(c) that is achieved through a combination of mutually presupposed formal and substantive elements.

If, moreover, we accept the distinction between the more substantively demarcated *private sphere(s)* and the more formally demarcated *public sphere(s)*, we have the building blocks for a theory of *communicative legitimation* of the law.

First, it is important to find the right balance (which may be partly time- and place-bound) between individualism and collectivism. With individualism citizens tend to be defined as atomised entities isolated from any community, as if they could really be "free", develop, enjoy life or even survive without at least some community. Classical freedom rights tend towards such an overly individualistic approach to law. Collectivism, on the other hand, tends to reduce the individual to a tool for constituting and developing the community. In this conception individuals are not fully recognised in their own right and may be sacrificed in the interest of the community. Here, freedom rights tend to disappear or to have a limited scope.

Secondly, one has to find the right balance between a purely formalist approach (positivism), emphasising only procedures and democratic pedigrees, on the one hand, and a purely substantive approach (natural law), emphasising primarily or exclusively the moral acceptability of the law.

Thirdly, in both cases it is not only about a balance between two (extreme) opposites. We have to understand these opposites as *mutually presupposing each other*. In other words, it is conceptually simply not possible to take one of the extreme positions in its pure form. There can be no community without individuals with a mimimum of autonomy, just as a human being cannot exist biologically, socially, psychologically, or intellectually without others. Purely procedural rules are necessarily based on substantive principles (equality, fairness, rationality), whereas law without any form, containing just substantive principles, is by definition impossible. Moreover, also at the level of substantive legitimation of the law one has to agree on values and principles and on their compatibility with the law. Such an agreement implies at least some kind of procedure related to participation, argumentation and decision.

Fourthly, we need a pluralist approach to legitimation in which a *private* sphere (with more room for individualism) is distinguished from a *public* sphere, that, by definition, is communitarian. Moreover, there is not just one large public sphere, but a plurality of public spheres, of which the, until now mostly national, *political public sphere* is the most important one for the organisation of society in general. It is mainly here that the legitimation debate takes place.

Fifthly, this legitimation debate requires a *communicative space*, not only negatively, by just offering such a space, so as to make the discussion not impossible, but also positively, by creating the best possible conditions for it and stimulating a broad participation in the discussion, based on correct and extensive *information*.

Sixthly, a plurality of public spheres, with a broad communicative space, means, in legal practice, a number of different, always larger, legitimation spheres, involving only the parties at the trial and the judges for publicly less important cases, and legal doctrine, the mass media, or even society at large, in case of a broader public relevance.

Seventhly, the different public spheres (politics, economics, culture, etc) are also mutually constituting, stabilising and legitimating each other. In law these are the spheres of the production of rules (law-making), of the adjudication of the law (courts) and of the scholarly description and systematisation of law (legal doctrine). Legitimation in one of those spheres is not possible in isolation from the other ones.

(b) Communicative Legitimation in Law

(i) Legitimation of the Legal System

As already argued, legal systems as a whole are only legitimated in a weak sense, although, exceptionally, clearly unjust legal systems may lack legitimation in a strong sense. In this case, it will be at the level of the *primary rules* of the legal system that the legitimation debate will take place, regarding unjust principles and rules, as applied in practice. Most notably there will be attention paid to freedom rights. Secondary rules may also be criticised from the point of view of procedural rights, as regards political participation (undemocratic exclusions) or access to justice (unfair trials)

But, generally speaking, when the legitimation debate is going on at the level of the *secondary rules*, it will be rather a sociological discussion on the actual functioning of the legal system, for instance in cases of revolution or civil war. If the legal system is by and large functioning, it will be considered to be "legitimate" in the weak sense of sociologically effective, without moral connotation.

For this, a mutual recognition and support of the diverging institutions of the legal system (legislators, executives, courts, legal doctrine) is of paramount importance. It is to a large extent this circular legitimation that constitutes and maintains the legal system (see above 3.6.1), together with a reciprocal recognition of, and by, other legal systems (see above 3.6.1).

It is obvious that, at the level of the overall legitimation discussion of a legal system there will be a key role for the mass media as a forum for communicative legitimation in the political public sphere.

(ii) Legitimation of Rules and Decisions

Legitimation discussions most frequently occur at the level of concrete rules and decisions.

At the level of rules enacted by a legislator (in a broad sense) the criteria used for checking their legitimate status may pertain to their pedigree, to procedure or to their content.

(a) As to the pedigree: Does the legislative body have the power to enact such a rule? Did it receive this power, in the appropriate way, from a competent higher body?

(b) As to procedure: Was the rule enacted according to the prescribed procedure? Was it in accordance with fundamental procedural principles?

(c) As to content: Is the rule coherent with the fundamental principles and values of the legal system? Is it in accordance with the dominant ideology in society?

In hard cases there will be no clear "checklist" on the basis of which some objective conclusion could be drawn. The legitimation will have to arise from communication among all those concerned within the appropriate public sphere. Such "ideal communication" requires extensive and correct information and rational and coherent argumentation.

At the level of the adjudication of the law there will also be questions as to the competence of the judge (or civil officer, or policeman, etc), the procedure followed and the content. As discussed extensively above, theories and methods of interpretation may be of paramount importance for determining the content of the rule and, hence, of the decision. Moreover, this will be intertwined with a (broad or narrow) conception of the role of the judge.

In all these cases there is a key role to be played by legal doctrine. In the case of a broader interest for society mass media will play at least some role, and occasionally even an important role.

Legislation and court decisions are not only subject to a legitimation debate, they mostly *anticipate* such a discussion by indicating the *formal basis* (pedigree) of the rule or decision and explaining the *reasons* underlying it. In view of a broad communicative legitimation it is also desirable that this is done rather thoroughly, with stronger demands for higher courts than for lower ones, and for hard cases than for routine cases.

Legitimation is a social construct, not only in the sense that the community determines criteria for the legitimation of law, but also in the sense that the point of view of the majority in society will be the point of reference for the acceptability of the law for disagreeing individuals. If people have been used to a harsh dictatorship a new, more liberal regime may be considered more legitimate than some democratic governments in other countries. When living in a society where there have been high taxes and a lot of welfare provision for a long time, this high tax may look legitimate for a large majority in this country, whereas in other countries a lower tax rate may be considered unacceptable by a comparably large majority. What is "acceptable" or clearly unacceptable for each of us is socially determined. As a member of a community there are quite a number of points on which we all agree, in the sense that they are never subject to "agreement" or "disagreement". Some hot points of discussion appear to be hardly debated in other societies. What seems to be an extreme position in one community may be very moderate in another one. Tradition and culture determine to a large extent our convictions and our expectations, and, hence, our view on whether we consider something to be legitimate or not. These traditions and cultures are established and developed through all kinds of communication in society. They create the paradigmatical framework, or, in Habermas' words, the common "lifeworld",[19] *within* which legitimation discussions may take place. The framework as such, however, offers the unconscious certainties for every member of the community that fall outside the notion of "legitimation". They are the "objective truth" nobody can deny in *that* community. This seemingly "objective" truth will also to some extent determine the (possible) subjective positions as to legitimation discussions on "intersubjective" truths of the majority.

[19] "From the perspective of participants the lifeworld appears as a horizon-forming context of processes of reaching understanding; in delimiting the domain of relevance for a given situation, this context remains itself withdrawn from thematization within that situation" (J Habermas, *The Theory of Communicative Action*, vol 2 *Lifeworld and System: A Critique of Functionalist Reason* (tran Thomas McCarthy, Polity Press, Cambridge, 1987), p 135. The notion of lifeworld is thoroughly analysed at pp 113–52).

9

Conclusion

From the systematic analysis of some of the major aspects of law it has transpired that the concept of communication is relevant, not to all, but to an important part of them, and probably to the most important ones. It has also appeared to what extent *psychological elements* are important in law, most importantly for the social acceptance of the law, and for its interpretation. These psychological aspects are to a large extent socially determined and formed through extensive societal communication processes. Communication related to law is thus not only a rational matter, but to a not unimportant extent also a psychological process.

Law regulates human interaction within (legal) communities. Sometimes such interaction occurs without any communication, such as most crimes and accidents. However, what is typical for human beings is their ability to communicate and to construct and develop complex relationships and societies. Here, law is of paramount importance, be it for the construction and main-tainance of a company, an association or a democratic society, or for economic, cultural or any other kind of development. Some parts of the law typically regulate and create frameworks for such interhuman communication: contract law, association and company law, part of human rights law (free speech, free asso-ciation, etc), procedural law, regulation on all kinds of political decision-making, etc. Hence, communication is at the heart of the law. It is one of its main objects and probably the most important one.

Above in 1.2, it was argued that human interaction and comunication have to be at the centre of any theory of law, rather than individuals or legal systems as such. In political terms, it means an intermediate position between (extreme) indi-vidualism and (extreme) communitarianism. In sociological terms, it means a bal-ance between (naive) subjectivism, in which the individual is cut loose from his environment, on the one hand, and (naive) objectivism, in which social systems are studied, cut loose from the individuals that are part of it.[1] I hope that the discus-sion in this book of several topics on law has sufficiently supported this statement.

---

[1] In its extreme version even the concept of "communication" is defined without any reference to individuals. According to Niklas Luhmann only communications, not individuals, may produce communication (N Luhmann, "Was ist Kommunikation?, in N Luhmann, *Soziologische Aufklärung 6, Die Soziologie und der Mensch* (Westdeutscher Verlag, Opladen, 1995), pp 113–24, at p 113; see also above 6.2.2). For an interesting analysis of Luhmann's conception of communica-tion as opposed to Habermas' approach, see P Guibentif, "Le chameau dans le laboratoire. La théorie des systèmes et l'étude de la communication juridique quotidienne", (2001) 47 *Droit et Société* 123–53, at pp 124–37.

From the investigation of the relationship between norm-sender and norm-receiver (above 5.2) and of language as a means for comunication (above 7.2.1) it has become clear that any message, including a norm, has to be located within a *communication* between sender and receiver, and even more, that such a norm is partly *created* in this communication process and not unilateraly and exclusively by the norm-sender (as assumed by the command theory) or by the norm-receiver (as posited by some "Realist" theories), or reduceable to the message itself, the norm-text (as is taken for granted by black letter theories of law).

Legislation has been circumscribed as a one-sided (at least meant to be so) normative communication process within a power relationship between legislator and citizen (above 7.2.2). The analysis of the interpretation of statutory law, however, shows how the adjudication of the law is governed by a multilateral communication process in which not only are the legislator, the judge (or, as the case may be, civil officers or other officials) and the parties involved, but also other courts, legal doctrine, and, exceptionally, even the mass media and the public at large (above 7.3, 7.4 and 7.5). The meaning of the law is never entirely determined by its author, but constantly refined and sometimes thoroughly changed through the interpretation and adjudication process, which is co-determined by its background of legal culture. This legal culture is the product of general culture (the world view(s) and dominant values of the involved community) and of the views, attitudes and practices of the legal profession. In particular, legal doctrine and decisions of the highest courts prove to be of paramount importance for orientating and developing legal culture (above 7.6 and 7.7).

From this perspective, an active role of the courts is not to be seen as a "democratic deficit", but rather as a democratic *benefit*. It is precisely by taking an active part in the discussion and communication about the content and meaning of the law that judges are fully assuming their responsibility as members of the legal institutions and as critical citizens. It is mainly the error of assuming that a strict separation between the creation and the application of the law would be possible that has widely created confusion over the legitimation of creative court decisions and on the demarcation of the role of the judges in modern societies.

From this perspective, legal systems with binding precedents are partly blocking communication and argumentation about legal issues and, hence, legal development. They are thus not recommended for modern societies. On the other hand, legal systems with a culture of dissenting opinions are beneficial for a broader argumentation and communication on legal matters, and should therefore be promoted.

That complex whole of *communicative actions* is not just related to informing people about the law, it is also *constituting*, maintaining and developing the legal system, and the rights it contains, through a permanent circulation of meanings within the legal community (above 6.2.2 and 6.3). Communicative action is opposed to strategic action, in which individuals use their environment, including the law, for reaching their own goals. As argued above in 6.2.2, human action cannot be reduced to purely strategic action. Setting up a company, concluding a contract, developing democracy, are typically *communicative* endeavours. They presuppose some common goals, to be fixed through a communication process among those involved in the enterprise.

The *acceptance of the law* (above 5.3) is not a purely individual matter. It is partly based on information on the behaviour of others and on the behaviour of law officials, as with "conditional" and "forced" acceptance of legal rules. Acceptance of the legal system as a whole (above chapter 8) is also based on a large exchange of information and ideas and political discussions on legitimation issues in society as a whole or in some circles within it.

There is a large deliberative communication in diverging public spheres, which include at least the parties, advocates and judges involved in the trial, but occasionally also other courts, legal doctrine, the mass media and/or the public at large. This deliberative communication is not only important for *determining* the exact content of the law, but also for its *legitimation* (above 7.6, 7.7.1 and 8). We concluded (above 8.3.3) that legitimation is a social construct, established through a communication process in which all human beings (should) participate on an equal footing, and that is achieved through a combination of mutually presupposed formal and substantive elements.

To this brief summary of the main communicational aspects of law, as discussed in the previous chapters, I would like to add some concluding remarks, as building blocks for a communication theory of law.

One should distinguish between *spontaneous communication*, which is not necessarily expressed through language, such as the actual behaviour in traffic that co-determines the "rules", or at least their interpretation, on the one hand, and *rational communication*, expressed through language, which is essential for argumentation and legitimation in modern societies.

A large communicative participation in the making of the law is important for (a) the quality of the law (more coherent, better adapted to the (changed) circumstances) and (b) its acceptance by the involved citizen, and, hence, its legitimation.

Europeanisation and globalisation are important for the broadening of the interpretive community, for increasing the shared lifeworld, the common factual, interpretive and ideological framework (eg human rights, international sale of goods, maritime and air traffic regulation, banking law, etc).

Within a plurality of legal orders (and a pluralist conception of them), an open vision of interpretation and a broad conception of democracy (not just "the majority decides") there is a need for permanent communication at all levels: for both the making and the adjudication of the law, at the local, regional, national and international levels, and in which lawyers as well as non-lawyers are involved. Participating through this communication in the making, the interpretation and the adjudication of the law is not only a right for those concerned, but also a *duty* for all those who have a relevant professional responsibility (members of parliamentary bodies, judges, scholars, journalists, etc). In a constantly changing and moving world of intertwined legal communities it is communication in view of mutual understanding which is "instituting" society, creating the appropriate public spheres in which the political debate takes place, but also creating all kinds of private spheres and social networks, and, most importantly, the feeling of *belonging* to that community, of having something in common within that community, as opposed to the external world.

In a complex, globalised world there is a decrease of common background knowledge and shared world view, or, in Habermas' terms, of a shared life-world. In the Western liberal tradition of the last few centuries this has led to an emphasis on individual liberties and rights, through which citizens may pursue their individual interests through the strategic actions they consider appropriate. However, in order to construe a new globalised community one needs a *communicative space* in which a new common lifeworld may be created. I agree with Habermas, when he posits that if complexes of interaction cannot be stabilised simply on the basis of the reciprocal influence that success-oriented actors exert on one another, *in the final analysis* society must be integrated through communicative action.[2]

The pluralisation of society and of communities with a decreased set of common moral values and principles has led to a *juridification of morals*. Parallel institutions, such as churches, have, in the western world, almost completely disappeared from the public sphere. Both at the national and international level a new common set of moral values and principles is built in the form of international treaties on human rights and constitutions containing such rights, and further elaborated in case law by international human rights courts and domestic constitutional courts. The broadening of the scope of "human rights", if not a banalisation of these rights, is responding to the need to establish a new common morality. In the field of less fundamental values and principles, law too is determining what kind of social behaviour is morally acceptable or not. Courts in particular have been playing an important role in this field, also in legal systems with so-called codified law. When deciding about someone's liability in tort law or when interpreting a contract a moral duty is often determined *a posteriori* and applied by the court to the case at hand. By introducing moral principles into the law "disguised" as "unwritten legal principles" courts have been able to sanction immoral behaviour with the help of principles such as the prohibition of "abuse of rights" or the duty to act in "good faith". Through a large amount of (published) case law a "code of social conduct" is gradually established. The rules it contains are nothing else but a set of moral rules, worded by judges and transformed into legal rules through their judicial decisions. Through this juridification of morals, the legal sphere has become the

---

[2] J Habermas, *Between Facts and Norms* (Polity Press, Cambridge, 1996), p 26. For an application of this idea to the European Union, see J Habermas, "Does Europe Need a Constitution? Response to Dieter Grimm" in J Habermas, *The Inclusion of the Other* (Polity Press, Cambridge, 1999), pp 155–61, esp. at pp 158–61.

main forum for discussing, establishing and refining a new, "official" common morality. It is obvious that this requires extensive communication within large circles and a wide acceptance to be legitimated. However, if this succeeds by and large, it should not be considered to be some kind of usurpation by judges (*le gouvernement des juges*) who interstitially impose their own world view on society, but rather the result of a necessary communicative action that we *need* for establishing and maintaining our changing society. *Someone* has to coordinate this communication process and the law is the only area which is sufficiently institutionalised for that purpose. For guaranteeing a wide participation in the public sphere, however, law necessarily has to be complemented by the mass media.

Of course, the conditions for a perfect communication in ideal circumstances are not fulfilled in practice, and never will be. However, some elements may well further its optimal realisation: (correct) information, (correct) argumentation, the establishment and improvement of spheres and concrete activities of communication and argumentation, such as elections, or reasons in court decisions, facilitating communicative actions, rather than purely strategic ones (creating a climate in which people are more inclined to reach a real mutual understanding).

As a result, two areas are of special importance from a communicational perspective: argumentation theory and theory of democracy.

9.1 ARGUMENTATION THEORY

When enacting law as a public body, deciding a case as a judge, or using legal rules as a citizen or a public or private institution, this may be part of a strategic action with the view of realising some specific goal and furthering some interest, but, by definition it is also always a communicative action, aimed at convincing others of the *truth* of one's statement and/or its underlying reasons,[3] of the *normative correctness* of the rule, decision or claim, and that the *intention* of its author is meant as it is expressed.[4] Any legal statement, sentence or set of sentences can be criticised if one of these implicit claims is not fulfilled. Hence, actually or potentially, *grounds* have to be given to convince the others of those underlying claims of truth, correctness and sincerity.

This requires rules for the validity of reasons and for the acceptability of types of reasons, in other words a theory of argumentation, or, in Alexy's and Habermas' terminology, a discourse theory of law. Such an argumentation theory will have to take into account the shift from *goal rationality* to *communicative rationality*. As we have seen above, there has been a move in legal practice from

---

[3] When enacting a rule, for instance, this rule cannot be "true" or "false", but the facts on which it relies or the proclaimed goals for which the rule is said to be made can be true or not.

[4] These are the three validity claims which, according to Habermas, must at least be raised by any actor who is oriented to *understanding* (J Habermas, *The Theory of Communicative Action*, vol 1 (Polity Press, Cambridge, 1984), p 99).

a vertical linear legitimation to a circular mutual legitimation. This development also has consequences for argumentation (see Table 9.1).

Table 9.1: Traditional versus communicative legitimation

Traditional legitimation	Communicative legitimation
Linear	Circular
Authoritative decision	Argumentation
Imposing	Convincing
General justice	Concrete justice

A linear legitimation imposes an authoritative decision in view of general justice and legal certainty. As for statutory law, general rules are imposed authoritatively by a legislator empowered to do so by higher norms and institutions. The validity of these rules is reasoned through a linear pedigree, which ends with some kind of basic norm or rule of recognition. The same goes for court decisions (or decisions by other officials), which have to refer to such general rules, both for supporting their own competence in the case and for adducing reasons for the content of these decisions. Here, arguments are basically authoritative ones: (higher) rules enacted by competent official bodies, previous decisions by (higher) courts, opinions of (generally esteemed) legal scholars[5]. Arguments tend to be formal as only the authority of the rule or decision has to be proven, not its adequacy for solving social problems. Therefore too, individual justice and equity are subordinated to general justice and legal certainty.

A communicative legitimation is circular, in that there is a dialogue with the social problems to which the rule or decision is meant to be applied.

Its social adequacy largely co-determines the content or the interpretation of the rule. Legal rules are no longer sufficiently supported by the authority of the enacting body and their systemic pedigree. They have to fit with general, even unwritten, legal principles, which are often morally laden (especially human rights) and escape the control of the legislative bodies, because of their supranational or constitutional character, coupled with control by a supranational or constitutional court. Moreover, the (linguistic, legal, social, economic) quality and efficacy of the rules becomes important: it is generally reviewed in advance (by the administration and, as for legal and linguistic qualities, by bodies such as a *Conseil d'Etat*) and often after some trial period too. If desirable or necessary the rules will be adapted, considerably changed or even withdrawn

As for judicial decisions, formal reasons as to competence and content remain important. However, mainly through judicial interpretation of the legal rules, there is a *dialogue between facts and norms*, which largely co-determines the final content and scope of the rules applied to the case at hand. There is also an

---

[5] In the United Kingdom traditionally judges (and preferably dead for a long time), on the continent (preferably old) professors at (preferably old) universities.

increasingly inevitable *dialogue between norms* for determining their exact scope and content: first, because of an inflation of legislation and the incoherences it creates, which have to be solved by courts; secondly, because of an increasing plurality of legal systems (regional, national, international, non-statal), which are not always (and seldom completely) in a mutual hierarchical relationship, but may be regulating the same, or a neighbouring, area. By this they are also creating potential incoherences courts have to solve (eg European Union directives and domestic law, rules of international sports associations and European human rights law). All this is not only a dialogue "between rules", it is a complex communication between legal systems, between legal rules, between legal rules and legal principles, between legal rules and principles and their underlying moral or political values, between the rules as enacted and the interpretation they received in previous court decisions, between the rules, their judicial interpretation and their evaluation in legal doctrine (and sometimes in the mass media), etc. From this perspective one could posit that there is a kind of prima facie duty to follow *precedents,* as judges have to justify their decisions within the framework of previous ones, because they are building blocks for the legal system that should be kept coherent. New decisions have to define their position in the light of such precedents. Following them will considerably limit the burden of justification. Not following them will require extensive reasoning.

Communicative reasoning of court decisions is meant to *convince* the parties, their counsel, the higher courts (which, at a later stage, may have to decide that case), legal doctrine and the legal community in general that the decision is both *legally correct* and *socially adequate and equitable*. "Convincing" does not just mean referring to authority and the need to follow the law, it implies an effort to take the position of the losing party, to look at the case from the point of view of a reasonable person who sees his interest fully or partly rejected, so that the reasons may convince such a person enough to make the judicial decision at least acceptable to him.

The combination of those three aspects of communicative argumentation leads to emphasising the *concrete justice* according to the specific characteristics of the case at hand, rather than general justice in view of giving rules a broad scope and an identical meaning in all cases and (at least apparently) furthering "equality" and "legal certainty". Here, both "equality" and "legal certainty" get a different meaning. Equality is no longer approached from a formal perspective, but from a substantive one (eg positive discrimination), thus eliminating the traditional opposition between "equality" or "general justice" on the one hand, and "equity" or "concrete justice", on the other. Legal certainty is no longer defined as some theoretical prophecy by a lawyer of how the rule will be applied, whatever the concrete characteristics of the case may be, instead is it perceived as how the citizen would expect the law to be (and to be interpreted) on the basis of a layman's knowledge of law and legal and moral principles, combined with reasonableness and common sense. By this interpretation "legal certainty" too is no longer opposed to "equity".

All this implies an important shift in argumentation. When emphasising substantive rather than purely formal reasons the scope of possible arguments broadens considerably. Moreover, not only purely legal reasons can be used but all kinds of factual, psychological, socio-economic, moral and political ones may prove useful according to the kind of case. Finally, there is a need for a much more extensive argumentation when enacting a rule or deciding a case.[6]

9.2 THEORY OF DEMOCRACY

In this work theories of democracy have only been briefly discussed, and in other contexts (above 6.3 and 8). It is not my aim to do it thoroughly here, but only to indicate some directions for further reflection and research, relying to a large extent on Jürgen Habermas's views.

In a complex plurality of legal systems, in the broad sense as it was defined above (above chapters 2 and 3), there are some of major importance, ie those who are structuring the *public political debate*. These legal systems structure *public spheres* in which decisions are made for the organisation of society as a whole and in which some common morality and world view is determined, valid within the whole territory governed by that legal system. These legal systems also demarcate the borders within which *private spheres* can function freely, whether these private spheres are structured as legal systems in their own right, or not. The concept of public sphere is broader than the concept of "state". It also includes levels such as the European Union or the United Nations, and, as these examples suggest, there may be an overlap of public spheres and a struggle to get the prevailing position. Moreover, public opinion does not stop at the borders of a legal system's territory, or may considerably diverge within that territory. So, according to the topic, the relevant public spheres may diverge, without necessarily fully overlapping the competences of the concerned legal systems. Theories of democracy have to concentrate on these public spheres, their mutual relations and their relationship with the private spheres.

The demarcation of these private spheres is now at the core of the scholarly, political and judicial debate: to what extent are Muslim headscarves to be tolerated in western society when, eg school regulation forbids head covering? To what extent can sports clubs freely "buy" and "sell" players within the ambit of the European Convention on Human Rights? What are the limits to state regulation of private sexual behaviour (eg homosexuality)? and so on.

---

[6] Examples of both types of argumentation are to be found in the case law of, eg the French Cour de Cassation and the House of Lords in the United Kingdom. The French supreme court is a pure example of traditional authoritative argumentation with no substantive reasons at all, but only formal legal arguments, if any. Particularly the possibility of giving concurring and dissenting opinions forces, or allows, the judges in the House of Lords to try to convince the other Law Lords and the legal community of the soundness of their interpretation of the law, thus bringing these decisions much closer to the model of communicative argumentation (much more substantive, and not purely legal reasons, and a much more lengthy argumentation).

The first discussion is about who has the power to regulate: may public authorities decide anything, with the only condition that the rule came about through a democratic procedure, as positivist, and to some extent also Republicans, would argue? or are there innate rights, as natural lawyers and Liberals posit, which escape from the competences of political majorities?

The second discussion is about how the content of such fundamental rights is to be determined: by a simple vote in Parliament, by a constitutional court, by a supranational court, through a large public debate?

In the ongoing discussion about the individual as opposed to the state, Habermas rightly posits that the current complexity of our societies cannot be covered by theories focusing exclusively on one of them.[7] Society is not just a conglomerate of atomised individuals and neither is the state an autonomous body that could exist and function independently of the individuals of the society governed by that state. Any theory of democracy will have to solve the opposition between both by taking an intermediate or dialectical position. Basic rights guarantee a sufficient private autonomy, which is the condition for creating a public sphere in which citizens can make use of their public autonomy. On the other hand, there is no public sphere without legally organised procedures and legally recognised individuals, legal persons:[8]

"A legal order *is* legitimate to the extent that it equally secures the co-original private and political autonomy of its citizens; at the same time, however, it *owes* its legitimacy to the forms of communication in which alone this autonomy can express and prove itself. In the final analysis, the legitimacy of law depends on undistorted forms of public communication and indirectly on the communicational infrastructure of the private sphere as well. This is the key to a proceduralist understanding of law. After the formal guarantee of private autonomy has proven insufficient, and after social intervention through law also threatens the very private autonomy it means to restore, the only solution consists in thematizing the connection between forms of communication that *simultaneously* guarantee private and public autonomy *in the very conditions from which they emerge*."[9]

For lawyers this distinction between private and public sphere and private and public autonomy is also an important starting point from which to rethink the traditional, but now somewhat obsolete, distinction between "private law" and "public law". In nineteenth-century Europe, private law was, undoubtedly, considered to be the main area of law, the core of the legal system. It was, of course, linked to the prevailing liberal ideology. Following emerging socialist and welfare state ideologies, the twentieth century has brought about a strong expansion of public law, interfering in all areas of traditionally purely private law (protection of workers, of tenants, of consumers, etc). The twenty-first century will have

---

[7] J Habermas, *Between Facts and Norms* (trans William Rehg, Polity Press, Cambridge, 1996), pp 1–2.

[8] J Habermas., *The Inclusion of the Other* (Polity Press, Cambridge, 1999), pp 260–61.

[9] Habermas, above n 7, p 409.

to work out a redefinition of public law and private law and their mutual relationship, in which public law is concentrating on matters of general interest, such as the structure of society, or ecological problems, and used less as a tool for protecting private interests of specific categories of citizen. In any event, it should be clear that public and private law mutually presuppose each other. They are not separate islands, but rather "a nexus of reciprocal connections".[10] Public law structures the field of private law in such a way that private law is possible at all, eg by creating the bodies for the creation and the adjudication of the law (legislators and courts). Private law, on the other hand, offers concepts, such as "legal person" or "property" that are used in public law too. In the past, some legal systems (eg in the Soviet Union) have considerably broadened the scope of public law, at the expense of private law, without however being able to eliminate it completely. Just as with the economy, it is impossible for any authority to arrange *everything* from above, leaving no space whatsoever for private actions. As soon as *something* is left for private initiatives, we need rules of private law that demarcate competences (the ability to act) and powers (on others and on goods) and rules for exercising these powers and competences, for the exchange of goods, for solving disputes as to property, liability, and so on. However, the possibility to act presupposes basic freedoms, such as freedom of expression, freedom to conclude contracts, freedom and minimal protection of personal property (including against expropriation). Many of such basic rights are part of public law (mainly constitutional law).

It seems important to pay special attention to the structuring of the political debate in the public spheres, to maintain and elaborate the links between the political level and civil society, to organise and support mediating organisations and institutions, such as political parties and the mass media (but also to control whether they fulfil their role more or less properly), as stated by Habermas:

> "The core is formed by a political public sphere which enables citizen to take positions at the same time on the same topics of the same relevance. This public sphere must not be deformed through either external or internal coercion. It must be embedded in the context of a freedom-valuing political culture and be supported by a liberal associational structure of a civil society. Socially relevant experience from still-intact private spheres must flow into such a civil society so that they may be processed there for public treatment. Political parties that have not become integrated into the state apparatus must remain rooted in this complex so that they can mediate between the spheres of informal public communication, on the one hand, and the institutionalized deliberation and decision-making processes, on the other."[11]

Just as with economics, a well developed "*midfield*" is important in politics and in law. Small and medium-sized enterprises are an important element for economic development and stability, including political stability, of a society. Political parties and mass media play a comparable role in politics, as they struc-

---

[10] Habermas, above n 7, p 396.
[11] Habermas, above n 8, p 160.

ture political communication, mediate between all involved citizens and institutions, and have a stabilising function. In law it is legal doctrine that plays this mediating and stabilising role. Legal doctrine mediates between legislation and case law, between isolated rules, statutes and legal decisions, on the one hand, and the legal system as a whole, on the other, between law in the books and law in action. By constantly re-interpreting and re-structuring the legal system on the basis of this mediating communicative function, legal doctrine is permanently changing, but at the same time stabilising the law.

In a theory of democracy, it seems important to demarcate the role of political parties and mass media in the public sphere and to limit their impact in private spheres. As both political parties and mass media play an important role in structuring the political debate in the public sphere, they also should bear some *responsibility* and, where relevant, *liability*. First, they should provide the public with correct information. Secondly, they should take up all important societal issues. They should criticise or support points of view and proposals related to those issues with correct facts and acceptable rational arguments.

Intrusion into the private spheres occurs with political parties, for instance, through the practices of clientelism, which, moreover, often goes at the expense of the public debate. With mass media it is mainly the problem of privacy that is at stake. When, eg, the press reports on an alleged offence, on the basis of secret information of the public prosecutor, it infringes on two private spheres, ie the privacy of the, probably innocent, suspect, and the sphere of public prosecution, which is private in the sense that it has to be secret in the interest of the investigation, which in its turn is of public interest.[12]

In the practice of constitutional interpretation in the USA and in the EU, courts now seem to accept not only the importance of procedual rights, but also the importance of *information* that should enable the individual meaningfully to use his rights to political participation.[13] However, this is still largely conceived as an individualised matter not as a socially constructed *communicative* space. Even the concept of "*deliberative democracy*" is often used in the limited sense of allowing the individual to participate in the democratic process, combined with a duty for public authorities to give account of their policy and a presumed concern about the *public interest*, not mere representation of private (group) interests,[14] but not the elaboration of the communicative political deliberation *within society as such*.

---

[12] An interesting analysis and criticism of the way the media intrude into the sphere of public prosecution is to be found in A Garapon, "Justice out of Court: The Dangers of Trial by Media" in D Nelken (ed), *Law as Communication* (Dartmouth, Aldershot, 1996), pp 231–45.

[13] Eg US Supreme Court in *Weinberger v Wiesenfeld*, 420 US 636, 650 (1975) (information about the reasons underlying an Act); in most European countries: an increasing requirement of access of citizens to information on administrative decision-making (eg the reasons why A has been nominated rather than B, etc).

[14] See, eg as to the discussion on the US Constitution: C Sunnstein, *The Partial Constitution* (Harvard University Press, Cambridge MA, 1993), pp 19–20 and 133–41.

* * *

Legal communication may take many forms: one-to-one communication, for instance in a trial, or with the concluding of a contract; one-to-many, for instance with legislative enactments, or with legal decisions, or with scholarly writing; many-to-one, for instance with elections or referenda, or many-to-many, as is typically the case with the general political debate, or with the establishment and development of a legal culture.[15] In some cases the communication will be face-to-face, but in law it will mostly be in writing. Hence, the importance of the interpretation of texts in law. The characteristics of each type of communication process may diverge considerably. When analysing and discussing them these differences should be taken into account. For our purposes it is mainly the broadest form of communication which is of particular interest. Specific topics to which attention should be paid in further research are, for instance, the role of opinion leaders (eg renowned professors, or judges belonging to the highest courts as for legal doctrine, or leading politicians or action groups in the political debate), or, what in communication theory has been called "gatekeepers", those who select the information for others[16] (eg boards of legal journals, when selecting court decisions to be published or not, or the managers of databases when linking legal sources to some entries or not). For public opinion-making the degrees of *involvement* and *control* of the involved persons in the communication process should reach some minimum levels.[17] The influence of the context on communication[18] should not be neglected, as we have seen most notably with statutory interpretation.

Of course, a communicational approach to law does not solve all problems. Many concepts, including "communication" itself remain, probably inevitably, rather vague. Ideal conditions for an optimal communication remain utopic. It may be that perfect communication can never be achieved.[19] Extensive inform-

[15] For a discussion of these different levels from the perspective of communication theory, see J Ruesch and G Bateson, *Communication: The Social Matrix of Psychiatry*, 2nd edn (WW Norton, New York, 1968), where also an "intrapersonal" level is distinguished (a person observing his/her own physiological and psychological "messages"), which is not of direct relevance for our discussion here.

[16] *"Gatekeepers* are persons, groups, or roles that can supplement a receiver's own direct knowledge of the communication environment. Officially or unofficially, they serve to monitor the range of messages that might be relevant to a given audience, to select and abstract the portion of that range they believe will 'fit' the audience's needs, and to relay those messages to the audience" (R Anderson and V Ross, *Questions of Communication* (St Martin's Press, New York, 1994), pp 238–39, with reference to BI I Westley and MS Maclean, "A Conceptual Model for Mass Communication Research", (1957) 34 *Journalism Quarterly* 31–38).

[17] On these fundamental dimensions of any communicative act, see LA Lievrouw and TA Finn, "Identifying the Common Dimensions of Communication: The Communication Systems Model", in BD Ruben and LA Levrouw (eds), *Mediation, Information and Behavior* (Transaction Publishers, New Brunswick, 1990), pp 37–65.

[18] "In any given communication situation the context may influence communication and vice versa" (Lievrouw and Finn, above n 17, p 55).

[19] Pierre Livet concludes his book *La communauté virtuelle. Action et communication* (Editions de l'Eclat, Combas, 1994) by stating three failures in communication in the broad sense: (linguistic) *communication* is problematic because it is impossible for linguistic acts to guarantee that they

ation and communication are also rather time-consuming, but sometimes decisions have to be taken in the short term. Moreover, not all matters can be discussed by everybody; some division of labour is necessary, even when one tries not to leave everything to professional specialists. On the other hand, developing a culture of communication about law and politics is also a *learning process*. The more developed such a culture is, the better, on average, the quality of that communication, and of the arguments used.

In the final analysis, the question is not whether a communicational approach to law is perfect, but whether it is better than other ones, or at least offers some additional useful elements that other theories lack. Worded in this way, I believe that the answer is positive.

---

achieve what they say; the weak point of (communicative) *actions* is the impossibility to define fully and determine the "intention" of an action; finally it is also impossible to guarantee that *cooperation* is free of failures (p 278). However, he does not see this as a handicap, as indecidability may be a fruitful element in trying to reach communication and cooperation. If one requires too many "certainties", as eg Jacques Lenoble does (*Droit et Communication* (Editions du Cerf, Paris, 1994), eg at pp 34–35), or Jan Broekman ("Communicating Law" in D Nelken (ed), *Law as Communication* (Dartmouth, Aldershot, 1996), pp 45–61) nothing is possible: no communication, no knowledge, no theories. Obviously such a view does not fit with our common sense and daily experience. Of course, it is, intellectually and philosophically, useful to question all kinds of apparent certainties and to deconstruct them from time to time, but we cannot escape the acceptance of quite a lot of "certainties" in order to make any kind of rational thinking and rational behaviour possible at all. This is a practical necessity and not necessarily the result of some kind of epistemological naivity or idealisation.

Index